Praise for
SEX TERROR

"Setting common sexual sense on its ear, Simpson's Swiftian proposals strike at an emotion dear to us: sexual desire. His anarchic mission is to free sex from sermonizing, convention, egoism, and cultural bias. But unlike Foucault, his deconstructing weapon is built of ribald humor and potshots at pretension. Simpson's essays produce rancor and hilarious laughter, disbelief and delight. Some call him wonderful, and some call him outrageous, but I call him a true original and you shouldn't miss this book."

—Bruce Benderson, Author of
Pretending to Say No and *User*

"When the culture of sex breathes its final breath, Mark Simpson will be there to deliver the eulogy with great zeal. And what a gloriously sardonic and insightful farewell it will be!"

—Glenn Belverio, U.S. Editor,
Dutch magazine

"With surgical precision, Mark Simpson peels away the layers of modern masculine culture, leaving few (if any) iconic figures unscarred. The complexities and contradictions of love and lust, examinations and manipulations of the body and mind, pop culture distortion and assimilation, are but a few of the topics handily addressed in this brilliant series of missives. These texts are certain to provoke, and likely to offend; we would expect nothing less from one of our most important voyeurs of contemporary man-sex-life. Exhaustive and exhilarating, *Sex Terror* is a must-read for those who long, for those who belong, and for those who like it wrong."

—Bob Mould, Musician, Songwriter, Producer
(Hüsker Dü, Sugar)

"Mark Simpson is a wit, a wag, a naughty old sausage, but always serious, even at his most teasing. A skinhead Oscar Wilde, his bon mots are both alarming and amusing, getting up people's noses and inside their trousers with equal aplomb."

—Philip Hensher, Author of
The Mulberry Empire

Praise for
IT'S A QUEER WORLD

"These unfaltering sharp and amusing articles and interviews take the piss out of Britain at the same time that they reveal its fabulous queerness." —*Out*

"Brits make better fags, and Mark Simpson is among the very best, pushing the envelope of what the hell faggotry is. Simpson's latest, *It's a Queer World,* is a biting and perverse journey through 90s pop culture. It further establishes Simpson as one of the most insightful and hilarious commentators on queer and straight culture—and all the grey areas in between. And did I mention he's a massive beauhunk stud?"
—D. Travers Scott, *Seattle Stranger*

"Snappy, wicked, infamous." —*Seattle Gay News*

"Like a very dry martini imbibed at high altitude. Giddy, ginny cynicism at its best." —Glenn Belverio, *Glue* magazine

"Erudite, sassy, fresh, hilarious." —*Publishers Weekly*

"Mark Simpson is one of the brightest writers around, as this collection amply proves." —*Time Out,* London

"With wicked, wacky humour, this book is one of the most entertaining ever written on popular culture and sexuality." —*Gay Times*

"Brilliant . . . Seriously funny." —*Scotland on Sunday*

"You'd have to be a chronic depressive not to laugh." —*New Statesman & Society*

"Provocative, irreverent . . . A valuable and entertaining read for those of any persuasion seeking fresh perspectives on the era in which we live." —*The Hot Press,* Dublin

"Perceptive and funny." —*The Scotsman*

"May bring a tear to your eye." —*Irish Gay Community News*

Sex Terror
Erotic Misadventures in Pop Culture

Sex Terror
Erotic Misadventures in Pop Culture

Mark Simpson

Harrington Park Press®
An Imprint of The Haworth Press Inc.
New York • London • Oxford

Published by

Harrington Park Press®, an imprint of The Haworth Press, Inc., 10 Alice Street, Binghamton, NY 13904-1580.

Cover design by Jennifer M. Gaska.

Library of Congress Cataloging-in-Publication Data

Simpson, Mark, 1965-
  Sex terror : erotic misadventures in pop culture / Mark Simpson.
    p. cm.
  ISBN 1-56023-376-1 (hard : alk. paper)—ISBN 1-56023-377-X (soft : alk. paper)
  1. Sex. 2. Sex in popular culture. 3. Homosexuality. 4. Gay men—Sexual behavior. I. Title.

HQ21 .S488 2002
306.7—dc21

                                                                                    2002024216

For Michelle

CONTENTS

Acknowledgments

These essays originally appeared in the *Independent on Sunday,* the *Guardian,* the *Independent, Vogue Hommes International,* the *Seattle Stranger,* and *Attitude.* The pieces collected in Dirty Words all appeared in *Attitude* between 1996 and 2000 in the Simpsonicity columns.

Thanks are due to Suzi Feay, Marcus Field, Richard Buckley, James Collard, Ian Tucker, Adam Mattera, Matthew Todd, Paul Flynn, David Keeps, Joe Dolce, David Arias, Dan Glaister, Claire Armitstead, Nick Haeffner, Alan Jackson, Ray Purtee, David Arias, Michael Blighton, Randy F., Steven Zeeland, and LadyFerry, alias Michelle.

DIRTY WORDS

The Crapsex Guide

Forget the choice between freedom and slavery. Forget the choice between tyranny and democracy, communism and capitalism. Forget, if you possibly can, the choice between Boyzone and Backstreet Boys. Now that the twentieth century is definitely over, it's clear that the only choice left to humankind nosing into the lonely, inexperienced, still-single-(digit) Miss New Millennium, is the choice between HotSex and crapsex.

Which, like democracy, isn't really any choice at all. We're now slaves to our desires rather than to our ideology. Who, given free and fair elections, would actually *choose* government sausage over Burger King Whoppers? In a world where the consumer is a queen, there is no choice but to indulge our appetites, even if we're not particularly peckish. It's our duty as subjects and our responsibility as regents to binge ourselves silly. However, the mundane truth that Häagen-Dazs adverts will never tell you is that while crapsex may not be very appetizing, you really ought to try it more often. Even if you are, like everyone else, already having it much more often than you admit.

But what precisely is crapsex? Well, crapsex could be bad sex. It could be sad sex. It could be sex with your hair net and slippers on while doing the crossword. But to put it succinctly, crapsex is sex which isn't hot.

Once upon a simpler, kinder, chillier time when people wore more, there was only one kind of sex, and it was crap. All other kinds of sex were illegal or practiced only by foreigners. But then came the 1960s and hotsex was invented, around the time of the Beatles, the contraceptive pill, and hair conditioner. Hotsex was a new concept: sex which wasn't simply hydraulic but *hedonistic*. A way of life rather than simply a way of continuing it. Self-expression rather than repression. Of course, gays were in the vanguard of this, rioting in New York in protest at attempts by the NYPD to force them to wear baggy clothes and settle down with that nice girl who works in the dentist's office, instead of getting on with the business of having as much hotsex as a person can have without actually melting.

Gays won this battle, of course, and triumphantly made the world safe for disco shorts. Having amended the Constitution of the United States to guarantee "life, liberty, and the pursuit of hotsex" they spent the 1970s having nonstop hotsex, usually to the strains of Donna Summer. In doing this, they showed straights how to (un)dress for the designer 1980s—when hotsex was branded and became HotSex. A ruthless propaganda campaign conducted by Hollywood, Calvin Klein, Versace, and Madonna, deploying *9½ Weeks,* Nautilus machines, *American Gigolo,* and lycra-cotton mixtures sold this new brand to the world and convinced everyone that any sex that didn't feature flawless bodies executing hours of sweaty gymnastics culminating in Technicolor multiple orgasms on black silk sheets simply wasn't worth having.

HotSex, not the condo, the white leather sofa, the home gymnasium, or the big hair was the ultimate 1980s' aspiration—if only because the condo, the white leather sofa, the home gymnasium, and the big hair were necessary props for achieving HotSex, the most conspicuous form of consumption of all. That epic, decade-long battle between Alexis and Krystle Carrington wasn't about who would make the best wife or even who had the best shoulder pads, it was about who could offer Blake the most high-class HotSex (mind you, everyone knew this was Steven Carrington's boyfriend—which is why he had to die).

As we all know, the 1980s never ended and since then, the worldwide branding success of HotSex has continued apace. HotSex is *everywhere*—even in Britain, that damp island fortress of crapsex. Here twitching suburban net curtains have been replaced with red lights, bridge clubs with wife swapping, Evensong with S&M. No longer something associated with an out-of-reach glamorous lifestyle, something to be found only on the big screen or in glossy ads, HotSex has hit the streets and everyone is a junkie for it. And just in case some pockets of resistance remain in the form of dowdy, once-a-month shaggers, sex surveys, sex guides, and sexperts fill magazines, newspapers, airwaves, and video stores with the shrill, evangelical, harassing message that HotSex is something everyone can have and, in fact, *should* have—unless they fancy being laughed at by the old maid next door.

But HotSex has advanced its perfectly manicured hand up the public's skirt quite far enough, thank you very much. In fact, if any of us knew what decency was anymore we'd slap it down, scream our tits off, and call the cops. Really, it's time to stop skipping to the whip of HotSex, put some clothes back on, drain that water bed, cancel that Viagra bulk order, and take some pride in sex that is *not* hot, instead of forever living in shame and fear of being outed as crap.

When this finally dawned on me—oddly, around the time I realized that I was no longer in the market for HotSex—I came up with the following ten, solidly persuasive, not say throbbingly irresistible reasons why crapsex is better than HotSex (and it only took me three minutes).

1. *You don't have to worry about your appearance.* During crapsex you're covered the whole time by your duvet. During HotSex, however, you're forever stopping the action in order to reapply your body make-up and adjust the position of the arc lamps for the video camera.

2. *Crapsex is cheap.* No Internet bills, no year-round tan, no gym membership, no silicone implants, no vacuum pump, no hay bills for the goat in the backyard. All you need for crapsex is a slightly elevated pulse. Well, a pulse.

3. *Crapsex is quick.* Whereas HotSex has to last forever. Crapsex takes no longer than it takes to boil an egg. HotSex will take over your life. Also, because crapsex frankly isn't very satisfying, there's always plenty of energy left over for important things such as building ships inside bottles. Or masturbation.

4. *Crapsex is easy.* HotSex is mentally fatiguing because it's an endless competition—with yourself. Each lay is meticulously compared with the last and rated on a personal-best score sheet. Crapsex cuts out this grinding stress cycle with the relaxing reassurance that sex *can't get any worse.* HotSex, on the other hand, is *bound* to.

5. *Crapsex improves relationships.* If you have crapsex long enough, you'll forget how enjoyable HotSex can be, so you won't see the point in risking your relationship to get it. But if you have HotSex with your partner it's only a matter of time before you work through every conceivable fantasy and realise that someone else will be able to offer you even hotter sex simply *because they're someone else.* All those better-sex guides for couples whose "spark" has gone out of their love lives are just hastening the end. Crapsex is what keeps people together, like a guilty shared secret. When sex is unfulfilling you

have to invest some of your unexpressed libido in that neurotic form of behaviour called "affection."

6. *Crapsex is safer.* Not only will you be having very infrequent sex if you practice crapsex, you will also be keeping your number of partners to an absolute minimum—partly, of course, because the definition of crapsex is "monogamy." And, because when you're used to having only crapsex it's sensible to avoid new partners because they might have been having lots of HotSex and will immediately spot you for a sad crapsexer and laugh at your untrimmed pubic hair, unpierced penis, and unsuppressed gag reflex.

7. *Crapsex won't wake up the neighbours.* (Or your partner.)

8. *Crapsex isn't gay.* Gays are, of course, still the greatest devotees of HotSex and the greatest enemies of crapsex. (These days, even lesbians, once the standard bearers of crapsex seem to have made the conversion to HotSex.) Homosexuals who make the mistake of admitting to their gay friends that they practice crapsex are immediately told that they are "letting the side down." Homosexuals who make the mistake of telling their straight friends that they practice crapsex are immediately told how disgusted they make them feel.

9. *Crapsex doesn't have to be with someone who is your "type."* Instead, it can be sex with someone you're almost quite fond of, when the lights are off and they haven't been eating onions. And it's their birthday.

10. *Crapsex is the real world and probably the only chance for real happiness that any of us has.* Unfortunately, this is also why HotSex will get you—and me—every time.

Attitude
April 2000

Girl Trouble

I recently saw my ex-girlfriend on *Oprah*. The show was called "Older Women with Younger Men." Several mature divorcées, including my ex, were lined up on stage with their boytoy boyfriends, explaining why three decades and a full set of prosthetics were as nothing between true lovers.

Bitterly, I realised that if only I'd played my cards differently it could have been me up there sitting next to "Deborah" (not her real name), with a tight-faced tan, bleached teeth, styled hair, and Rodeo Drive linen jacket pushed up to the elbows, insisting that this was the woman of my dreams. I felt like Chance Wayne from Tennessee Williams' *Sweet Bird of Youth* seeing Miss Del Lago on another hustler's arm at the Academy Awards.

Of course, Deborah wasn't exactly my girlfriend. Deborah was more of a dare. I met her at a party in LA in 1990. I was there because I was new in town and wanted to meet the "right" people and use them. She was there because she worked in Hollywood. So we had a lot in common. I liked her instantly—she was easily the most Beverly Hills woman I had met in LA.

Actually, apart from some lesbians at a karaoke night in one of the gay bars on Santa Monica Boulevard and the nice helpful girl at the car rental place, Deborah was the only woman I'd met in LA. And, to be honest, she was more Pearl Harbor than Beverly Hills. An armour-plated divorcee with a foghorn voice, she had great, conical, twelve-pounder breasts that seemed to raise and lower themselves, as if ranging their target in coordination with the deep-set eyes that swivelled continuously in their sockets, scanning the horizon for someone famous, or someone young, male, and desperate. She zeroed in on me in no time.

We chatted for some time. I hoped I'd made a splash—surely she would be able to pull strings on my behalf, perhaps mention me to a film director, maybe set me up with my own apartment, convertible, and expense account? Or maybe just a six-figure film contract with a major motion picture studio. I wasn't greedy.

Back at the apartment where I was staying with my gay friend, Dan, who'd introduced me to Deborah, we discovered someone had left a telephone message, the "message waiting" LED blinking away furiously. "Hello, Deborah here. *My,* what an *interesting* fellow that Mark Simpson is," she almost purred, managing somehow to reign back her collision-warning voice. "I wonder, is he . . . *available?* I don't want to poach on your territory, but . . . if he is . . . *available* . . . could you give him my telephone number?"

I've got it made, baby!, I crowed to myself in my best Paul Newman.

I met Deborah the next evening at her Beverly Hills home, complete with pool and grand piano covered in framed pictures of her with the stars—Arnie, Meryl, Sly, Dustin—her smile exactly the same and exactly insincere in every one. Then we went to the movies together to see *The Cook, The Thief, His Wife & Her Lover* (1990), a film about lust, greed, deceit, and cannibalism.

Every time anything slightly out of the ordinary happened poor, frail Deborah grabbed my arm or leg with a powerful pincer grip and yelped, doing her best to look scared instead of scary.

Slowly, slowly it began to dawn on me that Deborah might not be the shortcut to easy money and fame that I had imagined and that, instead, here was a woman who was unlikely to part with anything before she got *exactly* what she wanted, several times a night, every night—and even then she probably wouldn't. I had bitten off rather more than I, or for that matter a hydraulic car compressor, could chew. As Liz Taylor puts it in *Sweet Bird of Youth* (1989), when monster meets monster, one monster has to give way, and I could see that monster wasn't going to be Deborah.

After the movie, Deborah—who, was very much in the driving seat—swung the car toward Santa Monica, stood on the accelerator, and announced we were going for a "nightcap" at Gladstone's, the famous seafront bar, clutching my thigh even more often and even more firmly than she'd done in the cinema.

Gladstone's, I thought. The famous, *romantic* seafront bar. The famous, romantic seafront bar where you take your date before *banging* her. "It's such a warm evening," Deborah sighed, leaning toward me threateningly. "Who knows *what* a girl might do on such a night!" Not wanting to become another date rape statistic, I thought it best to disappoint her before we got there, before she worked up an unstoppable head of steam, and suggested that there might be a misunderstanding about the nature of this evening.

"What?" she demanded loudly, swerving and nearly hitting a parked car. "What kind of *misunderstanding?*" I had to think fast; I decided to blame my fag friend for the breakdown in communications. "Didn't Dan tell you I was gay?" I asked (I had in fact given him strict instructions *not* to tell her).

The car came to an immediate, neck-straining, rubber-burning halt.

"Gay?" She yelled.

"Er, yes," I said.

"But what about this evening? What about our *date?*" she cried, with a face like a drill instructor to whose parade you turned up in a tutu.

"Well," I sputtered, thinking that my only possible hope of surviving this evening was to appeal to this woman's wounded but immense ego, "I enjoyed your company *so* much at the party," I gushed, "and found you such a *witty, funny,* and *attractive* woman that I thought it would be fun to hang out with you. As *pals.*"

As the fact that I wasn't killed or castrated would suggest, the ploy worked, and another hour or so of obsequiousness saw me dropped off in the relative safety of West Hollywood.

So ended my last date with a woman and my only chance of making it big in the movies. Of course, unlike Chance Wayne, my hero, I didn't have a Heavenly, a golden girl from my golden youth, to redeem me from my gigolo mendacity. Although, come to think of it, there was Claire Wise, a nice girl I kissed on stage every night for a week in a school production of *The Winslow Boy.*

Claire was very pretty, with freckles and red hair, and I really did enjoy snogging with her, but, truth be told, I would probably have preferred her brother, Greg Wise, who played the policeman (something Emma Thompson would understand: she ran off with him during the filming of *Sense and Sensibility*). If I'd known that Claire was in fact destined to be a film producer, I might have kissed her a bit harder and never had to go on a date with a Hollywood divorcée twice my age.

On the other hand, if I'd known her credits would include *The Adventures of Priscilla, Queen of the Desert* (1994), I might not have kissed her at all.

Attitude
May 1997

A Rounded View

You know when straight men joke, "Backs against the wall, lads! You'd better watch that one, 'e's an arse bandit!'"? Isn't it just so *silly?* Isn't it *immature?* Isn't it *presumptuous?* After all, what self-regarding gay man would be interested in an icky straight man? I mean, they don't even floss properly and probably don't have a decent tan line. And anyway, it's not as if they're in dire danger of being buggered senseless when they lean over the pool table to pot a tricky ball, is it?

Well, yes, actually—if I'm in the room. You see, I'm the arse bandit they're talking about. (And lads, my cock can drill through walls.)

Of course, I know I shouldn't be interested in straight men. I know it's predatory. I know it's a sign of self-loathing. But I can't help myself. You see, I'm a bum man and I've tried loving gay men's botties, I really have. The problem is, I can't find them.

Really, it's all too tragic to bear. Where their legs meet their backs, instead of a nice round, firm, double-mound of muscle that you can grab, bite, maul, slap, bounce up and down on, and play a couple of rugby games with, gay men usually have nothing but vestigal buttocks, an ancestral memory of a time when men actually walked and ran instead of taking taxis everywhere.

Would that it weren't the case. Being a bum boy who is a bum man can be a bum rap if you don't fancy spending it hanging around pool halls or the prison showers.

The worst thing is so many gay men's arses are not only flat but, like cats, without any cleavage at all. Exploring men's bums should be like pearl diving: the jewel should be difficult to reach, requiring expert breath control and the prying apart of stiff, reluctant muscle: a precious and rare reward for skill and daring. Call me uptight, but I'm a teensy bit turned off when a man's sphincter winks at you through his jeans and offers to buy you a drink.

There are many theories as to why gay men don't have arses. But the most convincing one I ever heard came from a friend of mine who grew up next door to a bumless gay couple in Wales. As a boy, he pondered their afflicted state and came to the understandable conclusion that their derrieres were missing *because* they were homosexual. All that sodomy had worn away their rears. Understandably, this discovery put back his own coming out by years.

Whether bumless wonders are born or made I cannot say. Even in the gymnasium, where we homos usually hammer our pansy bodies into the image of someone we'd quite like to pull ourselves, the bottom half of the body is more often than not neglected—probably because in a crowded disco you can only clock the top half. But it's all a bit self-defeating; the showy superstructure of pecs, delts, lats, and biceps is turned into a bit of a camp, cartoony joke by the paltry pins supporting it. Squats, the Holy Grail of straight male bodybuilders, are just too much like hard work, and anyway give you terrible piles (as I discovered to my horror).

Straight men's bums, like straight men themselves (or at least the ones worth molesting), are sexy because they are the thoughtless, melony fruit of gritty, honest—and frankly stupid—labour. Arse beauty is in blank function and not design. The circumference and firmness of those featureless spheres is, perhaps, a measure of how thrillingly *out of touch* with his body and its pleasures and pains a straight man is, how it is subjugated to his brutish will. (Or maybe it's just that when he was a kid he never had a letter from his mum excusing him from gym for the rest of the term because of a rare but very serious allergy to contact sports.)

Sprinting footballers, yomping squaddies, hauling hodcarriers: their arses grow and their prostates itch, entirely unawares—until they've had ten pints and you promise not to tell anyone. You see, straight men's bots are so sexy because straight men make the best bottoms.

Of course, there are straight men who aren't sexy and whose arses I wouldn't like to bite, even if they were the only meat for miles around. The vast majority of them, in fact. And, of course, wishful thinking about thoughtlessness and brutishness aside, many of the sexiest straight men are not that "straight" after all. This isn't to say that they are "really gay"—just that they're not "really straight." There's a kind of polymorphous narcissism, a love of attention whatever the gender, that goes with a certain intensity of studliness.

But the bottom line—and one that most gay men seem unable to bring themselves to admit—is that the sexiest bums in the world are attached to men who aren't gay.

Which leaves homos like me in a bit of a quandary: You're a man who fancies men. Being pedantic, as is the modern habit, you decide you must, therefore, be gay. So you come out. Like the well-behaved, conscientious homo you are, you do everything that nice homos are supposed to do these days. You solemnly tell everyone that you fancy other men and that this is what you are, that you are "gay." Being of a tidy mind, you then go on the gay scene in search of other men who fancy men.

But then something rather curious happens. Instead of being rewarded for your good citizenship with happiness and as many beefy-buttocks as you can chew, it slowly dawns on you that the very men with the arses that it hurts to look at and who made you realise that you were a bummer are now out of reach—that in ordering your life around your homoness, you have cut yourself off from the very thing which made you homo in the first place.

As the old fag joke has it, "What's the definition of gay agony?" "A bottomless pit." Or a gay bar.

Or, for that matter, a pitiful bottom.

Attitude
October 1996

Bottoms from Outer Space

You might, especially after that last piece about gay and straight men's arses, think me obsessed with bottoms. And you'd be right. But if you want to know what a real bottom obsession looks like, one that makes my own look positively flirtatious, just visit the movies.

Take the summer blockbuster *Independence Day* (1996). Here's a film so fixated on bumholes that it can't see anything *but* bumholes. Bumholes so big and special-effected that they threaten to swallow up the whole world. Literally.

In this startlingly excremental movie, American civilisation is dwarfed by vast, round alien arseholes that saucily position themselves over the biggest, proudest, pointiest buildings in New York, LA, Washington, etc. After twenty-four hours of teasingly hovering above these phallic monuments, they open up their sphincters—deploying an anality so voracious, so *terrifying*, that it first demolishes the skyscraper below and then engulfs, destroys, and generally wreaks havoc on the nicely ordered American metropolis beneath it. That's some bottom.

In case we've missed the point, the gung ho U.S. pilots who attempt a counterattack talk a great deal about how they can't wait "to give it to those aliens up the ass!" However, they fail to penetrate the aliens' defences with their hot, hi-tech rockets—even the nuclear-tipped babies—because the cheeky aliens have a force field hymen protecting them from such unwanted attentions.

Fortunately, Jeff Goldblum's wily Jewishness saves the day, and mankind's reputation as fuckers not to be messed with, by craftily deciding to lower the aliens' defences with a *virus*. Jeff infects one of the smaller alien vessels and thence the mother vessel by "docking" with it, and soon the virus is transmitted to all the alien ships, whose force fields/immune systems collapse.

This allows Randy Quaid, playing a kamikaze love missile, to fly up the sphincter of an alien vessel, crapping destruction onto a city below, while shouting "Alien assholes! Up yours!" before exploding and destroying the alien ship, helpfully showing the rest of the

Earth's forces "Where the aliens' weak spot is." That is to say: in the same place as men's.

You can't get more botty-fixated than this. Except, that is, in the recent sci-fi blockbuster *Stargate* (1994). This film, made by the same team who made *Independence Day*, featured basically the same explosive anal ending in which an alien desert despot is destroyed by an American bomb, which is sent shooting up the arsehole of his spacecraft by Kurt Russell (who is much the same thing as Randy Quaid), shortly after Kurt has uttered pretty much the only expletive in this PG movie—"Fuck you, asshole!"

Men's bottoms are officially meant to allow only one-way traffic. Any reminders that bottoms can admit as well as expel usually make men uneasy—unless the notion can be projected onto something hated. *Stargate* begins with the discovery of a huge "ring" in the Egyptian desert, which turns out to be a "portal" to other worlds— which is fine and dandy. But it is also a point of entry to our own— which isn't. So Commander Kurt and his men are dispatched to plug that hole good and proper and protect Earthmen's virtue.

In an infamous interview Mel Gibson was asked whether he worried that people might think he was a homosexual because he was an actor. Pointing to his not-uninviting arse, he allegedly shouted: "This is just for shitting!" Quite right, too, Mel. All the same, it's just a little odd that his hard, manly, hairy performance of Scottishness in *Braveheart* (1995) in which he battled against the soft, smooth, nancy-boy English reached its "climax" during a scene in which he was publically *disembowelled* by the pervey-poovey Sassenachs without so much as *blinking*.

Of course, invasion, enslavement, and defeat have long been seen as analagous to male rape—a form of emasculation. Recent revelations of sexual humiliation practised by victorious troops in the Bosnian conflict on their male prisoners have only reinforced this idea. Perhaps this is why, in *Independence Day*, Randy Quaid, the man who finally "gives it to the aliens up the ass" on behalf of all Earth men, is an alcoholic Vietnam vet who, we're told, was once abducted by the aliens and subjected to "sexual experiments." The ending of *Stargate* also owed something to recent American history: A T-shirt popular with U.S. forces during the Gulf War depicted Saddam Hussein—that other scary despot the Yanks liberated desert people from—bent over with an American missile up his butt and the legend beneath it reading: "We're Gonna Saddamize Ya!"

The direct representation of male violation, like consenting male homosexuality itself, used to be a taboo. In the 1970s the play *Romans in Britain* was prosecuted for indecency because it featured a simulated male rape scene. The film *Deliverance* (1972) was considered controversial because it hinted rather heavily at male-male sexual assault.

Nowadays, however, in this arsehole-anxious era, male rape scenes are practically de rigueur in mainstream movies, popping up (and being held down) in films such as *Pulp Fiction* (1994) and *The Shawshank Redemption* (1994), while, as we've seen, the theme of forced, vengeful posterior penetration has even become the stuff of science fiction movies ostensibly aimed at kids.

This might just have something to do with the rising visibility of homosexuality and male passivity, as well as the inescapable fact that no matter how many aliens the guys blow away at the movies—and in *Stargate* and *Independence Day* saving the world is strictly a guy thing—they still keep losing the sex war with the aliens they live with: females.

So, without wanting to come across all Vito Russo, it's probably no coincidence that the *Stargate* alien, played by Jaye Davidson, who also played the tricky tranny in *The Crying Game* (1992), is surrounded by muscular young men in leather, and flies about in a spaceship that likes to sit on pointy pyramids. Nor is it, I suggest, entirely without signficance that in *Independence Day,* Harvey Fierstein, playing, as usual, an hysterically obvious attention-seeking gay who is constantly on the phone to his mother ("Oh, Mother it's *awful!* The aliens are getting *more attention than me!*") is the first character to be killed by the alien attack, eliminating early on (but not early enough for my money) the only Earthling who willingly takes it up the ass.

These days Hollywood science fiction is not so much about men's fear of invasion from outer space as that of the invasion of men's inner space. But then, maybe it was always like this: As Kevin McCarthy shouts to the freeway traffic in *Invasion of the Body Snatchers* (1956), "They're here already!" Standing behind you.

Attitude
September 1996

Cock Au Vote

Dame Democracy is a bit of a size queen.

Actually, she's a lot of a size queen. The vital statistics she's really interested in are not the size of the money supply or the rate of inflation, but the heft of a politician's inflatable. All those graphs, statistics, and "swingometers" on election programs are trying to answer the only question that anyone's really interested in: Which candidate is hung like a baby's arm?

And like a lot of size queens, Dame Democracy instinctively feels that men with faces like a bag of spanners are likely to be packing a bigger monkey wrench. This is why we vote for men—and they usually are men—who you might be forgiven for thinking that no one, except the occasional bimbo with ambitions of taking up "smoking," would lay if they were the last men left standing at the office party.

Of course, there are exceptions: Kennedy was a looker and still made the presidency of the United States. But the American public was swayed by the fact that his father had one of the largest penises in the American Underworld, and by Jack's encouraging habit of fucking everything that moved (including one or two things that didn't, such as Cuba and Vietnam).

Nixon was a man who strutted around like the proud possessor of a real tonsil teaser. Perhaps this is why he was inaugurated in 1969. However, a special Senate committee was set up to investigate the true dimensions of his masculine virtue, calling witnesses and threatening to subpoena certain tapes which, it was rumoured, would reveal the whole picture and the full extent of his naughtiness.

Exposed as a liar, Tricky Dick spent the rest of his life in disgrace, proving that there's nothing the public hates more than a pussy teaser who doesn't deliver in the luncheon-truncheon department. His successor, Gerald Ford, didn't measure up either, despite the encouraging impression conveyed by his habit of losing his balance and falling forward whenever he became excited.

President Carter, it goes without saying, had the smallest penis in the history of American democracy. Political scientists had to employ high-powered optical instruments to locate it. The American public was initially fooled by his lazy, self-satisfied Southern drawl and his intimate knowledge of farming practises, but Afghanistan and the Iranian hostage crisis soon revealed him for the short-dick man he was.

So the United States dumped Jimmy and plumped for Ronald "It's morning in America and I've got a woody" Reagan whose virility was so enormous that it even promised to reach out into space, where its vast, hi-tech dome would protect America from penetration by Russian warheads, and eventually cow the Reds into submission. Which indeed it did (even if it actually belonged to Nancy).

That his Republican successor was called "Bush" was hubris indeed. Despite his reaming out of Saddam Hussein in the (en)Gulf(ing) War, it was inevitable that someone called "Slick Willy" would force him to submit. By the same token, Dole never had a chance in 1996 because his name rhymed with "hole."

The last *British* leader to sport a world-class weapon was Winston Churchill, a man who didn't need to read foreign muck like Freud to understand what sucking on a Havana cigar could do for his public image. But then we lost an empire and gained Clement Attlee, someone Churchill once described as a harmless, penisless, grass-grazing creature in the clothing of a harmless, penisless, grass-grazing creature.

Sir Anthony Eden lost his dignity up the Suez Canal in 1957, but his successor, Harold Macmillan, thought he knew what the public liked when he crowed that we'd "never had it so good." Even though he was a promisingly tall man with large feet, the punters decided that they *had* had it better, actually, and dumped him for Harold Wilson who smoked a big black pipe.

But Wilson suffered a foreign exchange crisis that shrank the "penis in his pocket," and he eventually lost to Heath, who had the biggest nose in British political history but who led us into an unwilling threesome with Europe and its garlicky *vagina dentata*. Happily, he was brought to his knees by the stalwart miners (stiffened no doubt by being raised on Attlee's free school milk, which did much to ensure the full muscular development of the lower orders).

So Wilson won again but cut himself off after only two years into his term of office. Callaghan plugged the gap but, despite palling around with the Trades Union Congress big boys, he never quite got over this psychological blow and was forced into the hands of Jeremy Thorpe and the Liberals who massaged his frail majority for him.

Little wonder then that he was no match for Margaret Thatcher, a woman with the largest penis since Winston, her idol. Indeed, it is rumoured that her penis *was* Winston's (which after his death had been pickled in a jar at Conservative Central Office for the day when England would need it to rise again).

But Thatcher proved that even in the greedy world of politics you can have too much of a good thing. The Poll Tax and Europe had nothing to do with her downfall. In-party jealousy over her gargantuan Hampton Wick was to blame. Excessive endowment, you see, can blow up in your face (see also Alan Clark and Michael Portillo).

To appease the hummingbird tendency and heal the rifts in the party, Maggie's successor, John Major, was chosen precisely because, despite his bragging name, he possessed an even smaller penis than Jim Callaghan. After being trampled on for years by Maggie Stryker, Major was a leader that the Tories could at last look down to.

That he managed to defeat Neil Kinnock, a bald Welshman with a large nose who played rugby, is further evidence that size alone isn't always the determining factor. Sometimes the electorate will choose a leader with a smaller penis simply because he doesn't have red pubes.

Shape and symmetry also count for something. Despite a consensus amongst psephologists that Tony Blair's *membrum virile* is bigger than Major's minor, there does appear to be some anxiety as to the actual width and weight of his instrument, and whether it is one of those nasty numbers that has an unexpected bend to the left.

Whoever Britain's next prime minister is, and whatever the dimensions of his electoral tackle, it seems inevitable that Dame Democracy's attitude will eventually echo that of Michelle, a tranny friend of mine who always crows about the size of her latest amour's penis only to announce, usually about a week later, that she's no longer seeing him, saying, "Oh, I didn't like 'im anyway—'e 'ad a *really small dick.*"

Attitude
April 1997

Porn in LA

"You've got to meet my friend, Bo Garret," shouted my LA host, David, above the noise of rubber on concrete, behind the wheel of his oh-so Kaly-forn-i-a convertible Camaro muscle car as we sped along the airport freeway toward West Hollywood. "He's got this really awesome, *totally buff body.*"

Being jet-lagged and slightly intoxicated by the eucalyptus-scented evening air of LA, which always seems to promise so much, no matter how many times you come to this place and are disappointed, I couldn't help laughing out loud.

"What's funny?" asked David.

"Oh it's just so *LA*," I drawled.

"What is?" he asked.

"That expression," I said, *"'totally buff body.'* It tells you so much more than he works out or that he's athletic. I immediately have a vision of a man in a singlet, asking the waiter as if his life depended on it, 'Does that have any budder in it?'"

"Oh," said David. "Bo's not like that. He's a real studman. A real honcho. He's a *pornstar.*"

Ah, so Bo was one of the gay Olympians, a member of the Elect; someone who has been to the mountaintop, seen God, and fucked him—on a motorcycle or in the back of his pickup truck (whilst remembering, of course, to keep those tummy muscles tensed).

"Pornstar" is the only thing that is more LA than "totally buff body"—and, in fact, the two usually go hand in hand unless you happen to have a lens larger than the Griffith Park Observatory telescope. And then you might just get away with a body that's only been slightly dusted. LA is the city of dreams where everyone hopes to become an image, a glitter, a *shine,* to "buff" themselves until their dowdy, small-town selves dazzle the whole world. Especially if they're gay.

Later that evening I found myself sitting at a table with David and Bo in Numbers, LA's only gay bar worth visiting. It's a hustler bar with decor straight out of *American Gigolo* (1979)—smoked mirrors, lots of chrome, black-tiled bathroom—and an ambience straight out of John Rechy.

And, this being the end of the month, the place was also jumping with hunky boys with rent to pay, in haircuts straight out of a Matt Sterling movie circa 1983 (perhaps that's what people are still watching in Idaho and Budapest, the places of origin of most of the boys here), and charitable old men in toupees straight out of *Midnight Cowboy* (you know, the trick that gets a rolled-up newspaper rammed down his throat by Jon Voight) looking for a nephew to help out of his skintight designer jeans.

Bo, David's pornstar buddy, turned turned out to be about six feet four inches tall and about five feet wide, wearing a singlet that might as well have been a couple of shoelaces draped over his shoulders. He had tattoos from his wrists up to his shoulders so dense that he looked as if he had thrust his arms into a vat of multicoloured ink wearing a pair of gloves. He was, in fact, a real honcho, with a deep, vibrating voice and extrovert personality that, combined with his height and width, made him just a tad larger than life—just the ticket in the world of porn.

But, sure enough, when given a menu, Bo quickly scanned its contents and then pointed to an entrée and asked the waiter anxiously, "Has that got any budder in it?" David glanced sheepishly across the table at me while I bit my lip.

LA's "totally buff bodies" of course provide the raw material for the world's largest porn industry, which buffs concave and convex bits for the titillation of millions. Which is just as well, really, since having a "totally buff body" is like a full-time job which, funnily enough, can only be combined with the flexible hours and easy money involved in hustling and porno movie appearances (or writing).

In the 1980s, gay porn in particular became eye-wateringly big business, producing big stars—the biggest of which, of course, was Jeff Stryker, immortalised in half that decade's output of latex, now gathering fluff under the beds of thousands of (still somewhat sore) gays.

In fact, gay porn got so big in the 1980s that it swallowed gay sex and gay men altogether with a disgusting plopping noise. Desire is always the desire of the other, but gay desire became the desire of the VCR. Cheap video equipment combined with cheap exhibitionism to turn practically every gay man under thirty into a "pornstar." Gay sex wasn't really gay sex unless it was in extreme close-up on Super VHS tape. The gay obssession with "visibility" reached its reductio ad absurdum in the ubiquitousness and banality of gay porn. By the 1990s the images of gay porn were so exposed that they were absolutely mainstream. Hard-muscled, naked male bodies with bulging underwear, straight from the box covers of gay video porn, were plastered over the sides of buses and in Times Square. Gay porn wasn't a dirty, exciting secret anymore—just more advertising.

The day after I'd met Bo, David dragged me to see his latest movie which was "previewing" at a porno cinema on Santa Monica Boulevard. Gingerly sitting down on seats that probably hadn't been cleaned since Rick Donovan's penis last got fully hard, we dutifully watched the poor-quality video projection in front of us. The dozen or so other men there seemed to have decided against trusting their trousers to the fertile upholstery and instead were milling about silently in the dark, like extras from a George Romero movie.

The flick itself, a low-budget affair, consisted of a series of uninspired and uninspiring duos rehearsing the same routine—I suck yours, you suck mine, then I fuck you, ta-da! All accompanied, of course, by the same Jeff Stryker karaoke: *"Oh, yeah, you like that, dontcha?"* (I always wanted to see some guy, choking on Jeff's tool, take it out of his mouth and answer, "Well, no, actually, I detest you and *hate* big dicks, but I have a *really expensive* cocaine habit.")

Bad as the film was, the most striking thing about it was the way that nobody seemed to believe in *porn* anymore. Not the director. Not the models. And certainly not the men wandering around the auditorium without so much as a glance at the screen; they looked as if they were just trying to kill time before going home to the wife/houseboy and didn't fancy a round of golf.

In short, everyone was simply going through the motions—as if Pavlov's dogs had grown bored of the ringing bell and no longer salivated but felt like they ought to pretend they were drooling anyway. Eventually, Bo came on and strutted his stuff. In fact, he was quite something on screen; he had a smouldering machismo and presence that put him streets ahead of the competition, as well as a sadistic edge which always goes down well in gay porn (only slightly deconstructed by his habit of calling his partner "my li'l doggy").

Driving back to my hotel with David, along Santa Monica Boulevard through West Hollywood, past the gay bars thronged with gay men waiting to be discovered, or at least bleeped, we passed beneath a huge billboard promoting Ryan Idol's latest big-budget gay porno flick, looking just like an ad for the latest action movie or men's briefs line from Versace. It occurred to me that Bo, gifted as he was in the genital deportment department, was nevertheless simply born too late to ever become a real "porn star."

While the Ryan Idols of this world will continue to make money, and house-proud homos across the Western World will stain their sofas for some time to come, porn itself as an exciting or even vaguely interesting medium is finished. Washed up. Over. Porn has popped its wad, zipped up its fly, and gone home to read a book. Perhaps this is what went through the mind of Joey Stefano, a (rare) bottom boy star in the porno business, when he took a fatal overdose recently. He was, after all, famous for his responsiveness. And timing.

But then, because the distinction between porn and sex is gone, we're all overexposed and overdosed; self-conscious about our lines, actions, and fantasies, even if we're one of those rare, pathetic creatures: a gay man who has never actually appeared in a porno movie. In our pornolised world there's nothing left to show, nothing left to watch, nothing left to imagine, nothing left to *feel*. We've totally buffed sex and desire until there's nothing left but our own reflection.

And it ain't pretty.

Attitude
March 1997

Slick Willy

Now that the allegations about Monica Lewinsky and Bill Clinton have given new, explicit meaning to the expression "Head of State"—and, for that matter, to the president's nickname, "Slick Willy"—how can young people be expected to look up to the leader of the Free World without imagining his hand around the back of their head? How much respect can they have for the man who sits alone in the Oval Office, suspecting, as now they must, that there's somebody helping him with the French polishing under that big shiny desk? Well, at least in the case of young men, they probably have a lot *more* respect than they used to have. Now that the Oval Office has become the Oral Office, you can be sure that the young men of America are paying politics a whole lot more attention these days.

Once, becoming a rock star was the only way a young male could be assured of getting limitless—or, in the case of the Gallagher brothers, *any*—blow jobs from females, without having to pay. Blow jobs, not private jets, have been the reason why young men aspired to be rock stars above anything else. But thanks to Clinton, teenage boys everywhere are now practising making speeches, shaking hands with bewildered people in shopping malls, kissing babies, and making dodgy land deals. The "Elvis" of the White House and his alleged fondness for allowing someone else to play his saxophone has made politics the rock and roll of the 1990s.

Fellatio is the way to a man's . . . well, if not exactly heart then at least his *gratitude*. Even if, as many women will tell you, men are not always grateful enough to actually return the favour (the "sixty-eight," or "I'll owe you one," is a very popular position with straight men—come to think of it, it's a very popular position with *me*). Learn to suppress your gag reflex and you will be invited to all the best parties, even if no one will share your glass.

Most sex surveys show that the favourite sexual practice for straight men is receiving head. This is slightly odd, since oral sex is *perverse*. Biblically speaking, oral sex is sodomy, as it doesn't make babies. Legally speaking, oral sex of any kind is still considered an offence under the puritan antisodomy laws of some states in America (of course, if your partner has a womb transplanted into the back of his or her throat that makes it OK). J. Edgar Hoover kept a list of public figures who were suspected of engaging in "oro-genital" contact because he considered it a sign of subversiveness—and in case he found himself at a loose end of a Friday night.

To some people, a bit of a lick round the family heirlooms can be more shocking than other, more pungent perversities. Jim, my best friend at Junior School, after a surprisingly frank sex-education class in which we'd been told "what gays do in bed," including "sucking one another's penises" (I think our progressive biology teacher had a rose-tinted view of homosexuality as some kind of *mutuality*), sputtered, "It's so, so, so . . . *dirty!* I mean, I can understand putting it up someone's arse-hole," he said shaking his head in disbelief, "but . . . *that!"*

Looking back on it, his remarks made a certain kind of sense. Willies are dirty, bums are dirty, so a bum + a willy = something still dirty. On the other hand, mouths are supposed to be clean, so a mouth + a willy = angry Mummy.

Perhaps it was the "now wash your hands" dirtiness of pee-pees that caused the lad who used to toss me off in the Fifth Year in a darkened, deserted geography classroom every Tuesday afternoon after rugby to make an intriguing offer. "I'll suck it for you next time," he promised, graciously giving in to my increasingly frantic suggestions. "But only," he added, "if you bring some toothpaste to put on it."

On the other hand, maybe I just hadn't yet got the hang of foreskin hygiene. Whatever the truth of the matter, for years I carried a tube of Macleans in my pocket in case I got lucky. To this day I still get an erection every time I brush my teeth.

The idea of what is natural and what is perverse is not always as obvious as a knob in your gob. In renaissance Florence, in a healthy display of civic virtue Kenneth Starr would have approved of, they encouraged their citizens to anonymously denounce one another for crimes against God and nature via bits of paper slipped into a "Sodomy Box" (today, of course, this would be the name of a fashionable restaurant). Tens of thousands of denunciations were made every year. Apparently, most of the population of Florence, male and female, was accused at some time or other.

Some academic who doesn't get out much has spent years sifting through the records and discovered that there was a hierarchy of sodomy. Interestingly, and contrary to the mores that hold sway today for everyone except the president of the United States, it was thought a greater offence and shame to *receive* a blow job than to *give* one—whatever the sex of the participants.

Gore Vidal would have agreed. He has famously mocked the fond notion of the sailor receiving a BJ from a fag being in control and that the cocksucker on his knees as subservient. In fact, Vidal observes, the subservient fag literally has the sailor on the tip of his tongue. And this is a very vulnerable position to find yourself in, bearing in mind how cruel the tongues of fags can be. Interestingly, until the 1970s, homosexuals in the United States tended to be known as "cocksuckers." Which suggests that (a) American women were less interested in playing the hairy oboe in those days, and that (b) fags were probably much more popular after closing time than they are today, "cocksucker" being less a term of abuse than a user's guide.

Traces of the Florentine idea of cock*suckers* as being above the cock*sucked* in the infernal scheme of things survive in the old-fashioned euphemisms for oral sex that used to appear in personal ads— "French active" meaning you wanted to do the gobbling; "French passive" meaning you wanted to be gobbled. The French connection here probably has something to do with the fact that putting nasty things in their mouths seems to be an unnatural national pastime on the other side of *Le Manche* (e.g., garlic, snails, frogs, Gitanes, Pernod, and other people's tongues).

Not that any of this is much help for the compulsive gobbler. After all, who wants to be *actively* French, even if it means you're not the sissy?

The great and incontrovertible truth of oral sex is that no man would turn down the opportunity to suck his own penis. Which is, of course, exactly why God placed it where most men can't reach it with their own mouths. Homosexuality is a sin because it's a form of *cheating*. Sex isn't supposed to be so easy. God gave every man, except Jeff Stryker, a penis shorter than his backbone to make sure that men expended an awful lot of energy doing other things to get blow jobs, things that would seem rather daft and pointless otherwise, but without which the world would be a duller place—things like rock and roll, politics, cunnilingus, and odd jobs around the home.

If homosexuality wasn't discouraged, most of human history would have been nothing more than a man leaning against the wall in the back room of a gay bar in South London with his fly unbuttoned.

Attitude
May 1998

Homo Alone

Large bedroom to rent in nice flat with easygoing bloke with SOH. Suit someone who does a lot of travelling and needs a place to keep spare toothbrush, or non-UK resident looking for an address for tax/housing benefit dodge. No pets, no friends, no conversation. Paranoid introverts who keep themselves to themselves and are also invisible especially welcome. $100-800 pw (depending on how much oxygen you use).

Living with people is rubbish.

But you wouldn't know it to turn on the TV these days; it's full of propaganda about how great it is to have someone else drink the last of your breakfast milk and put toast crumbs in your margarine tub. Hit shows like *Friends* and *This Life* portray shared accommodation as such an incredibly cool, groovy, and exciting way of living that no one, not even yuppies who earn more money in the time it takes to pick their noses than you or I do in a month, would dream of finding a place where they can watch TV in their underwear and leave dirty dishes in the sink for a week without inciting homicide.

Let's get real. Roommates are not trendy or clever. *Roommates are a social disease.*

There is no such thing as *a* roommate from Hell. They're *all* from Hell. *Single White Female* was not a movie; it was documentary. As a *species,* roommates insist on doing irritating, thoughtless, selfish, antisocial, *psycho* things—like *using the bathroom* and *cooking.* They block up the hallway with their pointless to-ing and fro-ing, forcing you to either hide in your room until you're sure they've gone to bed or to manoeuvre around them whilst pretending they're not there (which, let's face it, isn't very dignified). They switch lights on and off—*click, click, click, click*—irritating you and wearing out the contacts in the switches. And they have the effrontery to encourage people to send their personal mail to your address, littering your doormat.

I've even had roommates who actually invite their friends around and sit drinking coffee and laughing in the sitting room, behaving for all the world as if they lived here or something. As if they didn't know that the only reason you allowed them to pay half the rent and use the spare set of keys was to change the bin liners and make the place look occupied when you're out.

Of course, you also get the occasional outright basket case. One loony ex-roomie of mine used to smile and say "Hello" whenever he ran into me. Creepy or what? Sometimes he'd follow me into the kitchen, freaking me out by asking me scary, leading questions like, "So, *how was your day?*" or "Turned out *nice* again, *hasn't it?*"

He lasted less than a week and he would have gone sooner if I hadn't made allowances for the fact that he was from the country.

Even when they realise that you're not interested in idle chitchat they don't give up. They'll try and get chummy another way. One bloke would leave cheery notes outside my bedroom door which I, of course, never replied to. Blackmail shouldn't be dignified with a response. Another used to try and bribe me by leaving Post-It notes on food she'd bought, saying things like "Eat Me!" But these attempts at being ingratiating just grate. Of course I'm going to eat her food. It's in my fridge.

You try vetting them at the interview stage, but it never really seems to work. People just lie. You know the ones: "Oh, I work very long hours and I'm seeing somebody who lives in Bristol—I go down there every weekend." Then, of course, you catch them sneaking in one weekday night *several minutes* before 1 a.m., or you hear them try to tell you that just because their partner died in a car accident they don't plan to go away on the weekends anymore. Yeah, right.

The thing is, you offer an inch and they'll take a mile. Show them a little consideration, such as not spitting in their orange juice or not keeping your dirty socks in the bread bin, and they'll take it as a green light for using the front door on days other than bank holidays and birthdays, instead of climbing up the rope you so thoughtfully hung out of their bedroom window.

There's nothing for it; you've got to be hard. Anyone who's ever had a flatmate will know that it's so easy to be taken for a ride. When you realise you've been had you feel so stupid and foolish, you could kick yourself, or rock backward and forward, your knees drawn up into your chest, moaning and muttering in the corner of your room with the lights turned off for a week or so. It's a frightening world. There are so many kooky people out there who want to move in, take over your life, and move your collection of glass coffee tables a whole inch out of alignment.

The worst thing about roommates is that they make you feel like *you're* the one with the problem. They go running around telling everybody that you're impossible to live with, or a fruitcake, just because you asked them to buy and label their own toilet seat. Really, some people have no concept of hygiene at all.

Or gratitude. I've lost count of the times I've tried explaining to people that the Calor gas stove and the basin of water and sponge in their bedroom are top-of-the-range models and that no one could ask for more. They also never seem to grasp why their door has bolts on the outside.

I once thought I'd found the ideal roommate. I rented to one of those corpses in cryogenic suspension. It worked out very well for a while and we were very happy together, but in the end we had to go our separate ways. We had too many rows about the astronomic electricity bills his frozen nitrogen pump was causing.

Getting rid of the roommate infestation once they've settled can be very tricky. Especially without communicating with them. So you have to resort to indirect methods. A kipper behind the radiator often conveys a helpful hint, as does the old horse's-head-at-the-foot-of-the-bed trick. But I generally find that walking into their bedroom naked in the middle of the night, arms outstretched, moaning, *"Brains! I need brains!"* is most effective. Come to think of it, just walking into their bedroom naked usually does the trick.

Why haven't I done the sensible thing and got a place by myself? Well, I suppose that, if I'm honest, I have to admit that as well as being too mean, in spite of everything I'm a bit sentimental and I sort of like having somebody around to avoid. See, I'm a People Person and I think I'd be a bit lonely if I lived by myself.

I mean, what would I do on a wet Thursday afternoon if I didn't have a roommate's underwear drawer to rummage about in?

Attitude
October 1997

Meat and Greet

Just saying "hello" to another bloke is a dangerous business these days. The reaction to a simple greeting can be so traumatic and terrifying that it takes months of therapy to get over. It's happened to us all at some time or another. But like most cases of senseless violence, it doesn't make the next time any easier. Worse, most men can't even bring themselves to talk about what's happened to them and just keep their feelings bottled up inside. They think that no one will take their suffering seriously.

I'm talking, of course, about being kissed. By *men*.

Time was when you ran into a chap you could rely on a good, firm handshake of the kind that could hand-crank a double-decker bus into life, some steely eyed contact straight out of a Clint Eastwood movie, and a suitably impersonal, gratifyingly emotionally retarded question about wall plugs or brake pads. Not anymore. For all this guff about New Lads, a chap you run into these days is quite likely to pucker up and give you a big, sloppy girly kiss.

Once, this oral intemperance meant that you were either gay, French, or Dickie Attenborough; now it just means that you're under thirty and live south of Watford. Personally, I blame Ecstasy and those Music and Movement classes they introduced in primary schools in the 1970s.

It's all a highly distressing state of affairs, especially if you are, like me, a Yorkshireman who finds the idea of kissing someone you're *in love with* slightly racey and continental, something to be indulged in only after several pints or on public holidays, and then always behind closed doors and curtains after putting the cat out. And definitely *not* when some media luvvie with halitosis and a ripe cold sore looms up in my face, lips flapping like a camel smelling a sugar lump.

Even many of those men who still resort to the old-fashioned hand tug don't seem to be able to execute it properly. Instead of a no-nonsense grip-shake-release routine, they seem to have succumbed to either the limp-lettuce syndrome, or—even worse—the novelty I-have-personality handshake.

These novelty handshakes take various irritating forms: There's the two-hander, popular with Tony Blair, Bill Clinton, and insurance salesmen, where you grip your partner's wrist, forearm, or upper arm with your free left hand and thus demonstrate your sincerity and bankability. Then there's the tricky jive handshakes, employing various combinations of open-palmed slaps, tickling fingers, etc., which are popular amongst black men, white boys who wear their baseball caps the wrong way round, and policemen.

The handshake is obviously in a bad way and slowly bidding us adieu. But how to replace it without getting slobbered over? Well, let's take a look at the options.

Hugs are increasingly popular and are admittedly a good way of avoiding being kissed, or at least forcing them to kiss you on the neck or, better, your collar, rather than on the face. But frankly, these manly clinches are best left to Men's Movement weekends and stag nights, not least because there's always the gruesome conundrum of groin grazing—should I lean into that hug or go for full pelvic contact?

Mooning is also on the up; it's down to earth and carries a low risk of being kissed (unless you have a very pert bottie), and it certainly works for chimpanzees. But for humans it has the drawback of requiring incapacitating amounts of alcohol. Plus, bending over and showing another man your anus can be read as being a little bit too forward.

Rubbing noses suits Eskimos fine and has the advantage of cutting out the hand middleman and getting those respiratory infections straight from source, but it really only suits men of a uniform height in cold weather (in the heat, snouts can slide dangerously out of control on nose shine). Besides, given the proximity of mouths, the danger of being kissed during this maneouvre is altogether too high.

Tweaking nipples has its attractions—it's sporty, it's direct, cheeky, and an effective way of determining whether someone is still alive or not. Unfortunately, it isn't a reliably standardised way of greeting: some men's nipples are impossible to find, while other men's nipples require winching gear and steam traction to get to grips with.

The fascist or Roman salute, right arm erect, palm vertical and facing outward, is smart, businesslike, and masterful. It also signals quite effectively to other blokes that you're not up for the kissy-wissy stuff (unless you happen to be Eric Rohm). Disadvantages include hailing unwanted taxis and having to invade Poland.

Some men, particularly those living in American inner cities and Hulme, like to greet one another by drawing and cocking automatic weapons. Although this does look rather cool in Tarantino movies, and you're probably fairly safe from being snogged, it's somewhat socially limiting in real life and may result in your having to kiss a large hairy cellmate's cheesy penis every morning.

Of course, there's always the strategy of running up to your mate, leaping into the air, and ramming your groin into his face. Mind, this behaviour is generally frowned upon if you haven't just scored a goal. In which case, you'll probably be Frenchied by ten men as well.

Patting buns, particularly when they are large and firm, is satisfying without being sissy and very popular amongst rugby players and American footballers and all those arenas where rumps rule. But there is, of course, always the danger that your hand will slip on an unseen patch of K-Y and end up giving your buddy a tight handshake in a place he won't forget.

Sniffing bums, as man's best friend loves to do, has much to recommend it: you don't have to look at their faces and—well, you don't have to look at their faces. But until more British bathrooms are built with bidets and buttock waxing becomes more widespread, this practice is unlikely to become more popular.

So, all things considered, perhaps the best greeting between men is the one that was employed at my all-boys school. This consisted of grabbing each other's packet and giving it a good, hearty shake. It's direct, it's democratic, it's undeniably friendly, and it's definitely manly. It's primate-tive and antibourgeois. It's practical in cold weather. It's also the very essence of male bonding without any of those nancy niceties. Both men make for the root of the thing they are really hailing—each other's maleness—and making sure that it's still there and hasn't been replaced by some bulky press-on towel. Grabbing one another's goolies gives you the real measure of a man. If the handshake began as a way of proving you didn't have a sword in your hand, why shouldn't it become a way of making sure you have *his* sword in your hand?

True, there is no guarantee that the groin-grab greeting will save you from being kissed, but chances are that the other bloke will have his mind on other things.

Attitude
November 1997

Surprised in Sodom

There is only one gay joke in the whole world. It goes like this: Two gays are shagging away. As they reach their climaxes they get a bit verbal:

> Top to bottom *(basso profundo):* "Tighter! Tighter!"
> Bottom to top *(falsetto profundo):* "Bigger! Bigger!"

This joke tells you everything you need to know about anal sex. I wish I'd told it to my Dutch friend, Hans.

Recently I got a late-night call from this man who looks and sounds exactly like John Lithgow in *3rd Rock from the Sun*. Only more neurotic and more Dutch. He is straight(ish), middle-aged, and with several kids, but is very camp—something which I've always thought suits straight men better (with the exception, of course, of Jeff Banks). Hans' camp is more foppish than effeminate; he approaches everything with a charming self-consciousness and vanity, exactly as if he were an alien performing humanness. Which is, after all, what being Dutch is all about.

"Mark," he says in his delightfully strong accent. "There is shomething I tell you have to. I have shomething very important dishcovered. You must your readers tell."

"What is it, Hans?"

"Anal shex work does not!"

"Sorry, Hans? Can you say that again?"

It turns out he was recently picked up by a Thai boy on the train to work. The lad eyed Hans up casually for about half an hour, "like he was choosing a three-piece suit," then sauntered up to him and said, as if asking for a light, "Would you like to go to bed with me?"

"Well, Mark, my firsht reaction was to think, 'What kind of pershon do you me take for?' And then, I remembered that I am precishely *that* kind of pershon. So, I went home with the boy and I fucked him. And, I might add, I've seen him sheveral times shince."

"I blame you, Mark," he says. "I have obvioushly been listening too much to your talk of a univershal 'bishexual potential.' But Mark," Hans says, sounding like a boy who got knitted socks for his birthday instead of a mountain bike. "You didn't tell me that it really hurts your kidneys!"

I pause before asking quietly, "What way are you doing it, Hans?"

"Well, I lie on my back and he shits on me, facing. Is that not right? Should he shit the other way facing?"

"No, that's OK. But why does it hurt your kidneys?"

"Because he has bones in his ash which into me shtick!"

"Ah, yes. I see. You *are* doing it wrong."

"In what way, Mark, pleash tell?"

"You shouldn't be fucking a boy with a boney ass. It's depraved and should be illegal. Even in Holland."

"You are right! Now I begin to shee why you boysh with big ashes like!"

"Yes, upholstery helps a lot. Get yourself a football player; someone who runs around a lot and eats beef, someone who has a better-sprung ass. Ditch the rice queen."

"But Mark?"

"Yes, Hans."

"I also try letting him me fuck, because I have never been fucked, not even when I was bishexual like everyone else in Holland in the sheventies. And it was *awful*. It wasn't at all like in the books. The first bit was correct. There was pain. But eventually the pain went, as they shaid it would, and I waited for the ecshtasy they about talked, the pleashure-like-you've-never-experienced-it-before moment—but you know, *it never came!* I felt like a turkey which is for Chrishtmas being shtuffed! Shage, parshley, and onion, and cheshtnut—everything. All at once. I don't think I can turkey ever again eat! Anal shex work does not!" Hans is getting agitated now. "You need the world to tell, Mark. *Anal shex work does not!*"

"Anal sex isn't meant to work, Hans," I reply. "But you're not allowed to say that. Everybody, gays and straights, homophobes and homophiles, has too much invested in the idea that anal sex is the most fun you can have with something pointy. Who am I to take that away from them?"

"But shomebody has to say it, Mark! The books," Hans' voice cracks with emotion, "they told me that being fucked would give me the most intense orgashm I've ever experienced. . . . I was so forward to it looking."

"The books are written by tops, Hans."

"Musht be," sighs Hans, sounding like the last gasp of air from a deflating bouncy castle at the end of a rained-off summer fete. "But," he adds brightening a little, "I did shomething during anal shex enjoy."

"What was that?"

"Poppersh. I really like them, you know. At first I thought they were a bit weird, 'Why this shmelly shock thing under my nose during lovemaking am putting?' I thought, and then I really began to have fun with them. Opposhite to what my Thai boyfriend told me, they don't make being fucked any better, but I dishcover they make much more enjoyable *fucking*. Are they unhealthy, by the way?"

"Only if you sniff them."

"Ah. Anyway, I have decided that gay anymore I'm not, but my Thai boyfriend giving up I shan't be. He's too nice, even with his bony ash, Mark. I think he is so beautiful, and who am I to turn him down if *he* wants like a turkey to be shtuffed? It is a very nice thing to offer shomeone, no? Even if not actually that nice to shomeone shtuff."

"It's the nicest thing anyone could do for anyone else, Hans." I concur. "It's real love."

"You are right, though," he muses. "Anal shex appeals precishely because work it doesn't. My Thai boy may not be the best fuck in the world, but at least I know he has no plans for a breakfasht bar, nurshery, and mortgage hell. We are not anywhere going—and when you've had three marriages and children from all of them, that is nice to know, you know? Pusshies are nicer, but they can deshtroy you, Mark. The homoshexual univershe is completely empty and uncomfortable—but I like it that way.

Besides," adds Hans philosophically, "the poppersh my mind off the pain in my kidneys takes."

Attitude
January 1998

Brave Hearts

"WHOAAAAAAHHHHHH!!!!"

Andrew is very, very pissed. I know this because he is doing that dance that some men do when they're very, very pissed. He has his arms in the air, his legs are bent, and his hips are thrusting and gyrating—about six inches from my face. I wouldn't mind, except I've only just met him, it's only 8 p.m., and I'm stone-cold sober.

I've been invited to Andrew's twenty-fifth birthday party by Martin, Andrew's boyfriend. Andrew is, obviously, Scottish. Even if he wasn't very, very pissed, his Scottishness would have been betrayed by the party snacks in the kitchen—cubes of pink Spam on cocktail sticks and garnished with pickled onions.

He lives in a small, forgotten ex-town outside Glasgow. To be precise, an ex-mining town where, like a lot of Scotland, the 1980s didn't really happen, except in the sense of ending the 1970s and putting everyone out of work. No train station, no real shops, except for a Spar market with a long queue for lottery tickets, three off-licences, and a very large sweet shop supplying the local Scots' sugar habit. But the town isn't completely stuck in a time warp; every single person on the streets, including the OAPs, is wearing the latest Umbro.

In Andrew's well-kept council flat, Martin, the square, has taken exception to his boyfriend lap dancing for me and pulls him off. Andrew rushes into the bathroom and locks himself in. Martin hammers on the door, making various threats. Andrew ignores these, remaining in the bathroom and calling out for someone named "Huey" for the next hour.

After admiring the textured wallpaper and the big-patterned carpet while listening to Sínitta's "So Macho" and "Time Warp" from *Rocky Horror* (disco remix) for the umpteenth time, I decide there's nothing for it; I'll have to mingle with the other guests who have begun to arrive. I chat to a stocky, fey forty-five-year-old with a halo of permed red hair around his bald pate. He has "L-o-v-e" and "H-a-t-e" tattooed on his knuckles. He tells me that he worked in the now-defunct local pit from the age of sixteen until it closed ten years ago. Since then, apart from a stint DJ-ing with a mobile disco, he hasn't found another job. Poor bloke, I think in my patronising, Sassenach way, he must be feeling doubly redundant: a miner in a postindustrial era and middle-aged at a gay party. (Of course, he left the party three hours later with two pretty laddies on his arm.)

Chris, Andrew's flatmate, is a lanky, good-looking, dark-haired young man who seems perfectly at home with postindustrialism. He works in a clothes shop in another town (which actually has such things), and his bedroom is a shrine to Girl Power. All four walls and the ceiling are covered in Spice Girls posters and clippings.

"Do you like strong female characters, then?" I ask him.

"Oh yeah," Chris laughs, "definitely. I blame my mother." I *like* Chris, I decide. And this is only partly because he shares with me his secret whiskey stash (at the bottom of a trunk with a picture of Geri— Ginger Spice—on the lid).

It's now chucking-out time at the pubs and a flood of guests arrives, including James, an eighteen-year-old cutie who works in an electronics factory; Fernando, a tubby friendly Spanish Glaswegian travel agent in his midthirties; and, curiously, a family from Essex: Mum, her husband, their twenty-year-old attractive, blonde daughter, Jasmine, and her even more attractive and even blonder fiancé, Jason. A Spice Girl compilation tape is pressed into action and the dancing really gets under way, Chris and James demonstrating the fiendishly complicated routines they've developed for each song.

Essex Mum chats to me in the hall. "We spent ovah five 'undred quid comin' to this party," she boasts. (In Scotland, people from Essex feel like American tourists in Cold War Eastern Europe.) Before I can ask why they'd blown all that money to come to a pouf party in a two-horse town outside Glasgow, she confides in a low whisper, glancing up at my short hair, "You look like a Nazi, you do!"

This may not have been intended as a criticism, however, as she then "accidentally" brushed her hand against my packet. I decide it's time for more Spam on a stick.

A few minutes later all hell breaks loose. *"I'll fackin' kill you!!"* Mum is screaming at the top of her voice. Jasmine has been caught in the loo with one of the dykes by her fiancé, Jason. Apparently, he hit Jasmine and then Jasmine's mum hit him, twice, and, for good measure, threatened to cut his balls off and feed them to him. All in all, it's just as well she didn't know that, by all accounts, Jason had been canoodling in the same bog with young James earlier.

It's interesting, in an academic sort of way, to note here that until the eighteenth century sodomy was thought to be caused by drunkenness. I think this is still the case in Scotland. All the same, despite probably having drunk more than all of us put together, Mum the Essexian remains impervious to the charms of another lesbian, who pretends to be sympathetic and consoling all the while staring at the Aryan Mum's ample bosom.

Jasmine sobs. Jason sobs ("I'm so *sorry*. . . . I *really* love 'er!"). Mum growls. Dad, a nice, affable man, engages me in a blokish chat—as if he weren't married to a woman who made Attila the Hun look like Pee Wee Herman and who wasn't still threatening genocide on the other side of the room. "Great party, innit?" he says, his back to the mayhem.

Chris finally manages to restore order and bundles the Essex drama queens and their ostrich dad out of the door. Perhaps feeling upstaged by the heteros, Jamie and Steve, a gay couple in their early twenties, started shouting and hitting one another. Jamie: *"I fookin' hates yoos!"* Steve: *"Fine, coz I hates yoos, too!"* Jamie storms out of the flat, slamming the door behind him. "They're nae right, those ones," Chris tells me in a confiding tone. "They hit each other with pots and pans."

No sooner is Chris out of the door than Andrew is out of bed, Lazarus like, and drinking again, as if he hadn't been in an alcohol-poisoning coma for the past five hours. "Come in here, Mark," he says, motioning to the bathroom. "There's something I wanna ask yer."

Once the bathroom door shuts it turns out the question he wants to ask is addressed to my tonsils with a tongue still flavoured with puke. At that precise moment the door bursts open and Martin, Andrew's very possessive boyfriend—and my host for the weekend—charges in. Nice timing. Fortunately, the situation is easily defused in the traditional Scottish manner—by refilling everyone's drinks.

It's going on 3 a.m. now and I've had more fun than I've had since I was a teenager. More fun in fact than a thirty-year-old snobby Londoner deserves. These lads are real *pals,* I think, finishing off the last of Chris's whiskey and trying to remember how many people I've snogged this evening and what sex they were. It's so nice to meet a whole nation of people who are nearly as mad and slaggy as me after a few drinks.

I wake up on the sofa the next morning. Blearily, I look at my watch. It's 9 a.m. I have an ache in my balls which I put down to the previous night's drinking. Then I notice a large pair of feet next to my head. Propping myself up and looking blearily and gingerly toward the other end, I make out fat Fernando's head by my feet. His eyes are closed, a contented smile on his face.

He has his right hand between my legs, pulling on my balls.

Attitude
July 1997

Walk Like a Man

Putting one foot in front of the other is a tricky business when you're a bloke. There's so much scope for things going wrong. Seriously wrong. You might be a Dennis Wise on the pitch, but if you walk off it like Frank Spencer you might as well hang up your boots.

How a man moves through the world is the most important and most serious thing he can do. Even though the map of human evolution seems to have gone from quadripedal to bipedal to couch potato, how a man perambulates his pegs is the key to his masculinity. Walking on two legs is, after all, still man's greatest achievement, next to which all his technological triumphs are dwarfed. Neil Armstrong recognised this when he uttered those immortal words: "One small step for me; one giant blokish stomp for mankind."

Unfortunately, Armstrong went and spoilt it all after he stepped off the lunar module by prancing like a fairy in slow motion. The only reason anyone bothered to fish him out of the Atlantic after splashdown was because NASA scientists explained at great length that it wasn't Armstrong's fault, that it was the moon's reduced gravitational attraction that made him walk like a total pranny.

By far the most dangerous part about walking is that it seems to be something, after you get the hang of it and solid foods, you can do without having to think about it. But this is a fatal error. Any man who lets his concentration lapse while walking and begins to allow himself to notice the world around him is bound to come a cropper. For men, the whole point of walking is not to actually get anywhere, but to demonstrate that they never for a moment forget the deadly *seriousness* of what they are doing.

This is why new recruits have to spend so much time square-bashing. In being taught how to walk like men instead of boys, recruits are taught how to move like they mean business—that's to say, how to look like they have rather fewer joints than females and pansies.

But for a lot of civilians, and all off-duty squaddies, the key to successful walking is remaining concentrated on the task in hand but af-

fecting a casual, happy-go-lucky air while executing it—sort of the
walking equivalent to riding a bike without gripping the handlebars.

So we have the "Squaddie Spring," that jaunty little bounce that
TV squaddies do when going down the pub or on leave—elbows out,
hands balled up near their chest or in their high jacket pockets, head
moving from side to side while doing some excessive heel-toe calf-
work. The Squaddie Spring signals that you're full of beans and/or
spunk, that you know how to have a good time, and that you're carefree in a determined, cocky kind of way (see also Persil Skinhead—
"Ahhh, *Mum!*"—walking down the street in a freshly washed white
shirt). This cracking amble is particularly effective if you have a
sports bag/kit bag slung over your shoulder with "Head" or "Man U"
on the side. This look is popular with cheeky chappies everywhere,
such as comprehensive schoolboys—and public schoolboys wanting
to avoid getting beaten up by comprehensive schoolboys.

For those who want a walk with more gravitas, there's the "Bodybuilder Bowl," the key to the successful execution of which is imagining that your limbs are so muscle-bound that you can barely move
them. Arms and legs must stick out at an angle of no less than 45 de-
grees. Note: Head is not allowed to turn without the whole upper
body moving as well (otherwise people might think you have a neck).
Arms are not allowed to move at the shoulder, but are permitted some
movement at the elbow. Legs cannot simply move forward and backward but must move in semicircular, robotic jerks. This lets the world
know that your glutes are so huge they cause friction burns and also
hints that you still have something resembling testicles, despite your
massive steroid abuse. The BB Bowl is popular with bouncers, wrestlers, male masseurs, and lesbians.

For those looking for something with a bit more élan, a bit more romance, there is the "Wide Boy Waltz," very popular on North and
East London housing estates, on football pitches, and in the City. This
requires the same 45-degree angle of the limbs as in the BB Bowl, but
the action is quicker, smoother, suppler, and it advertises *attitude* not
muscle. However, it is absolutely essential that you keep your hips
and arse *completely immobile.* The head, however, *may* move around,
but only to clock birds and nice motors and generally proclaim a
cock-o'-the-roost demeanour. One drawback to the Wide Boy Waltz,
of course, is that it requires hours of practice walking with an XXL
butt plug up your arse.

Another drawback to the Wide Boy Waltz is that it often turns into the "Daddy Dribble" within just a few years. The Daddy Dribble is best achieved by imagining your stride restricted by a pushchair or pram or shopping trolley full of Pampers. Also useful in achieving the right effect is changing your Nike trainers for Hush Puppies and imagining yourself trying to remember what sex with the lights on must be like.

Once upon a time the Daddy Dribble was something that made you respected by men, attractive to women, and guaranteed a lifetime's supply of Marks & Spencer socks every Christmas. Nowadays, it earns you nothing but contempt from men and women alike (although it might get you a date with Melanie Phillips).

Of course, there is a genus of men's walks designed to announce the fact that you are never going to have children or wear Hush Puppies. This is gay walking. Gay walking comes in two different but immediately recognisable styles. First off is the "Mary Mince." To achieve this, walk as if you were negotiating a narrow tightrope in heels whilst trying to describe a perfect circle around your hips with a lighted cigarette. It is also very important that your shoulders should appear attached to your feet by some invisible string. Alas, the Mary Mince is less popular than it used to be with gays and tends to be practised nowadays only by ex-husbands of Sandie Shaw and the lead singer of Suede.

What has taken its place is the "Compton Street Swagger." This very intense form of walking retains within it the ghost of the Mary Mince but is now overlaid with elements of the Wide Boy Waltz and Bodybuilder Bowl (the Squaddie Spring is usually omitted—perhaps because most gays wouldn't be seen dead carrying Head sports bags).

The Compton Street Swagger is, needless to say, very, very alarming and is very, very difficult to describe since it is impossible to identify quite which joints remain rigid and which are allowed movement. In the Compton Street Swagger, rigidity and passivity blend into one versatile action (£70 out calls; £50 in). The overall effect is Graham Norton crossed with Dennis Wise crossed with Rhona Cameron crossed with a black DJ bag and lots of Celtic rings.

Because the Compton Street Swagger is really at least three walks at once, it is by far the most serious and businesslike of all the serious and businesslike walks practised by men today. Perhaps this is why most afternoons British Army drill instructors can be seen on Compton Street taking notes.

As a visibly shocked Armand reassures his extravagantly queeny partner in *The Birdcage,* after witnessing him trying to butch up by attempting to walk like John Wayne, "No, it was . . . fantastic. I just never realised that John Wayne walked that way before."

Attitude
March 1998

Chaste Around the Bedroom

"Marriage has many pains, but celibacy has no pleasures," famously wrote Dr. Johnson back in the eighteenth century, a kinder age when the marital bed was a place of carnal knowledge rather than lesbian bed death. By the early nineteenth century British attitudes toward abstinence had not improved. "Marriage may often be a stormy lake, but celibacy is almost always a muddy horsepond," declared Thomas Peacock, a minor poet who read too much Johnson and had the writing style of a stormy horsepond.

Nowadays, marriage may be less fashionable than furry slippers, but abstinence has never been less popular, and not just with dissolute scribblers looking forward to bedding their next salon groupie. Today *everyone* mocks the idea of a life not ordered around groinal hydraulics. Especially those who aren't getting any. The triumph of eros in the modern world has been so complete that even the famously stiff British upper lip has migrated lower down the national anatomy and ended up as an even-stiffer member.

A nation whose gloriously fucked-up sexual mores used to be epitomised by the smutty, stifled postcard humour of "Carry On" films is now just . . . carrying on. (Or at least that's what they'd like you to think they're up to.) The British are no longer repressed and instead have become what they mistakenly think Americans are—"sexually liberated." The very word "celibacy" is now a national joke, evoking a dirty, Sid Jamesian laugh in everyone who hears it. In fact, the only thing funnier than "celibacy" is a "celibate," a creature considerably more preposterous than unicorns and bug-eyed aliens—or, for that matter, Anne Widdicombe and Britney Spears. In the sexplicit age, chastity has gotten a skinful and fallen flat on her back in the street with her legs in the air and everyone is queueing up to take advantage.

The beginning of the end, of course, was the breakup of Take That. For years these fine, fit, pure young lads travelled Britain, entertaining swooning crowds of single women under twenty-five and single men over thirty-five. Inevitably, the cynical media relentlessly pressed them to answer questions about their sex life and girlfriends. Time and time again the Mancunian angels made it clear that they had no time for such distractions, that they preferred to concentrate on their vocation—demonstrating how sublimation improves your skin tone and muscle definition by selflessly dressing up in uncomfortable leather harnesses and slapping their pert buttocks on stage.

But then, as we all know, Robbie was led astray. He left the holy circle, stopped slapping his buttocks and shaving his chest, took a girlfriend and some drugs, and Take That fell apart. There have even been reports that Gary Barlow is now living with a woman who is not his mother.

The impact of this latter-day Fall cannot be underestimated. Stephen Fry, someone almost as famous for being celibate as he is for the promiscuity of his chins, was obviously shaken. He recently declared that he had met someone and fallen in love, and consequently he could no longer describe himself as celibate. His friends tried to bring him to his senses, telling him that he shouldn't be so silly, that he was just acting in a film and Bosie wasn't really his boyfriend, just a historical figure. But to no avail.

Which is grave news indeed. And not just because it means that someone other than his doctor must now see Mr. Fry unclothed. With the members of Take That being chased around their bedrooms instead of being chaste, and Stephen dipping his nib instead of quipping, what future has frustration? Kenneth Williams would be spinning in his lonely grave, if his nose didn't get in the way.

Nowadays everyone has to at least pretend to be porking somebody, or preferably some*bodies,* and the details of who, how, where, and with what accessories have, by federal law, to be splashed across the front page of national newspapers, or else you risk being intimately and relentlessly probed by Kenneth "No Vaseline" Starr. Celibacy is no refuge; in fact, it's simply the biggest sex scandal of all. Even priests aren't allowed to be celibate anymore. Especially priests. Any self-respecting sky pilot these days has to fiddle with choirboys' cassocks, elope with his housekeeper, and get caught being gang-banged by navvies at their local sauna, preferably in the same week.

Which is also bad news for bachelorhood. There are now only three kinds of men permitted—gay, straight, and in the closet. So films like *A Bit of Scarlet* "out" Sherlock Holmes and Dr. Watson as gay lovers. Of course, this is laughable. If they'd been gay lovers, there would have been no classic genre, just one, unfinished short story—they would have had a flaming, furniture-thowing row by page three and separated by page four, Watson bitterly contesting custody of Holmes' tobacco ash collection.

It's no better news for women. Granted, they were never really allowed the dignity of bachelordom—they were either nuns or just old maids. But nowadays they are old maids at fourteen if they haven't already serviced the entire football team. Worse, with the advent of "lesbian chic," girls can't even be friends these days without being expected to jump into each other's cargo pants. To be indecent in this climate of filthiness requires real inventiveness. If punk happened tomorrow, it would be a pop band called The Nice Girls singing, "What I really, really want . . . is a cream bun and a good book," or "Two Become a Game of Whist."

And so the last remaining genitally continent Brits are left looking to is Sir Cliff "Lucky Lips" Richard, the Rorke's Drift of celibacy, the Maginot Line of chastity, the Berlin Wall of bacherlordom, a man whose abstinence is a national institution—an institution which will undoubtedly persist at least as long as the Royal Family (he's already the Queen Mum's official understudy), the Church of England, and Sterling. Well, hopefully a bit longer.

But all men are mortal, even our Cliff. About a thousand years ago, just before the Norman Conquest and the last craze for tapestries and eye patches, it looked for a moment as if he would be tempted away from his lifelong partnership with the well-known show business manager J. H. Christ by tennis ace Sue Barker's powerful service. Fortunately, Cliff managed not to rise to the challenge. Perhaps he gained inspiration by listening to his own very wise, very insightful song of experience, "Devil Woman."

But for all fleshly creatures, mortality takes its toll, one way or another. We are all implicated in the original sin of those sex maniac nudists in Eden and must pay the price, even if we don't actually get to enjoy doing it ourselves. Even Cliff, uncontaminated by contact with any womb other than the one which delivered him, and now almost completely fleshless, can't live forever. Eventually, the surgeons will run out of skin to staple and his face will implode, taking with it England's last celibate.

Only then, when his body is laid in state at Madame Tussaud's and millions of inconsolable housewives, mums, and grandmums queue around the block to pay their last respects to the Young One, will the nation understand what we have lost.

Yes, it's currently fashionable to sneer at Sir Cliff's audience, to dismiss them as foolish old frustrated women who don't know any better. But actually, who knows better than housewives, mums, and grandmums how overrated sex is? What its costs are? How frustrating satisfaction can be? If they were around today, Mrs. Johnson and Mrs. Thomas Peacock would agree, I'm sure, with the early Boy George that sometimes they'd rather have a cup of muddy horsepond.

Attitude
July 1998

A Fireman's Hosiery

"Why are the firemen in Paris so popular?" I ask my host as he speeds me from la Gare du Nord down Blvd de Magenta in that hair-raising nonchalant Parisian way which conclusively does away with Princess Di conspiracy theories.

He shrugs, taking both hands off the wheel as we approach a hair-pin corner at high speed. "Beecause they all look like pornstars. They are all veery feet, young, clean-cut, and with short 'air." (Even in France, "porn" is defined by Matt Sterling rather than Pierre Cadinot.)

"In Britain they are usually fat and forty," I whine. "Except for the twelve who like to pose for calendars."

"Eef you go out of Paree eet ees the same," he says, screeching to a halt at a red light. "But 'ere the firemen are run as a branch of the meeleetaree. They are 'and-picked from the other serveeces, and 'ooever does the 'and-peeking 'as great taste."

At that precise moment, a big, shiny fire engine draws up next to us at the lights, throbbing seductively. A smooth, meaty forearm rests on the top of the red cabin door. Behind that, an anonymous square jaw and chin juts out beneath a fetching blue cap, brim pulled rakishly over the nose. Suddenly, I understand why my host drives so reck-lessly. And why Princess Di's ugly death was not without some re-deeming beauty. After all, her horribly battered body would have been lifted out of the twisted wreckage of that Mercedes by *pompier* forearms guided by a *pompier* chin.

Everyone in Paris—women, men, dogs, street furniture—wants to shag *les pompiers*. Maybe this metropolitan-wide infatuation with men who hold big hoses is why you see a fire engine rushing down the middle of the boulevards, lights flashing and horns sounding, ev-ery five minutes. Everyone knows that the French are an accident-prone race—look how they managed to lose most of their aristoc-racy's heads. And Canada. But for all this national clumsiness, no amount of *frite* pan fires, *crimes passionel, coups,* and pussies up trees can explain the fact that Paris seems overrun by firemen.

No, the Parisian fire department answers a call much deeper in the Gallic psyche than mere ineptitude. *Les pompiers* are really answering a cry for help that is as much metaphysical as literal. Parisians, you see, want to be rescued from Paris.

This is something that most visitors to Paris cannot grasp. They see the grand architecture and opulent museums; they taste the fine food; they mingle with the busy, well-dressed, sophisticated, ever-so-slightly smug natives on the wide streets, in the efficient Metro, the bustling bars and cafes, and believe the myth that Parisians want them to: that they are happy being Parisian—that, in fact, anyone not Parisian is an unfortunate wretch, perhaps deserving of pity but certainly not accurate directions to the Eiffel Tower.

But no one is ever so sophisticated or so happy being what they are that they don't want to be rescued. Especially by a square-jawed man in a big shiny fire engine.

The city's love affair with *les pompiers* is something Edmund White overlooked in his book about twenty years of shagging men in Paris, *The Farewell Symphony.* But then, perhaps this isn't so surprising. As George Orwell put it, to an American, Paris is a cross between a museum and a brothel. Paris is perhaps the only place in the world where you can shag yourself clever. *Les pompiers* are far too American, far too nobly dumb, for someone who's travelled all the way across the Atlantic to get away from jocks and get into Proust (or at least, get away from jocks who weren't into poufs who read Proust).

Ironic, though, that White should be the biographer of Jean Genet— someone who wouldn't have overlooked the charms of Paris's firemen. Covering the infamous police riot at the 1968 Democratic Convention for a left-wing magazine, Genet famously praised the "strong thighs" of Chicago's finest as they enthusiastically truncheoned demonstrators. Nor did he shrink from praising the cruel Teutonic appeal of German troops on the streets of Paris and his urge to service them during World War II either.

When the Wermacht left, the U.S. Army arrived and this time the whole of Paris could open its legs unashamedly. Like Genet, Paris is a city of ill-disciplined bottoms looking for uniformed tops that will order them around the bedroom but not around the living room when they have friends visiting. The marvellous thing about the paramilitary chic of *les pompiers* is that since they carry no guns or power but *look* like they do, they are a politically correct repository for politically incorrect fantasies.

Emerging out of the Metro the day after my encounter with the forearm fire engine, my eyes immediately caught a sexy stud in natty, tight-fitting, navy-blue dungarees and a cute cap pulled down over his snub nose ambling toward me. With a utility belt around his waist, which managed to look like a gun belt (nicely framing his pert ass which swaggered sexily as he walked), he was clearly as much in love with the idea of being *un pompier* as I was with the idea of him. We passed almost lingeringly, and our eyes met two or three times as we both turned to check one another out again (and check that we were still checking one another out).

Steely Anglo-Prussian discipline and presentation struggling with, and not quite containing, a basic Gallic tartiness underneath. *Much* sexier than any pornstar.

I hovered on the pavement for a minute or two or three, watching him restore order and safety to Château d'Eau with perhaps an extra little swagger in his gait, which I'd like to think was his gift to me. And then, whatever local emergency or neurosis had summoned him and his noble pals dealt with, they climbed back into their engine, which revved into life with a sexy, stupid, but splendidly competent roar, and sped him out of my life forever.

The next day, however, I have lunch with my own little *pompier.* I expect he's actually far too bright to be a *pompier,* but he looks like one, with his strong chin, boyish face, clean-cut looks, and suedehead haircut. In his midtwenties, J has the sort of laugh that you could listen to for the rest of your life. He throws his head back and lets out a little chuckle—"Ha-ha!"—like a terrier pup that wants his tummy tickled. He has no shame and talks to complete strangers at the next table like they are old friends; they look at him slightly bemused, until he does that laugh, and then they know that they have always loved him too. Like those boys in blue, my J knows he is adorable and that all of Paris wants him.

Alas, J isn't my little *pompier* at all. He has a boyfriend. Who calls him on his mobile during lunch. Twice. Long, awkward, intense conversations, with head turned downward and half away. J's untroubled face clouds over like a shower in August. Finally, it dawns on me that J isn't going to rescue me after all. That, in fact, he's being rescued from *me*.

Tant pis.

Attitude
August 1998

Le Sex Club

"Le sex club" is the happening thing in Paris, so I'm told, with a new one opening practically every week. They now almost outnumber gay bars. Parisian gays, apparently, are fed up of chatter about the latest boy band and Brad Pitt's abdominal muscles and are instead into *chaud* cock action.

The particular sex club I find myself in this afternoon is probably the place to find *le chaudest* cock—it's a sauna. F120 (c. £15) purchases you the use of first-class steam rooms, Jacuzzi, weight room, and solarium. None of which I've used. Instead, like most of the clientele here, I'm pacing the rat-run network of corridors, nothing but a towel around my waist, holding in my belly and puffing out my chest, sliding past dimly lit rooms with the door ajar revealing men reclining, propped up on one elbow, playing with themselves and staring at you in what I suppose they imagine is a seductive way. Or flat on their stomachs, bums exposed to the world and the unkindness of strangers.

As I pass, again and again, men with towels tied around their waists, holding their bellies in and puffing out their chests, no one says anything. Instead, blank eyes rake up and down my body as if considering it for lunch. My eyes return the compliment. It feels like I am an extra in a George Romero zombie movie, set in ancient Rome.

At least, I think, this place doesn't smell too bad. My Anglo prejudices had led me to believe that French men—even gay French men—weren't the most profitable of markets for personal hygiene products. In fact, despite being very warm, this place smells quite pleasant; by a lucky nasal coincidence, everyone seems to be wearing the same aftershave—some Davidoff-type scent. Then, hearing a strange clicking noise behind me, I turn around and am squirted in the eye by some Davidoff-type scent from an automatic air-freshener dispenser.

In few areas of life is the gap between words and what they purport to represent so painful as in the area of commercial sex. "Le sex club" is turning out to be very unsexy indeed. I feel strangely sheepish, like a man dying of thirst in the midst of a flood. Once you pursue "sex" with relentless zeal it is bound to elude you. When men go chasing

cock they literally end up chasing their own tail. The agonising boredom of le sex club is the very same quality as its appeal—that there is
no mystery at all about what everyone is there for. Sex in such a place
is so inevitable, so expected that it becomes impossible. At least on
Hampstead Heath, a place where as yet there's no admission fee, you
can suspend disbelief and kid yourself that the lad you happen across
tied to a tree, with a condom dispenser surgically attached to his leg,
at 3 a.m., in the rain, has just got lost on his way back from the local,
or is walking his dog.

But after an hour or so of this aimless wandering around le sex
club, a funny thing happens. You feel so foolish at having spent so
much time in such a foolish place that you become desperate—not
for sex itself, but not to leave le sex club without having had "le sex"
that you've spent all that time and money pursuing. The humiliation
of leaving such a place with full seminal vesicles is much greater than
having sad sex with someone you can only find slightly attractive if
you focus on one part of his body *to the exclusion of everything else.*

So I begin to rescan the bodies and faces of the by now too-familiar
men as they pass, hoping to find some previously missed characteris-
tic or detail that will trigger some kind of sexual response or, better, a
porn video memory that will permit me to perform the hydraulic act
that will release me from this Inferno of *ennui.* Eventually I decide,
with a pathetic lack of imagination, on a young man with very large
pectoral muscles that look very "porno."

Of course, words are out of the question. So looks are exchanged
instead—just enough to lead me to believe that there is hope, but con-
veying just enough guardedness on the part of Le Tit Boy to let me
know that his interest shouldn't on any account be taken for granted,
and that, anyway, he has to see who is around the next corner and
whether his biceps are bigger than mine. So I follow him around the
maze at a discreet distance—close enough to signal my interest, yet
far away enough to bail out if necessary, feigning disinterest.

If you've ever played pocket billiards (the game, not the self-
abuse), you will be familiar with the scenario of trying to get three
tricky silver balls into their corresponding holes simultaneously. Le
sex club is a life-size version of pocket billiards. Somehow I have to
arrange for Le Tit Boy, myself, and an empty room to be in the same
place at the same time so that I can shove him into it, slam the door
shut, and jump on him before he has a chance to change his mind. Not

an easy task when there's only a limited number of rooms and they're all occupied by people who, judging by the length of time they spend in there, seem to be doing a spot of redecorating,

"But," I hear you say, slightly puzzled, "wouldn't it be easier speaking to the lad and then looking for a vacant room together?" Yes, it would be much easier. But it would also be cheating and result in your immediate expulsion and disbarment from Le sex club (besides, he's French, and the accent would make it more difficult for me to *faire le* fucking).

After what seems hours of trailing Le Tit Boy around the circles of sodomy, I finally happen across an empty room, leap into the doorway, and lean against the doorjam nonchalantly. Or as nonchalantly as you can, standing practically naked in the doorway to a room with no windows or fittings except a sticky plastic mattress. And I wait for Le Tit Boy to make another circuit.

Of course, he chooses this exact moment to vanish. After half-an-hour of excruciating and pointless leaning nonchalance, I begin to get a cramp in my shoulder and decide that someone else with bigger biceps and rather better at pocket billiards must have beaten me to it. Finally, I screw up the resolve to leave. But I need to shower off the air-freshener cologne, which by now is coated to my body like, well, sperm. Opting for the privacy of a shower cubicle, I suddenly notice a hole in the wall at waist height that must be at least four inches in diameter. I find this quite shocking—after all, there are rooms here for this kind of thing.

But shocking isn't that different from aroused, especially in a place where everything is so predictable. So I peer through the hole. On the other side a young man with his mouth open beckons to me with his finger. Since I am a guest in Paris and it never does to offend one's hosts, I gingerly stick my dick through the breach in the partition. He seems to appreciate this. And why shouldn't he? Amongst other things, it's an extraordinary act of trust, sticking your dick through a hole in a wall.

As I orgasm, my cheek pressed against the cold, wet Formica partition, unseen but expert lips working overtime on the other side, it occurs to me, for some unknown reason, that I might just possibly have a problem with intimacy.

But at least, I think to myself, that means I'm *fashionable*.

Attitude
September 1998

Love Thy Neighbour

Relationships are difficult things to maintain in this day and age. Especially in the metropolis, where people are too busy with their own lives to find the time to share them with someone else.

But not for me. I've been successfully seeing someone for years. We recently had our tenth anniversary. And you know, I feel so proud of us and so superior to those sad singles out there who just can't get it together. We have the perfect relationship. We never row. We give each other space. We don't get jealous or possessive. We don't ask too many questions. In fact, you could say that we live our own lives. And yet we always look to one another when one of us feels lonely or a bit blue.

The secret of our success? Well, apart from the fact that we're obviously just much luckier, happier, less dysfunctional people than most, I think it has something to do with the fact that, like a lot of modern couples, we don't live together and aren't always round each other's flats, even though we're just a stone's throw apart.

Or maybe it's something to do with the fact that we don't know one another's names. Or that we've never spoken. Or that we've never had sex. Or that we've never actually met.

The man in my life is my neighbour.

Looking back, it's easy to see now that we were meant for one another. We have so much in common! For instance, we have the same postcode and we shop at the same newsagent. Spooky, eh? But the real clincher, the incontrovertible evidence that we were meant to share our lives, is that he lives directly across the road from me on the same floor.

And he's middle class. Of course, our relationship wouldn't be possible if we lived in a working-class neighbourhood. Common people have these antisocial things called curtains in their windows. They treasure their privacy. It makes them feel middle class and semidetached. Middle-class people, on the other hand, like to feel aristocratic and landed, or at least a bit bohemian. They let their windows stare arrogantly and unblinking because they want to affect disinterest in the opinion of the world and don't want to acknowledge that there might be other people living within voyeuristic distance of them, even when they're training zoom lenses on their neighbours' bedrooms themselves.

It took me a while to learn this class fact of British window life. When I first moved into this neighbourhood I used to *draw my curtains,* twitching them the way I'd been brought up to when I wanted to spy on the neighbours. If I was actually caught at the window staring at someone—like, for instance, my silent-movie boyfriend across the road—I'd duck beneath the sill and then crawl out of the living room on all fours. Or I'd suddenly pretend to be trying to remove a minute mark on the window pane with my fingernail. But no longer. I've become naturalised upper middle class. I had my curtains removed and I stare at my neighbours in broad daylight, scratching my balls while they stare back picking their noses.

Of course, I only really have eyes for one neighbour, my see-through sweetheart directly opposite. Thanks to a happy combination of topography and sociology, we have shared each other's lives for the past decade. We've witnessed each other's triumphs and traducements. We've redecorated at least three times. We've seen our middles thicken and our hair thin. We've eaten pizza in front of the telly together in our underwear.

And never a bad word—or, in fact, a word of any kind—exchanged. Although we've passed in the street many, many times, we've never actually met. I don't think we've even looked one another in the eyes. The moment we see one another coming we become very interested in the pavement design or stoically fix our eyes on the middle distance and walk quickly past, holding our breath. In other words, we've managed to incorporate some of the fun games into our relationship most people only get to play *after* they split up.

But yes, sometimes it hurts having to deny our love in this way. Sometimes I want to speak to him, to ask him his name, his star sign, what kind of music he likes, and why he bought *that* sofa. But I realise that it would be a mistake. Our love is conditional upon never knowing the answers to these questions. Even acknowledging that we know one another would be social disaster. Not least because if we ever spoke we'd have to put up curtains.

And then, of course, I have to think of his situation. He's not ready to tell the world about Us. I think his family would find it hard to accept our relationship. And I suspect his girlfriend wouldn't under-stand it either. People can be very narrow-minded and traditional, even in London. There's so much prejudice directed at the love that dare not draw the curtains. People think that just because there's a couple of panes of glass and a major road between you, your relation-ship is somehow invalid, or not quite "normal."

And before you accuse me of being a doormat here, let me just say that we both need our freedom; he has his girls and I have my boys. But when all's said and done, we both know that these people we do humdrum, silly things with, like talk and touch, will come and go and that it is mute, chaste us that endures. (And besides, we both like to watch, if you know what I mean.)

Anyway, I don't *fancy* the guy. Please. Just because you spend ten years staring at someone in their living room doesn't mean you find them attractive. Ask any ordinary, non-window mediated couple. Our relationship isn't about sex; it's about mutual respect, genuine admi-ration, and a deeply shared fear of commitment.

Oh, I'd be lying if I said I haven't tried flirting with others from my window, like a buzz-cut Rapunzel. I've even tried to catch the eye of Les Dennis, who also lives on the other side of the road. But it isn't the same. It doesn't feel so special. Millions of others can watch him through glass in their living rooms and never get to speak to him. Plus, he's a couple of doors down and I can't see much through his window.

Then there's the guy with the odd floppy haircut and the beanpole body. For years I watched him come and go, fringe waving from side to side like one of those car-wash brushes after they stop spinning, and thought, "Oh, he's a bit of a Bernard Butler clone." Then, one day, I saw him with a guitar case and realised that he actually *was* Bernard Butler. Which explained those antisocial shutters on his win-dows. Only a *pop star* would stoop to such a thing.

So I stick with my pane pal across the way. If only because I see more of him than anyone else. But I have to say I don't approve of his new girlfriend. She looks the kind that shops at IKEA.

In the blinds department.

Attitude
December 1998

Monkey Business

Grief these days seems to come easier when it's attached to the death of celebrities. Especially when it's seen as the end of not just a media relationship, but an age of innocence. For some it was the death of Diana, Kennedy, Lennon, or Martin Luther King. For me it was the death last year of that international icon, superstar, and chimpanzee, Roddy McDowall.

What TV giveth, TV taketh away. BBC1 Sunday lunchtime news, to be exact: "Roddy McDowall, the British actor best known for his role in *Planet of the Apes* (1968), has died of cancer at his LA home, aged seventy-six. He never married." I was eating some toast and Marmite at the time and began to choke.

You see, I'd grown up with Roddy. In the 1970s, during the long, tedious summer holidays (alcopops and incest hadn't been invented back then), they would show kids' programmes in the mornings. Mostly it was 1950s schlock that didn't cost them too much: stuff like "Casey Jones," about an extremely unpunctual engine driver who, when he wasn't being delayed by pesky logs and landslides, red Injuns, and cute, lame ponies, used to lean out on the window of his footplate, beaming and winking at the camera while pulling on his whistle.

But the jewels in the crackerjack crown of morning kids' TV in the 1970s were *Lassie* and *Flipper*. And Roddy had the unique privilege of being both Lassie's *and* Flipper's best friend. How I wanted to be Roddy! He never went to school; his parents drove him around in huge estate cars with big picnic hampers in the back; his mother was always perfectly turned out in a hoop skirt, smiling and cooking pancakes or pouring out frosty glasses of homemade lemonade. His dad was a lumberjack/park ranger/fisherman with a very square jaw who grinned a lot and wore check shirts rolled up to show off his big arms. Best of all, Roddy lived in the mountains or on the beach and was always in barefoot and shorts, and his best friend in the whole world was a devoted animal that would communicate extremely important information about forest fires or missing persons with some barks or squeals that only he could interpret.

Yes, Roddy had it all. His was the fantasy 1950s lifestyle that any 1970s British suburban kid would aspire to. For years I fiercely resented my parents for not making my life just like Roddy's. (And, by the same token, the retro 1980s is to be blamed on cheapskate 1970s BBC children's programmers.)

How weird, then, to watch TV with the grownups in the evening back then and see Roddy himself grown up and wearing a monkey suit in the dystopian science fiction film series *Planet of the Apes*. Apparently, man had destroyed himself in some apocalypse and buried the Statue of Liberty up to its elbow. The animals, in the form of apes, had taken over and Roddy was playing a cross between Flipper and Lassie, befriending the last humans, led by Charlton Heston, whom the apes had caged. I particularly remember the odd way Roddy had of cocking his head to one side while looking up at Moses with his big brown eyes, begging for a petting that never came (at least not before I had to go to bed).

Years later, when I was grown up, too, or as grown up as I'll ever be, I had the pleasure of looking into those big brown eyes myself when I was interviewing a has-been Hollywood actress for a glossy American magazine.

I was sitting down with Ms. X at Orso's, a swanky Italian restaurant in Beverly Hills, when suddenly she gasped, "Oh! There's *Roddy!*" and waved at a table close to ours where a brown, skinny, elderly man was sitting with another slightly less elderly and much fatter man and lots of papers. It wasn't until he came over to our table to introduce himself, and I could see those monkey-yet-strangely-human eyes, that I realised it was Galen. He shook my hand a little too firmly and a little too long and gave me a brazen once-over with those glittering round eyes that had once reflected the miniaturised and slightly humiliated image of Charlton.

"What a surprise to see you here!" Roddy trilled to my companion in that charmingly singsong, syrupy voice of his. "I'm just lunching with my agent." Ms. X introduced me as "a journalist from *Glossy American Magazine*. He's interviewing me!" she said, a bit too surprised at the idea herself.

"A journalist, eh?" said Roddy, looking me up and down again. "That's a good one! I've never seen shoulders like that on a journalist before!" He leaned toward me and hissed in a stage whisper, liver-spotted hand held to the side of his face, "Watch her now, Mark! She's *wicked!*" And with a lascivious wink and a leathery grin, he sauntered back to his table. My audience with Galen was over.

Meeting a legend like this—probably the only celebrity I've ever wanted to meet—was shocking enough. But I was even more shocked by the way he was quite obviously and openly *fag*. It was like having Casey Jones make a pass at you. Call me naïve, but I never thought of Galen as having any kind of sex at all.

Looking back and rewriting history as we do, I can now see, *of course,* that Roddy's entire Hollywood career was queer as a coot (a creature which I think actually makes an appearance in one of the *Lassie* films swapping Judy Garland stories with Roddy). The boy with the perfectly mad nuclear family, who had no real friends, who developed overintense relationships with animals, who grew up to be an ape with twinkly eyes, identifying with humans stranded in a world where they were now the oppressed minority.

Then there's *It!* (1967), a reworking of the Frankenstein story, which is probably the queerest movie ever made. Roddy plays a meek assistant museum curator in London, living with his domineering mum. His boss's death lands him the job of running the museum and ownership of a two-thousand-year-old statue, which comes to life to do his bidding. Naturally, it all goes to poor Roddy's head (he can't negotiate that pesky oedipus complex), and he destroys half of London trying to impress an uninterested woman, who knows a Lassie when she sees one. Roddy is finally locked up but escapes after he hears his mother has died, hijacks a hearse, kidnaps the girl, and heads off with the golem and the trophy bitch to the cemetery where his mother is buried.

I think most of us, one way or another, have been *there.*

Roddy's greatest asset was also his greatest giveaway—his eyes. In person, they were the faggiest eyes I've ever seen—that bright, alert, hungry quality which in its innocent form is mostly found in children and small animals, but which in adult men is the nearest thing to a reliable indicator of inversion.

On TV they just looked very friendly.

Attitude
February 1999

Dear Hero in Prison

"Hello? Is that the *Crimewatch* Grass' Em Up Hotline? Yes, well, I was watching that item about that evil, thickset young man with short hair in the Adidas top who callously raided that 7-Eleven in Wolverhampton at gunpoint, giving a pensioner angina, sending a pregnant woman into labour and scaring a small furry puppy . . . ."

"Oh yes, sir, a very nasty business. Do you have some information about the crime or the whereabouts of the suspect that you'd like to share with us?"

"Erm, well, no, not exactly. I only wish I did."

"Well, what is the purpose of your call then, sir?"

"Umm. I was sort of hoping, y'know, that you might let me know when you've caught him."

"Ah, keen to see him behind bars, eh? I'm not surprised. A particularly vicious villain."

"Mmm. Yeah. An absolute *menace*. I definitely want to see him *banged up*. But I was wondering if you could let me know—once you've caught the little thug—where you're holding him?"

"And why's that, sir?"

"I'd like to visit him. And smuggle drugs to him in a rolled up condom when we French-kiss good-bye."

Click.

"Hello? *Hello?*"

Those TV snoop shows are such a tease. They tell you all about these young crims, their naughtiness, and their violent ways, give you a detailed description of their shady appearance, arrange for beefy lookalikes to reenact their heinous crimes, or even show actual CCTV footage of them in shifty action—behind the wheel of stolen Ford Escort Cosworths or romantically holding up the Texaco garage at 4 a.m. And then they ask YOU how to get in touch with them. The cheek!

There's something about a boy with trouble in his eyes, a swallow on his neck, and an arm almost as long as his record—one with those couple of veins running underneath the forearm up to a thick wrist attached to a large, callused hand with nicotine-stained, sovereign ringed square-ended fingers, and bitten, dirty nails. . . .

Sorry, I got a bit carried away there. Is it just me, or are all those TV true crimes shows turning anyone else into Jean Genet? Oh, right. Just me then.

Maybe it's a sign of a sheltered life, but I never seem to find those "suspect" descriptions they read out on *Crimewatch* as alarming as I do arousing. Even the photofit pictures of suspected rapists they flash on the screen seem vaguely erotic to me. Not that I have any fantasies of being raped, mind—just fantasies of raping some rapists. My "have a go" heroism isn't inspired by an exaggerated sense of justice, more an exaggerated sense of lustiness. Rapists are understandably usually described by their victims as "swarthy," "powerful," and "well-built," and tend to choose the most bestial, brutal, bruiser attributes available from the photofit kit. (I wonder if you can get those kits through mail order, in full-body versions? Oh, right, yeah, I forgot; it's called gay porn.)

Or maybe it's just the glamour of it all that gets me. Crime is, after all, just a bit rock and roll. At least from a safe distance. To a nice boy. As that Last of the Famous International Niceboys Mozza famously put it, "it's written all over *my* face." More than one friend of mine has said to me lately that I should go to prison—and without my even confessing my *Crimewatch* fetish. "You'd just *love* it there," they've asserted, sending me down to a long stretch with complete conviction. Okay, okay, I'll admit there's a certain appeal attached to the idea of sharing a cell and bad food with a young villian from Romford called Dean, winning his trust, helping him with his appeal, teaching him to read, introducing him to the metaphysical poets and the literal meaning of "arse bandit." But I spent ten years at boarding school so I feel I've done more than enough time inside, thank you very much.

Being on the outside looking in as a prison visitor or pen pal seems to have more going for it. And I'm certainly not the first to notice this. After all, it's probably quite sensible to fall in love with someone whose whereabouts you can be sure of for the foreseeable future. People mock those women who marry cons doing life. But these women aren't stupid; they understand the nature of desire better than most. Not only is disappointment and disillusionment postponed possibly forever (if you're really lucky they might die inside), but also your man is already being punished for being the complete bastard that he'll undoubtedly turn out to be. You don't even have to call the police in tears at 2 a.m. on a Sunday morning, having barricaded yourself in the bathroom, or even go to the trouble of separating; it's all included in the package.

However, I suspect that I wouldn't get very far as a prison visitor. The authorities would spot my game straight away and only let me see seventy-year-old jailbirds with no teeth and halitosis. I need a subterfuge. I'd become a probation officer if I wasn't such a pushover: "Sorry I didn't call today or for the last three weeks, Mark," they'd say. "But I 'ad to look after me dear old mum. You know 'ow it is. D'yer want to massage me back again?"

I could, I suppose, if I was really desperate and totally without shame, become a policeman. It is, after all, a way of making chasing villains and feeling their collars into a career. But it would be too much like giving in. Plenty of people think I'm fuzz already. More than once I've been offered free drinks by the management in gay pubs, and would I like to take this wad of fifties and buy some for my mates down the nick? (I think this has something to do with looking repressed, uptight, and homophobic.)

Hanging around pool halls used to do the trick, but that bloody injunction they put out on me is still in force. I could get a job in a building society in Swindon or a sub-post office in Uxbridge (which is where, as you'll know if you follow *Crimewatch*, most holdups happen) and wait to be done over. But I was hoping for a relationship that was a bit more than wham, bam, hand over the jam, y'know?

Or I could just move to Kilburn and "forget" to lock the steel shutters when I'm at home of an evening. But that sounds a bit too real and a bit too scary to me. What if the thieves should turn up when I haven't brushed my teeth or done the hoovering? Sod's Law dictates that crimes never happen when you want them to (e.g., that very long, very uncomfortable, VERY LONELY night I spent on a Liverpool housing estate, hiding under the backseat of my unlocked red GTI with go-faster stripes and fog-lamps, engine running).

All in all, I think I'm best off watching the young crims on telly. My relationship to outlaws, like most things in life, should never really go beyond the voyeuristic. For everyone's sake.

I just wish they wouldn't electronically blur those young thug's faces on those *Police Camera Action!* programmes. Do they have *any idea* how *frustrating* this is?

Mind you, there is something about an anonymous, buzz-cut meaty body in sports casuals with trouble in his pixels. . . .

Attitude
March 1999

Bad Apple

*"Yoo can't stop the myoo-zik
No-body can stop the myoo-zik."*

I'm singing acapella, out of tune and fighting against a Pet Shop Boys ditty whining and clattering on the PA in this tiny, pre-Stonewall, retro New York fag bar with the fabulously cheesy name IC Guys, the show-stopping, pull-out-all-the-stops-and-wear-something-glittery big finale number from Nancy Walker's epic Village People movie *Can't Stop the Music*. I'm trying to infect my native New Yorker friend Glenn, the artist formerly known as Glennda Orgasm, with my out-of-towner enthusiasm for that 1980 box-office bomb and show why it is my cultural compass for my first visit to New York since the 1980s.

He's not impressed. In fact, he looks at me with a textbook rendition of "askance," with a side order of wariness and concern, and says dismissively, "It's just a bad movie, Mark." I put this down to my bad singing and embark on an intellectual exposition instead.

"Look," I plead, trying to ignore the skinny, queeny barman-cum-go-go-dancer (I told you this place was small) who is coquettishly counting his ribs for us, *Can't Stop the Music* is a tour de force! The 'music' that 'can't be stopped' is clearly desire—something that vibrates in everyone, choreographing them to its own plan. One that has little rhyme or reason. The opening number alone, with its kooky collage of the Technicolored, steamy street life of Manhattan—roller-skating, boom-boxing, jogging in leg warmers, or just showing off their baskets—is so exhilarating, so chaotic, so . . . *Vital*. Even the giddy contrast between the high camp of the big production numbers and the low-rent bathos of the script is movingly apposite to. . . ."

"Yeah right," interrupts Glenn, staring openly in disbelief at our skinny stripper who is now jiggling his bones in time to Sylvester's "Mighty Real," like something escaped from a Ghost Train ride, wearing nothing now but a thin, lascivious, slightly vengeful smile (in any other bar in New York no one would even see him; here you can't avoid him). Glenn finally manages to tear himself away from the harpie Skeletor, "Whatever. All I can remember is that I wasn't able to sit through that film."

"But—but," I burble, crestfallen that Glenn of all people—the Glenn who once told me that "old movies are all I have"—isn't with me on this one, "the 'YMCA' Busby Berkeley pastiche! With the young men falling into the pool like a line of muscular dominoes, even more perfect when you hear that apparently they were hand-picked serving U.S. Marines who . . ." But Glenn isn't paying any attention.

So I try another tack. "Well, my other New York reference point is *On the Town,* 1949, starring Gene Kelly and Frank Sinatra as sailors determined to have a good time on twenty-four hours shore leave in Manhattan. The energy and . . . *spunk* in that film is breathtaking. *'Noo Yawk, Noo Yawk, it's a wonderful town / the Bronx is up and the Battery's down.'*"

Glenn looks even more bored. "Just because it's got *sailors* in it. . . ."

"But," I protest, "Gene Kelly's bell-bottomed thighs are historic. An exquisitely curvaceous counterpoint to the rigid phallicism of the 1940s' Manhattan skyline. . . ." But Glenn isn't listening to me. Now he's decided I'm being ironic.

But I'm not. Actually, like IC Guys, I'm being *nostalgic.* I feel that both those films capture something about New York that has been lost—something that made New York the centre of the world in the 1940s and again in the 1970s—before the election of a 1950s film star as President in the 1980s saw the West Coast eclipse the East, private spaces eclipse public ones, safe sex eclipse the dangerous variety, and shallow visual values eclipse lyrical ones. Until that time New York— the city of cities—was synonymous with a crazy, edgy exuberance, otherwise known as "song and dance" or just "life." As "Sound of the City," the opening number in Nancy's Village People *meisterwork* has it: *"Listen to the sound of the city / Listen to the sound of my town."*

Even this much was clear to me as a whiny sprog visiting New York in the early 1970s with my suffering parents, on holiday from my hometown of (Old) York. The smell, the heat, the dirt, the noise, the steam escaping bafflingly from the street, the perpetual motion of six million driven souls, and the giddy grandeur of the skyscrapers; New York was literally a city where you couldn't crick your neck enough trying to take it all in. Everywhere you looked, including heavenward, there was human vanity. In hindsight I can see that New York was the key to the 1970s: funk, disco, Kojak, punk, leg warmers, *The Godfather,* bankruptcy, bisexuality, the last gasp of liberalism, and, of course, the band who changed the world, The Village People, all had their origins here. New York even invented the end of the 1970s—AIDS. But back then, both me and the 1970s were in short trousers and it was a confusing, terrifying experience for a small-town boy, perhaps all the more so because it bore clearly and garishly the traces of something rarely seen in suburban Yorkshire: passion.

A quarter of a century on, I'm ready to embrace that confusion and passion, at least for a couple of days. But New York, dammit, has gone and cleaned up its act. As everyone knows, drugs, disease, crime, scandal, and vice are all on the wane. The Disney Corporation has been stamping all over Manhattan, flattening Times Square, biting the heads off street hustlers, and scaring away more interesting monsters. Everyone is now very sensible in New York. Even the junkies have pension plans, and gay leaders like Larry Kramer and his earthly representative Michaelangelo Signorile call for gay men to abandon the messiness of promiscuity, public sex, and shameful shags with straight men, and go for hygienic, orderly, proud gay monogamy.

At the gay nostalgia bar, IC Guys, Glenn and I are joined by the writer and connoisseur of bohemia Bruce Benderson, Camille Paglia's inspiration and the author of a book advocating downward mobility called *Towards a New Degeneracy.* He thinks that artists have a duty to live with the people of the streets (a duty his yen for street hustlers makes less onerous a burden than for most). Bruce is a very laidback middle-aged Jew whose brain is, nevertheless, always very much leaning forward. He has a very placid, congenial expression but appears to have a cheeky smile perpetually playing around his eyes. I complain to him that Glenn is blind to the genius of *Can't Stop the Music.*

"Oh," he says, matter-of-factly, "there is *no question* but that it is a *marvellous* movie. Its surrealism borders on high art. It conveys the absurdity of life *very well.*" Bruce has a voice that seems to be perpetually threatening, albeit ironically, to add "Mary" to the end of each sentence, but rarely actually does.

"I love you, Bruce," I say simply, hugging him and directing gloating looks at Glenn. "But what," I say, disentangling myself, "about *On the Town?*"

Bruce's eyes cloud slightly, almost imperceptibly. "Well, now, *On the Town* is more *difficult*. I was never much of a fan of Gene Kelly's dancing. I've always preferred the *French* school myself. I have little time for that, that . . ." Bruce trails off.

"Clean-cut, large-thighed, vigorous virility?" I offer.

"Precisely."

"Ah, I'm afraid I have little time for anything else," I confess. "I wish it weren't so. But then, that's what a Northern English public school education does to you."

In an attempt to rescue me from my sexual lack of imagination, Bruce whisks Glenn and me off to one of his favourite haunts, an Upper Upper West Side Latino hustler bar: "One of the last, sadly," he laments during the long, long yellow cab journey. "There used to be many more. But the cleanup of Manhattan and the pillage of Times Square has put paid to that." He sighs forlornly. Inevitably, Bruce now searches for illicit, messy, self-hating sex on the Internet. He's just written a book about cybersex, which is being published only in French. He researched it with a video camera atop his computer monitor. "I spent weeks sitting naked in front of that computer, having a whale of a time, before I realised that it wasn't only the people I was talking to on the Net who could see me. I really should have drawn my curtains."

As we stagger out of the cab and into the hustler bar, I mention out loud that Glenn walks like a puppet who has had two strings cut. "Do I really?" inquires Glenn, more curious than offended. "Is that true?" he demands of the assembled group. Silence. "Well," he says, resignedly, "I guess it *must* be true. Ohmigod! I walk like a puppet whose strings have been cut! Not one, but *two*!"

"Well," I say, putting on my best American talk-show voice. "In our own way, we *all* walk like puppets who've had two strings cut."

"Oh, shut *up!*"

In the hustler bar, a grubby little shack perched on some disused dockfront, there turns out to be rather more hustlers than punters. Which is especially bad news on a Friday night when a working boy is hoping to pay off the subs he's chalked up during the week. Four of them in their skimpy shorts and goatees stand in a line on the small stage facing the oval bar in the centre, go-going in their decidedly un-clean-cut Latino way. Everyone recognises Bruce and they are clearly happy to see him; hardly surprising since he is probably single-handedly responsible for keeping this place open.

One in particular, a short, bleached-blond number, exquisitely beautiful, hops off the stage and prowls toward us in that swishy-but-not-faggy catlike walk that Latin boys do, something very alarming bouncing underneath his shorts, tenting them out. He smiles easily and convincingly as he allows us to pull his waistband out far enough to get a glimpse of his salami-sized penis, which is somewhat purplish as it is tied off at the base. "Oh," exclaims Glenn nonchalantly, *"that's* where one of my puppet strings got to."

We stuff some dollar bills down the boy's waistband and he smiles even more easily and convincingly. As he rhumba-sashays off back to his perch, the back of his neck passes under my nose and I smell a sudden, all-enveloping sweetness. I ask Bruce about this. "Yes, they have that nutmeggy smell even when they've been on the streets for days," he explains. "Whereas white boys, well, they just have this really acrid, *ammonia* smell."

"Is it diet or temperament?" I ask, as if we were discussing a breed of dog.

"Oh, I think diet has a lot to do with it," ventures Bruce, scanning the chorus line. "But," he adds, "maybe Catholicism has something to do with it, too. The marvellous thing about Southern Catholics is that they have very poor memories. They forget. Which always makes the next morning so much easier."

"Ah, yes," I agree. "There's nothing more off-putting than *eau de regret*. Which is why I should really get into the Latin thing instead of the Anglo-Celtic schtick I've got going. I have enough ammonia in my life to clean kitchens with."

Glenn, who is a bit worse for wear now, is pointing at one of the hustlers on stage. *"He's no Latino!"* he shouts. *"He's just some muscle Mary from Chelsea with an instant tan!"*

Another Bruce we've been expecting, the Canadian filmmaker Mr. La Bruce, finally shows up. "Are you Catholic, Bruce?" I ask him as he joins us.

"Certainly not. I'm of Celtic Protestant stock," he says proudly, but won't allow Bruce and me to sniff him. After a quick round of drinks, we bid our farewells to Bruce #1, leaving him happy as Larry in Latinoland. Bruce #2 then whisks Glenn and me away to another hustler bar, one which he promises will be "less *Night of the Iguana*." On the way into the club Glenn bursts out laughing and points at Bruce who is trotting ahead of us. "Well, I may walk like a puppet who's had two strings cut, but Bruce walks like she thinks she's Jean Shrimpton in platforms on Carnaby Street, wearing a *big floppy hat!*"

Bruce pretends not to hear the evil laughter behind him.

The second hustler bar isn't quite so Latino. More Northern European and black, with just a smattering of Hispanic. As I'm talking to Bruce, one of the black dancers walks up to him and puts his cucumber-sized penis in his pocket. Bruce tips him ten bucks. (Well, what else can you do?)

Much, much later, over blueberry and cream cheese blintzes in some SoHo diner, Glenn tells us he has a confession to make. He looks at us anxiously. "Promise not to laugh. Okay?"

"Confess away, my son."

"OK. Here's the thing. My dad was a big fan of the Village People. He even joined the YMCA. And bought poppers." Glenn grimaces at the memory. "I was very worried about him for a while. What made it worse was . . ." He trails off.

"Yes, Glenn?"

"He was in charge of a factory making uniforms."

Bruce and I break our promise. Loudly.

"Yoo can't stop the myoo-zik. . . ."

                                               Attitude
                                               July 1999

Summer Loathing

Strangers in a strange land end up in bed together. Everyone knows this. It's self-evident. Contrary to what we're taught in biology classes, *Homo sapiens* does have a mating season. It's called August.

What, after all, is the point of splashing out on a new wardrobe, losing weight, trimming your pubes, plucking your nostril hair, travelling all that way, and talking to people you have nothing in common with about charter airline food, the price of property in Solihull, and the really strange noises the hotel plumbing makes in the middle of the night if you don't pull?

Holiday romance—that's to say, lots of desperate, filthy sex and a lying promise to "visit very soon"—is the most important, if unspoken, part of the deal we're looking for at the travel agent's. It's the only kind of package anyone is seriously interested in. When we enquire, "So, is this full or half-board?" what we really mean is: "So, will I get a good shagging from someone I never have to see again?"

It's why gays have such a fondness for "gay" vacations. The most awful thing that can happen to homosexuals is to travel somewhere where there are actually people they haven't already slept with, only to find them using the pathetic excuse, "Oh, sorry, I'm straight" to get out of going to bed with them.

But it isn't just gays. Everybody but everybody, including retired nuns using their air miles awards from bulk purchasing Roman candles, knows that only extremely tragic people come back from their holiday unlaid.

So perhaps you can understand why it's taken me so long to come to terms with something about myself, and why I hope you'll applaud my courage in deciding to share this shameful secret with you. A secret that even Jerry Springer wouldn't let me talk about on his show. You see, I'm a vacation virgin.

Every time August came around I used to go through the same tarty preparations as everyone else. I wondered whether to book a sunbed course to pump-prime my tan. I wondered whether to buy swimming shorts that went down to my knees or Speedo briefs (though I never, ever contemplated thongs). I wondered whether my sunglasses made me look pop-star mysterious or just junky photosensitive. I wondered whether to have my shoulders waxed or just braided. I wondered whether to stop eating for a week or to try and use the vacuum cleaner in a spot of DIY plastic surgery. Like most people, I never actually *decided* anything, but I did spend a lot of time wondering in front of a full-length mirror.

And every year I carefully packed two cartons of condoms. And every year I unpacked them again, the seals still as pristine as Pat Buchanan's cherry. Which, along with emptying the sand out of your shoes into the bin of a flat a hundred miles away from the sea, is one of the saddest feelings known to man.

For a long time I used to feel ashamed. I used to lie to my friends to conceal my hideous, flesh-rotting embarrassment, concocting stories of romantic conquests involving whole legions of lifeguards, fishermen, ski instructors, taxi drivers, and the man in passport control (I drew the line at flight attendants; even I had standards about the people I pretended to have sex with). I dreaded their mocking laughter should they discover the truth: "*What?* You went on holiday *And You Didn't Get Laid?* What kind of *loser* are you?"

"B-b-b-but," I pleaded with these accusing voices in my head, "I tried, really I did! I did everything you're supposed to do! But it just didn't work!"

And *how* I tried! I lay around on beaches, splayed out like a lab rat, or tethered bait for some large carnivore, waiting to be dissected or devoured. But nothing even nibbled. I followed the prescribed rituals to the letter—raising my head whenever someone under forty and penised walked past, tipping up my sunglasses and moving my head from side to side, just the way you're meant to, pretending to be checking that the sea was still there and that the horizon was still level. To no avail.

I'd dive into the pool from the highest board, making sure everyone was watching me, executing a fiendishly complicated backward somersault. Then I'd haul myself out of the water and lie on a sun lounger, my legs apart, all the better for everyone to get a butchers at my wet packet. And most important of all, *I never wore the same pair of swim shorts two days running.* But nobody seemed to notice.

I struck up flirtatious, borderline-hysterical conversations with overworked waiters, whose grasp of English wasn't quite up to single meanings, let alone double ones. They'd just laugh nervously and take an hour to bring the bill.

After the sun set, I'd dutifully visit the local bars and discos in my box-fresh shirts and jeans, some with the price tag still attached. I'd sip lots of long, sickly-sweet day-glo drinks with overgenerous measures, poured by a man who couldn't pick up herpes without tossing it up in the air and catching it behind his back, while I stood under the UV lights to make my throbbing red sunburn look brown.

But nothing happened.

For the longest time I couldn't figure it out. I degraded and humiliated myself in all the appropriately alluring ways. I objectified myself for a fortnight in the hope that a complete stranger would objectify me in my hotel bedroom for half an hour, which didn't seem much to ask, really. But it was all for *niente*. I still scored less than England in a European cup qualifying round. I didn't have *that* much trouble being slaggy at home, so why should it be so difficult when I was on holiday and when everyone was more up for it than the last dodo on earth must have been?

Finally, I twigged what it was. I didn't have sex on holiday because I was Trying Too Hard. And nothing is less appealing than a whiff of desperation.

It was like a weight off my shoulders, this revelation. Because it made me realise that having sex on holiday is actually a very bad idea precisely because it's expected. Like back rooms after last orders and visiting the supermarket on a Saturday morning, having sex on holiday is really something best left to other people. It's saved me a lot of trouble. Nowadays, before I go abroad I take a different kind of precaution than the one I used to. I always try to remember to pack a couple of packets of that antisocial substance that travel agents advise you to leave at home when you go on holiday, and armed police employ sniffer dogs to detect on your arrival.

It's called self-respect.

But you know, like they say you always forget *something*. . . .

Attitude
August 1999

Morosexuals

My mostly hetero but increasingly bi-curious, middle-aged, divorced Dutch friend Hans (John Lithgow in *3rd Rock from the Sun* with a Dutch accent) rang me the other day. "Mark!" he said, in that slightly surprised voice he puts on when telling me of his latest discoveries in the world of MAN SEX, "I have discovered a completely new kind of homoshexuality!"

"Oh, yes?" I say, only mildly interested.

"Yes!" replies Hans. "It is called Moroshexuality!"

"What," I say. "You mean not having any sex and not eating meat?"

"No, no," says Hans, "my reference is not to your favourite British cult pop star, but to North Africa. I was staying in a hotel in Morocco lasht month and one of the waitersh there invited himshelf to my room. He was quite attractive, sho mind I didn't. We were chatting and drinking, when suddenly he took out his erect cock—which was quite large by the way. 'What are you doing?' I asked in a friendliesht way I could manage.

"He just sat there with his legs apart, his erection looking very erect, and said, very factly-matter-of, 'You can shuck my cock, but it will cosht you five hundred dinari. And you will not touch my arshe or I will hunt you down and cut your throat.'

"'Oh,' I said, 'that's nice.' And I chatted to him for a while with his cock completely erect, shticking out of his troushers. He sheemed very proud of it.'"

"As he should be," I say. "I think that men should show off their erections more. Well, straight men anyway. My tranny friend, Michelle, agrees. The other night she was walking her dog and a group of agitated women approached her shouting, 'Don't go down there! There's a man FLASHING!' Michelle didn't miss a beat. 'How *terrible!*' she exclaimed. 'I didn't bring my TORCH! How big is his COCK?'"

"Yes," said Hans, "that shounds like your Michelle. But, getting back to *my* shtory, I have to shay I was intrigued, but not aroused, by thish very big North African erection in my hotel room. I wasn't intereshted in the schenario he was for me painting. It wasn't flattering enough to my own vanity, you undershtand. I pay him to shervice him? I think so don't."

"Oh, Hans," I laughed, "you're so . . . *bourgeois*."

"Yes, well, that may be, Mark. But one must have shtandards. Even in the homoshexual univershe."

"But Hans, you're missing the point, I think. You are supposed to pay him to be the Other—to be the dark, unyielding, unresponsive phallus. Something which a lot of people go for, apparently. Including Joe Orton and Kenneth Halliwell, who probably stayed in the same hotel."

"Yes, and I am one of those people after the Dark Phallush, Mark. But my narcisshism won't let me pay them for that, I'm afraid. They must be unyielding, but not unintereshted. Anyway, it turned out that of courshe he does thish with many of the male hotel guests and that they usually take up his offer. Whether they are married or not. Apparently it is the same for his friends, who also make a lot of money being—how you shay? Blued. They have no problem about another man shucking them, sho long as they are paid. But the arshe thing is very shpecial to them. I don't doubt that he meant it when he shaid he would shtab me if I touched his arshe. There was something in the way he said it that was very convincing, Mark."

"Hmmm," I say, "I can believe that he probably meant it. Or at least, that he meant that it would cost you one thousand dinari extra to touch his arse."

"Well, yes, you may be correct, Mark," agrees Hans sighing, "as sho often you are about the homoshexual univershe. On the other hand, you are not *always* right. I seem to remember that you once told me that you were—how you shay?—'dogmeat' in the gay world if you were over thirty. I am in my forties, and I have had a lot of shuccessh. . . ."

"Yes, you're right, Hans. But you see, I already suspected you wanted to dip your toe, or whatever, in the queer demimonde, and I was probably just trying to put you off the idea. It's really not to be recommended, you know. Which is why I respect the way your Morosexual draws the line at his bottom, saying, 'You can't touch this and this is why I'm not a faggot, even if I let men suck my cock.' God knows I've used that line often enough myself."

"I see," says Hans sceptically. "But isn't that hypocritical?"

"Well, maybe. But then, so is most good sex. And it isn't as if the 'truth' were very straightforward anyway. While some straight men will insist on being only active, some men will let you fuck them, but don't kiss—because that's for faggots. Some men will get fucked *and* kiss, but not suck your dick. Some men will suck your cock but not look you in the eye. And some will kiss you with their eyes open, sleep with your dick in their mouth, and do your housework with a butt plug with your name on it up their arse—but whatever you do, don't send them a Valentine.

"You see, Hans," I continue quickly so he can't interrupt, beginning to really enjoy my smug riff, "most men who have sex with men have something that they don't do. Or say they don't do. Which is fine, isn't it? I mean, why should we all be versatile? Or even honest? If everything is permitted, and there are no boundaries and no secrets, why would anyone bother to fuck? I mean, you might as well shag your *boyfriend.* At least this 'hypocritical' way there's always something to try and talk them into, some further level of corruption to introduce them to."

"I shuppose, Mark," laughs Hans. "But it can be frushtrating. My Moroshexual told me that they will fuck anything—women, men, cows, trees. I asked him, if all Morrocan men want to fuck but won't get fucked, and Morrocan women won't let you, who is it they fuck?"

"What did he say?"

"'The Germansh.' Anyway, we talked and talked, very friendly and very intereshting, but not about his proposhal. His erection finally began to fall, with a regular beat. Like a shecond hand on a clock, between twelve and shix. Eventually it was flopped completely, he put it away, buttoned his trousers, and got up to leave. We said goodnight at the door in a friendly fashion and that was that.

"I thought about the incident all day and decided that when I see him the next evening in the reshtaurant I would ashk him if he would like to come up to my room for some more drinks and to continue our convershation."

"And?"

"He shaid, 'No, it is forbidden for shtaff to visit guests in their rooms.'"

"Obviously, Hans," I sputter trying not to laugh too bitterly, "this man draws the line at letting tourists fuck with his head for free."

Attitude
September 1999

Fannyphobia

Anyone fancy a bacon sandwich? How about some chopped liver? A fuzzburger, perhaps? A slice of hair pie, maybe? Possibly you'd prefer some tuna? A smattering of trout? Or some nice live snapper?

No? Oh, well. Suit yourself. Hang on, though, some of you seem to have gone a bit green about the gills at the back there. Crikey. Anyone would think I'd asked you to have sex with a *woman* or something. You remember women, don't you? They're those people that have V-A-G-I-N-A-S where they're supposed to have cock rings.

However much they might like to pal around with them, especially if they're famous and rich and called Madonna, most gay men just can't deal with the very bits that make a woman a woman. Lots of fags' faces screw up at the merest mention of the V word, as if they had discovered a week-old kipper under their pillow. I once knew a gay who used to actually retch at the mention of female genitalia. I've known several who dismiss the whole female sex in one word: *"Fish."* Obviously gay men are all strict Catholics for whom every day is Friday. But maybe this shouldn't be so surprising, since gay men aren't defined so much by their phallophilia as their fanny*phobia*.

This is why bisexual men often come in for such stick from gay men, when they're not sucking their cocks in lavatories and lay-bys. When gays complain about bisexual men's "hypocrisy," they're really complaining about what they perceive as their lack of hygiene. It's a dumb reversal of society's attitude toward homosexuality: "Why do they *have* to insist on sticking their dicks up *there,*" gays bitch, "where it's nasty and smelly, when they could be sticking them up *here,* where it's all lovely and nice?" Most of gay male culture is built around the disavowal of sexual difference. Bum fucking is considered more "natural" and "homely" than fanny fucking because

---

In Britain "fanny" is slang for "vagina." In the U.S. its meaning is reversed—i.e., U.S. gays have fannies, too.

gays have back bottoms but don't have front bottoms (which are, of course, alien and evil). At best, fannies are merely ridiculous. As one queen put it to me only half joking, "How am I supposed to get a fanny up my arse?"

While gay male culture may worship the mother goddess that brought them into the world and ruled (and usually continues to rule) their lives in the form of their endless tribute to "divas" and "icons," they try to deny the existence of the very organ that made Mummy Mummy and not Daddy, the organ which Daddy penetrated to make them, and Mummy squeezed them out into the world with. Gay culture, in its pumped, primed, phallic smoothness, is forever trying to forget that that we all came from a hairy hole and we're all headed for one. That we can either choose the womb-tomb and its promise of a kind of immortality, or just the tomb.

Naturally, the only thing dafter than a vagina is another one. To gay men, lesbianism is the most absurd idea ever conceived. One famous veteran London pub drag queen's act depended on one joke, repeated over and over again: "L-l-l-l-l-l-l-l-l-l-l-l-l-l-l-lesbians!" "she'd" say, with an exaggerated lapping of her tongue and reduce the gay men in the audience to helpless, disgusted snickers every time (cunt licking is, of course, gross and utterly distasteful, whereas licking shit holes is, well, rather nice, actually). In fact, most pub drag queens' jokes centre on their imaginary minge and its mysteriousness, its illnesses, and the notion that, like Mrs. Slocombe's pussy, it has a life of its own.

Fannyphobia is not, though, something exclusive to gay men; it's just more pronounced. All men, and even some women, display it. As the old joke has it, "How can you trust something that bleeds for seven days and doesn't die?" And as feminists have ceaselessly pointed out, most of the words for penis are fairly affectionate, while most of the words for vagina aren't—"you prick" just doesn't have quite the same "ring" to it as "you cunt." In fact, you don't have to be Camille Paglia to realise that much of Western civilisation is built on fannyphobia. Architecture attempts to raise man ever higher above cloying Mother Earth, and science and technology seems to be intent on designing an antiseptic future, where cloning and genetic engineering will do away with the need for all that messy womb-based reproduction altogether. I even read recently a report that some scientists are planning to impregnate a man's lower colon with an embryo (I think this experiment was scheduled to be conducted at The Hoist).

Science fiction presents a fannyphobic future. The idea of anyone having a period on the spotless *USS Enterprise* is absolutely unthinkable. Jean Luc Picard would have a hissy fit. Data would faint. *Alien* is of course an essay in fannyphobia; those hydraulic-jawed monsters are nothing less than walking vagina dentata. In *Return of the Jedi* Jabba the Hutt tries to throw Luke and his pals down a hairy toothy hole, where "you will be digested in agony for over a thousand years" (which sounds like marriage to me). You could even argue if you were in a cod-freudian mood that space itself is the original vagina that spewed us forth from the conception of the Big Bang, and that starships are merely swimming spermatozoa, attempting to reconquer it. Certainly it would explain the significance of all those scenes where some poor sod is sucked screaming through an airlock into the vast inky vacuum of space. (Not everyone shares Prince Charles's ambition of being a lost tampon.)

There's a short story by Stephen King that illustrates the general fear of the voracious vagina very well. A man meets a woman who appears to be pregnant. After a few hours her "pregnancy" subsides and disappears. The couple take a shine to one another, but when they begin to have sex he finds himself sucked into her vagina *in toto*. Once again she appears "pregnant," and rather radiant. I don't think that Stephen King is gay, but. . . .

And my own relationship to the vagina? Well, I don't wrinkle my nose at the mention of the word, but it speaks volumes that the first one I've seen close-up in a long, long time belongs to my tranny friend, Michelle, who has recently had the op (or rather the split—the penis is actually sliced in half and turned inside out). Of course, a tranny's vagina isn't a "real" vagina, its a vagina created by science and technology. It's "sterile." It's *man-made*. Like science fiction, of which Mich is a great fan, it's a special effect.

Operation Pussycat was, fortunately, a total success. "I now have a seven-and-a-half-inch fanny!" Michelle declared the day after, through her morphine haze, lying flat on her back, her legs apart, and her groin packed with more dressing than a Marks & Spencer salad. "And in about six months, Mark, it will stretch to *nine inches!*"

I cracked. "More like one month, in your case," I said. Michelle pursed her lips (the old pair).

On Fanny Day Three the packing came off and she insisted I look at what she proudly called her "car-crash vagina," giving new and literal meaning to the word "gash." I found myself worrying that I might not look sufficiently impressed or interested. I needn't have. I was spellbound. Michelle's *faux* fanny looked impressively convincing to my decidedly nonexpert eye (or at least it would when the swelling had gone down and the hair had grown back).

"Oh, Mark!" Michelle declared after the catheter came out on Fanny Day Four, "I can now wee like a woman! It's *fantastic!* Myron has finally become Myra. Aren't you *excited?*"

That was some months ago. Now Mich is fully recovered and "on line," but ironically finding it more difficult to find men than when she was a chick with a dick—i.e., without a vagina. She probably just has to change her social circle, but she's come to a different conclusion.

"Men," she snorts dismissively. "They're all *PUSSIES!*"

Attitude
November 1999

One-Hander

"WANKER!"

A bastard blue Mondeo has just pulled out suddenly from a side street right in front of me, forcing me to brake hard. So I respond in the customary way: winding down the window, leaning out and calling him, at the top of my voice, an Onanist. Rolling the window up again I feel peculiarly pleased with myself.

Accusing someone of being a player of pocket pool is a highly satisfactory insult. "Wanker" is, after all, a great Anglo-Saxon word which can be relished in its pronunciation. Especially if you deliver it—as most people do nowadays—with an Estuarian English twang, as in, "WAN-KAH!" Even better, it's possible to drive this insult home *visually,* by making that cute jacking gesture with your half-closed fist (though when I do this to other men I sometimes get a bit confused whether I'm offering an insult or an invitation).

The best thing about calling someone a "wanker," though, is, of course, that it's a crime you're just as guilty of. As the jigging fist does rather hint, the man accusing another man of being a hand galloper is no stranger to Rosie Palm and her five daughters himself. Unlike, say, "motherfucker" (for most people not living in Thebes), calling someone a "wanker" as a term of abuse is a tad self-incriminating. It's a bit like calling someone a "pisser" or a "nose-picker." Everyone does it. In fact, for the entire human race, "wanking" is the normal form of sexual behaviour and intercourse is the deviation. After all, if God hadn't wanted us to wank, would he have put our hands at crotch level? As any anthropologist will tell you, when *Homo erectus* stood up, the first thing he reached for was his tool. (The original obelisk scene in Kubrick's *2001,* in which an apelike man grabs his "bone" for the first time, was cut by 1970s' censors and had to be reshot in its current, allusive form.)

Of course, once upon a time having a Jodrell Bank was somewhat shameful. Not anymore. Nowadays, there's a whole TV channel devoted to it, called Channel Five. Everyone talks incessantly about it. Wanking has come out of the cubicle (with some toilet tissue stuck to its shoe). George Michael might have been arrested for it, but then he did turn it into a hit pop single celebrating it (and the discovery that he was gay was *almost* as surprising as the revelation that he was a wanker).

In the good old days, masturbation was regarded as a sin and a sickness, an enervation of the nation's manhood, and a waste of its precious jism. Boys were solemnly told that it would make them go blind/deaf/grow hair on their palms—which of course was all true. They just forgot to mention that it would take about fifty years. It may have made lads a bit anxious, but you can bet it made the slightly sad business of autoeroticism more fun and more masculine because it made it *naughty* and *dangerous*. These days it's as rebellious as a side parting. Boys are given videos by their mothers called "How to Pull Your Pud Properly," featuring Toyah Wilcox, on their seventh birthday. *Not* masturbating is now considered pathological.

Public schools in the nineteenth century were as obsessed with preventing their boys from jerking their gherkin as we are today with encouraging them. They developed a whole way of life which we called "Britishness," designed to stamp out "self-abuse." Cold showers, thin blankets, bad food, soccer, and rugby football were all deployed to ward it off. (Of course, the idea that after playing rugby all afternoon with the lads, you'd be too knackered to bang his bishop backfired spectacularly—as anyone who has attended a postmatch piss-up will tell you.)

Crackdowns on monkey spankings were not, however, exclusive to Britain. Apparently, the reason American men are circumcised is because it was thought in the earlier part of this century that circumcision would discourage masturbation by removing that naughty, oh-so-slidey bit of skin. A notion that was, for some reason, promoted most enthusiastically by the Crisco vegetable oil company.

Predictably, these anti-fiddling campaigns didn't work. Male adolescence is just too irresistible a force. When you're fourteen, everything gives you a hard-on—sitting on a bus, fizzy drinks, strong breezes, the smell of pencil shavings (oh, was that just me?). And almost anything can bring you off. I fucked pillows, mounted my mattress, and even managed to turn the cold showers so beloved of my public school into a masturbatory device by allowing water from the shower head to drip onto the end of my dick, in a pervy variation on Chinese Water Torture. Each large drop of water brought me tantalisingly closer to the edge (though I'd usually caught a nasty cold by the time I came).

It goes without saying that this method of self-abuse wouldn't work for me today. Now that I'm in my thirties and the hormonal frenzy has long since receded, it would take a water cannon to bring me off. If boyhood was a time when you masturbated four times a day despite your best efforts to curb your habit, adulthood is when you masturbate only once a fortnight, despite your best efforts to do it more often.

Naturally, one of the reasons why masturbation used to be so heavily discouraged was because it was rather too close for comfort to homosexuality. After all, at its minimum, homosexuality is no more than a wank shared with a friend. All men, however straight they might consider themselves, know what it is to feel a hard cock in their hands and how to please it (it's just that usually it's attached to them). Of course, homos have an unfair advantage in the masturbatory game, as they don't have to use much imagination or even pornography when they wank—just the fact of wanking is itself exciting to homos. Actually, it's debatable whether homos ever wank at all since, for them, Woody Allen's line that masturbation is "sex with someone I love" isn't a joke; it's just a fact.

But times change. Not so long ago, adult men with girlfriends or wives would rarely admit to having a J Arthur, unless they were separated from their missus by war or the law. The whole point of being an adult, being a *man,* was that you didn't have to play with your pee-pee anymore—you now had a woman to do that for you. But these days hen-pecked, feminist-badgered men want to advertise, or at least pretend to, their independence from women. So all those glossy lad mags which have replaced those glossy men's magazines I remember from my youth, which were full of fantasies about women giving them hand-shandies on buses, are full of pieces by men bragging about giving *themselves* hand-shandies. It's not just cheating on the girlfriend, you see—*it's cheating on the whole female sex.*

In fact, lad mags are all about public masturbation. With their fashion, chatter, celebs, and consumerism, they are, like all glossy magazines and like postmodernism itself, a load of new old wank. Unlike the old glossy men's magazines, today's men's mags are not something that anyone would actually wank *over,* maybe because they're already *full* of it. In fact, *FHM* and the rest are incontrovertible proof that those Victorian headmasters were absolutely right to believe that Western civilisation would collapse if masturbation wasn't held in check.

The much-touted next evolutionary leap for humanity, the Internet, is of course all about wanking, too, though less metaphorically in this case. The Internet has been described by the decadent American writer Bruce Benderson as a fulfilment of the Protestant vision of each man at home alone with his God. In fact, it's more a case of each man at home alone with his cock.

And yes, people in sex chat rooms do actually use the word "wanker" as an insult—even when they have to type it with one hand.

And I should know.

Attitude
December 1999

God Save the Queen

Gibraltar, otherwise known simply as The Rock, is the full stop to the sentence of Europe, and sometimes, it seems, history itself. It has been besieged no less than fourteen times. The Ancients thought it was a pillar holding up the end of the world. In the Middle Ages, Jews fled here from the red-hot instruments of the Spanish Inquisition. Aeons ago, the last survivors of the ancestors of *Homo sapiens* also retreated to this toothy promontory of the Iberian peninsula, lasting a few, increasingly lonely, thousand years more in the dark caves that abound here, before being finally snuffed out by Progress.

Even today, rare and exotic creatures survive here that have long become extinct elsewhere in Continental Europe. Off one of the narrow, steep, cobbled streets, down some worn steps, there's a dingy cellar bar, with red vinyl-covered banquette seating, no draft beer, and no natural light, that holds out against not only the twenty-first century but much of the latter half of the twentieth. This is the domain and refuge of the last of the Sea Queens, Lovely Charlie, run aground in the last corner of the British Empire.

It's also quite clear that this is the last bar on the Seven Seas. The decaying brick walls and damp vaulted ceiling of Charlie's cave are completely covered in battered Royal Navy Ensign flags. All of them have personal messages scrawled across them in Secondary Modern hands: *"To Lovely Charlie, from the lads on HMS Sheffield—We think you're magic!"* (dated 1981, the year before it was sunk by an Argentine Exocet in the Falklands), *"Donkey Nob Was Here—1979"* and *"Royal Marine Commandos do it in boats—1989."* Signed photos of sunburnt, laughing young men with cans of lager in their hands and their arms around each other's shoulders cover the wall next to the bar, together with postcards from Hong Kong, Belize, Brunei, and Kuwait.

Tonight the bar is completely empty, except for Charles himself, a well-preserved, handsome middle-aged man with glittery ear studs and immaculate hair, who may or may not be wearing a touch of makeup, sitting at the bar sipping a G & T, and his big old black pointer dog lying across the banquette, heavy eyelids sagging. "Well, come in, luv," he says, happy to see a face. "Sorry it's so quiet tonight. The Fleet's out. Mind, it always is these days. Are you a matelot? No? What's that you say? You're looking for one? Aren't we all, luv!" he laughs, and gets me a bottled beer. His dog yawns.

"It was best when the frontier with Spain was closed," he reminisces, in his effortlessly camp colonial English accent (comically spiked with some coarse, regional expressions he's obviously picked up from his clientele). "When Franco shut the border in 1967 that was the beginning of twenty years of bloody *bliss,* y'know. When hundreds of sailors have been out at sea for weeks and they dock here, they're not going to let the fact that there aren't enough women on Gib to make a football team stop them having a fookin' good time, luv!

"And they didn't mind their mates finding out; they'd just say, 'I bet you had a fookin' good time with Charlie gobblin' yer last night!' and everybody would laugh. Of course, who gobbled whom wasn't always the way they painted it—but that was something private between me and them. Things aren't the same now. I still get offers—but they're much more furtive; they're afraid that everyone will think they're gay just because they had a bit of fun with Charlie. And also, in 1987 they opened the fookin' frontier, didn't they? Now most of the lads head off for the bright lights of Marbella. I can't compete with dolly-birds and disco, can I, luv?

"But it isn't about sex," explains Charlie, freshening his G & T. "It's the company. The camaraderie, luv. It's my *duty* to run this bar. I'm a legend in the Royal Navy, y'know. I've been to Portsmouth and Plymouth. They treated me like a real queen. There was nothing they wouldn't do for me. I was really moved. I was in Edinburgh once, and a lad came up to me and said, 'It's Lovely Charlie, isn't it?' He was very sweet. He whispered, *'Look, Charles, you can't wear that much jewellery around here. They won't understand.'*

"I'm passed down, father to son. I had an eighteen-year-old sailor come in here last month, his first time. He said, 'That door's new,' pointing to that door over there to the poolroom, which I had installed about ten years ago. 'How did you know that?' I asked. 'Oh,' he said, 'my dad's got a picture of him sitting on your knee. It was the year before he met me mum.'"

"They like to tell the young ones that they're going to sell them to me for a round of drinks, y'know. Of course, that doesn't happen. I'd never take advantage. But they like to wind up, the young ones. One lad came here with his dad—the Navy has a fathers' week where they fly fathers who were in the Navy out here to travel home onboard ship with their sons. He said, 'Well, 'ere you go, Charles, you can 'ave your wicked way wiv 'im if you keep the drinks comin'!' I laughed and said, 'Well, you're his dad, so I suppose that makes it legal!' You should have seen the poor boy's face!

"Oh, yes, occasionally you get troublemakers. They come here saying how much they 'ate fuckin' queers. Everyone goes quiet because they know he's going to get a tongue-lashing from me. I usually say something like, 'And I 'ate fookin' ugly cunts like you, luv!' Everyone usually pisses themselves laughing. And more often than not," adds Charlie, smiling, "they end up staying the night. . . .

"I can't go on forever, though, y'know. I'm getting on, luv. And," he sighs, "matelots are fewer and farther between in these days of bloody Navy cutbacks! When my baby is gone," he glances over at his pooch snoozing quietly, "there won't be much left for me. I think I shall retire to the U.K. Most of my friends are there. But the matelots, bless 'em, they don't notice any of this decay! They always say, 'Oh, Charlie, you never change!' and I say to them, 'Well, no, but the wattage does!'" Charlie laughs. "Every year a bit less. I started off here with one-hundred-watt bulbs. Now I'm down to a bloody ten-watt! And *tinted*.

"Why do the lads love me? Oh, it's because they know I love them," he explains with a shrug. "And I'm always here. Unlike barmaids, I don't regard them as a problem or as a meal ticket. And, of course," he smiles, winking, "they do like my outrageous behaviour. They always insist that I wear *all* my jewellery when they come to visit."

A few hours and a crate of beer later, I leave Charlie, surrounded by his flags and memories and guarded by his old dog. Staggering back to my hotel I can't help thinking that the reason the sailors treat Charlie like a star is simply because they recognise one when they see one. Lovely Charlie is, well, *lovely*. And priceless. When he finally calls last orders, or runs out of wattage, a little but precious piece of British marytime history will be lost forever.

Attitude
March 2000

Casual Pickup

A couple of miles past Newark, bored and hot on a sticky August afternoon, I zoom past a crop-haired, sexy young lout in a T-shirt and jeans with his thumb out. I eye him in the rearview mirror as he shrinks into the distance.

I don't give lifts to hitchhikers. It's asking for trouble. Okay, so I used to hitchhike everywhere myself years ago, when I didn't have the price of a bus ticket to my name. But now that I have my own car, a nice, sporty little soft top, things have changed. I now realise that hitchhikers are layabouts and bad news. Only loonies, drug addicts, and convicts hitchhike *these* days. So, really, letting a complete stranger into your car and your life is a bad idea. It's dangerous. It's messy. It's daft. Unless, of course, they're cute.

I brake, hard.

The lad sees me pull over but seems hesitant. I twist around and shout over the back of my car, "Well, c'mon then, mate! *Do you want a lift or not?*" He runs up to the passenger-side door.

"Where are you headed?" I ask.

"London, mate," he says.

I look him up and down. In his midtwenties, he's not bad looking, but he isn't as cute as he was at 60 mph (but then, who is?). He could do with a bath. And he looks like trouble.

"Get in," I say, leaning across and opening the door. "I'm headed for Cambridge," I lie. "I can take you another thirty miles."

"Nice one!" he says with a wide grin, jumping in.

Rejoining the flow of cars southward, we chat the casually polite chat of hitchhikers and drivers. I introduce myself; he introduces himself as "John, but me mates call me Jonno." He tells me he was in Newark "visiting relatives" and now he's on his way back home to Dover, "I'll catch the train in London." He tells me about his wife and his three-year-old kid in Dover. "I love that kid to bits—I live for her, mate." We pass a sign:

London: 60 miles

"I'm really glad you stopped, mate," says Jonno, for the third time.

"Yeah?" I say. "S'funny. You seemed a bit reluctant at first. Thought you were going to run away!"

Jonno looks a bit sheepish. "Well, the thing, is mate, to be totally honest wiv you, there are some people after me. I owe money to some geezers in Newark. I thought you might 'ave been sent by them—not being funny, but you look a bit of a bruiser, mate!"

"Don't worry," I reassure him. "My bark's much worse than my bite. What do you owe them money for?"

"Oh. This and that."

"Drugs?"

Jonno shifts in his seat, looks down, and shakes his head. "No—no way, mate!"

"Look, it doesn't matter to me," I explain.

Jonno looks down at his hands. "Well, to be totally honest wiv you, mate, it *was* drugs. But only speed, and a bit of hash. Nothing 'ard. I'm trying to get off the shit, you know? I'm trying to get clean. I've gotta think of me daughter man. I can't be fucked up around her, can I?"

"No, Jonno. Not a good idea."

London: 30 miles

"Mark, mate, 'aven't we passed the sign for Cambridge?"

"Yeah. To be totally honest with you, I'm going to London, not Cambridge. I usually don't tell hitchers how far I'm going in case we—er . . . don't get on."

"Oh, right, mate. I understand. So you're going to London? Sorted!"

"So . . .," I probe, "what were you *really* doing in Newark?"

"You're not stupid, are you? Well, to be totally honest wiv you, I was on remand there for a week."

"Really?" I say casually, trying not to look too interested.

"Yeah. Nothing serious, though. Just nonpayment of a fine, like. Never again. It was disgusting in there, mate—'ottest week of the year in a shit hole with no showers or change of clothes. I fucking stink, mate."

"Yeah, I had noticed! So what was the fine you didn't pay?"

"Well, to be totally honest wiv you, mate, I was done for breach of the peace and criminal damage. I kicked my ex-wife's door down because she wouldn't let me see my kid. I was really drunk at the time; I didn't know what I was doing."

"So, you're not with your wife anymore?"

"No, mate. We separated a couple of years back, and she lets me see my kid once a week. But she wouldn't that night coz I was steaming.

"I 'ate prison. I was sent to borstal when I was thirteen and had the shit kicked out of me. It was that bad I tried to top meself." He holds out his hands, wrists uppermost, revealing a pair of ropy white scars across his dirty wrists.

"I only ended up in borstal coz me stepdad used to knock me about. He used to kick the shit out of me mum and I tried to stop 'im, and so he turned on me. The worst of it was, she was egging 'im on! Didn't spend much time at home after that. Fell in wiv a bad crowd."

London: 20 miles

"I've got some mates who live in London," Jonno announces, as the tired and dirty sun lowers itself into a peach melba bath on the western horizon. "They live in Soho. Is that anywhere near you?"

"No," I say. "I live a very long way from Soho—as far as you can get without actually leaving London. Your friends must pay a lot of rent to live there."

"Yeah, but they don't care. They make a packet." Pause. "To be honest wiv you, they're on the game, if you know what I mean."

"Yeah, I know what you mean."

"They're gay," he adds, driving the point home. He looks at me anxiously. "You don't mind gay people, do you?"

"No, I don't mind gay people," I lie. "Actually, some of my best friends are gay."

"Really? Sorted. I was a bit worried there, coz some people really hate gays."

"Terrible, isn't it?" I say.

London: 10 miles

"Are you sure you don't mind gay people?"

"Sure."

"Okay. Well, to be totally honest wiv you, right, I swing both ways." Jonno steals a sideways look at me.

"Really?" I say.

"Yeah. That's not a problem, is it?"

"Nah," I say. "Not at all. Everyone's thought about it, at least once, haven't they?"

"I like women and that, but I also like, y'know, a really good seeing to by someone who takes control. Well," he laughs, "in the bedroom, not in real life like me mum!"

Like your true destination, you don't tell a hitchhiker your real orientation until you're certain you want to go all the way with him. Mind, I can see that this lad has the measure of me and where this car journey is headed. It's a balmy evening; it's sort of spontaneous; he's rough and he's certainly ready. But I'm reluctant, and not just because he's not washed for a week. It's because I've heard much too much for it to be casual. We've come too far.

It's dark when we arrive in London—without any unplanned stops at bushy lay-bys. I drop him off. He shakes my hand firmly. "Cheers, Mark, thanks for the lift," he says, a flicker of disappointment crosses his face. "It was good talking to you." And he's gone.

I drive off. A minute later, I suddenly feel I have to speak to him again. Maybe to lend him some money—I'm sure he hasn't got any for the train to Dover. Maybe to be "totally honest" with him. I turn the car around, but there's no trace of Jonno. He's dissolved into the warm but unfriendly London night.

Like I said, it's a bad idea letting a complete stranger into your life.

Attitude
February 2000

DIRTY THOUGHTS

The New Naff

In the recent BBC2 gay comedy series *Gimme, Gimme, Gimme*—the show that put the "h" in "sitcom"—one moment stood out as being especially inept in an almost surreally unfunny programme. The fag and the hag are trying to establish the ownership of a strange man lying on their kitchen table. "Quick! Check the cooker!" shrieked the fag thing. "If there's a quiche in the oven, he must be gay!"

Quiche. Remember when this egg-based flan savoury was gay? Remember when quiche was exotic, poncey, and aspirational, and not merely a tired mainstay of pub lunches and school dinners? Remember when real men didn't eat it, let alone cook it? Wasn't it called The Sixties? Turn on the telly today in the Nancy Nineties and you'll find at least three cookery programmes featuring men busily engaged in preparing foreign, exotic, poncey dishes who wouldn't even think of making quiche because it's far too *straight*.

Time minces on, even if gay sitcom writers don't. Change channels and you'll catch one of those legion interior decorating programmes where men rouche the curtains and dapple the plaster of gasping (hetero) couples all over the country. Or an ad for IKEA, which sells their designer furniture to the masses as part of a religious renunciation of ordinariness ("Chuck out your chintz!"). Or one of those myriad dating programmes for single, promiscuous, self-obsessed heterosexual people. Or one of those countless confessional talk shows, where straight people feel the need to "come out," parading their private neuroses and perversions.

Or perhaps the return of *GayTime TV*, recommissioned despite critical pastings because it was one of the most watched programmes on BBC2. By straights. Or maybe a rerun of *Queer As Folk*, Channel Four's smash-hit soap opera about gays in Manchester's Gay Village, played by straight actors and watched by millions of straight people and one gay person who doesn't get out much.

There's no question about it. The TV ratings confirm it. The straights—or "naffs" as 1950s homos used to call them—have gone "gay."

According to letter writers to the *Daily Telegraph,* in a cleaner, more fragrant time long since polluted by permissiveness, decimal money, and free school milk, "gay" meant simply colourful, carefree, and happy. This was before, of course, it was hijacked by sodomites and became a byword for buggery. However, this poor, much-maligned word is now in the hands of even more unsavoury characters—marketing men, spin doctors, restaurateurs, and TV presenters. Now "gay" has little or nothing to do with buggery at all. It just means "mainstream aspirational" or "mass aestheticism"—otherwise known as "shite."

This was Robbie Fowler's faux pas with *Le Saux.* Northern nostalgic Robbie was absolutely right to consider southern smoothie Graeme "gay"—but, sadly, absolutely wrong to think that this meant that Graeme would oblige him and fuck his large Scouse arse. Hilariously, the other "big spread" that followed, in which Graeme paraded his lovely wife and lovely baby in *Hello!,* may have confirmed his heterosexuality—but the shots of his lovely Habitat home, his Lavazza Pininfarina espresso machine and six-ring brushed-steel Smeg cooker just proved that Graeme was as gay as a Waitrose goose (with a piquant lemon baste and tasty walnut-and-dates stuffing).

The titanic struggle of the twentieth century turned out to be not against Nazism or Communism but against naffism. But this struggle, in which gays were the hot-pink shock troops, is over. And the naffs have lost. The Fowlers of this world are conducting a literally "rearguard" action. Everything has been aestheticised, including the "beautiful game." Expression has triumphed over repression, Calvin Klein over Y-Fronts, designer over authentic, Metro over suburban, emotionally incontinent over emotionally blocked, IKEA over MFI, Islington over Essex, roquette salad over frozen peas, slagginess over sincerity, soap opera over seriousness, loft apartment over semidetached, show business over sport, aspirational over conventional, interior design over class. Britain is a nation of shopkeepers no more. We have become, instead, a nation of hairdressers.

And I'm sorry, but I don't think there's much to pop a bottle of Veuve Clicquot over, or even a bottle of Marks & Spencer's Premium Sparkling (you can hardly tell it from champagne you know, and it's *so* reasonably priced). You see, "gay" is now the new naff. The lifestylism and makeover mania which gays largely pioneered, and with which they seduced the straights, has become as dominant and as dull and dreary as the Old Naff once was.

Worse, where the Old Naff merely demanded your conformity, the New Naff commands you to "have fun" (or else), "be individual" (just like everyone else), and "enjoy" its fucking awful "Modern Italian" cuisine. In the days of Old Naff you had to eat what was put in front of you, but you weren't expected to praise the fruitiness of the extra virgin olive oil you're supposed to dip your *ciabbata* in, over-tip the waiters, and buy a bottle of overpriced sun-dried tomatoes in the restaurant shop afterward.

There is no escape from the New Naff's aesthetic totalitarianism. The very expansion of media and consumerism which helped see off the Old Naff has made the New Naff omnipresent and all-enveloping—even fucking is now just a branch of interior design. If television is riddled with the New Naff, the print media is addled with it. All the glossies are by definition New Naff, since they exist only to deliver fashion and lifestyle advertising to their wannabe readers. And now the crusty old broadsheets have gone "gay," as is advertised by the profusion of "Metro," "Space," and "Living" sections with tips on where to find cast-iron bathtubs with clawed-feet, leather sofabeds, and 100-percent-cotton duvet covers.

Even the tabs are at it. *The Sun,* once the impregnable, tightly clenched organ of Old Naff and the scourge of anything poncey or lah-dee-dah, seems to have been slipped some rohypnol. Now officially homo-friendly, design-led, and increasingly interested in cuisine, fashion, cinema, and furnishings, *The New Sun* is almost as "gay" as *The Old Sun* used to be "straight." Remember that infamous Barrymore coming-out headline—"WE'RE RIGHT BEHIND YOU— BUT NOT TOO CLOSE!"—of a few years back? Well, now *The Sun* has grabbed the "gay" thing from behind, is chewing its neck, and enjoying some very heavy, but highly tasteful, *frottage.*

New Naff is also in government, which is a sign of both its hegemony and, well, its *naffness.* New Labour is New Naff (as indeed is anything that has the word "New" in front of it—e.g., "New Lad," "New Britain," and "New Mr. & Mrs."). That politics has been replaced by aesthetics is bad news for both politics *and* aesthetics. It goes without saying that Tony Blair is *très* "gay." The drag queen smiles, the slaggy No.10 parties for pop celebs, the Italian-cut suits, the "classlessness" (really an upwardly mobile hairdresser's desire to distance himself from his party's working-class past), the air-kissing embrace of Terence Conran, the moisturiser—*the moisturiser.* Tony Blair must have the shiniest, most hydrated face in international politics, now that Mandy, the man who introduced him to Clinique for Men, is no longer in the public eye. Ironically, it is precisely because New Labour is so "gay" that Makeover Mandy, the party's interior-exterior design and fashion consultant, could never come out as homosexual and why the Labour Party is so unlikely to deliver homosexual equality. (Gayness plus gays equals "gay mafia" headlines.)

Not all Labour MPs aesthetic preferences conform to the party line, however. John Prescott is a closet straight, but his Old Naffness is even more of an open secret than Mandy's homosexuality, and most people seem willing to overlook it. (The most openly straight Labour MPs are, of course, Nick Brown and Ron Davies.) Then there are those rumours about Gordon Brown, whose gayness is, it has to be said, somewhat unconvincing—however, I suspect that his secret straightness won't stop him introducing a tax on sports jackets and Jeremy Clarkson in the next budget.

Open straightness can have a terrible political price attached to it. William Hague is an obvious ungay—he has a Yorkshire accent, wears wellingtons, speaks his mind, is Europhobic, and is bollock bald. And so naturally he is hugely unpopular. His recent public appearances with soap opera stars and on chat shows hasn't fooled anyone. Meanwhile, the Queen Over the Water, alias Michael Portillo, has noted which way the disco smoke is blowing and has shrewdly succumbed to his latent gayness. After years of struggle against his tendencies, he has allowed his interest in hair mousse, lip balm, and the experience of being thrashed by Stephen Twigg get the better of him and has apparently become a TV presenter.

Europe is, by definition, way gay—which is why Blair can't resist it (and why *The New Sun* will eventually abandon its opposition to it). But only to someone from Britain. In truth, Europe is in many ways Old Naff. The Germans, for instance, are the straightest people on the planet, even if half of them dress up in leather harnesses and peaked caps and invade Gran Canaria every summer. Sorry, *because* half of them dress up in leather harnesses and invade Gran Canaria every summer. It's all about perspective. The Swedish appear to the Brits as the gayest country in the world because they produced ABBA, Absolut vodka, and flat-packed frosted glass coffee tables with a lovely gunmetal grey frame. However, the Swedes are rather ungay in the flesh—they still live in a social democracy, belong to trade unions, and tend to be rather earnest people who get all—the horror of it!—maudlin and introspective after one Absolut-with-a-hint-of-blueberry too many.

And of course, to heteros, homos themselves are much 'gayer' than they actually are. Heteros watch gay programmes religiously, hoping to pick up some fashion, home furnishing, or kinky sex tips. This is why gays in gay soap operas have to live in fabulous loft apartments, have lots of glamorous sex, and why everyone wears very nice, fashionable shirts instead of those nasty, tight, white vests that gays actually wear (they make you look tanned under the ultraviolet).

This is why the Mao suit of New Naff, designer combat trousers, are everywhere—heterosexuals think that homosexuals wear them. And it's true, about three years ago a couple of Soho gays did wear them. But within a year they were worn by every male under thirty in Central London. A year later they were worn by every male under thirty-five in the South East. Today, every British male is given a pair with their BCG vaccination, while, in accordance with new local government regulations, corpses are laid out in silver Moschino combat trousers.

New Naff has blood on its hands. It killed pop music by making sure that *it doesn't matter anymore.* The reason Glam, Punk, or New Romantic couldn't happen now is because in the New Naff era the aspirations of young people are carefully channelled, exploited, and commodified from the earliest stage and can't explode into the frustrated abandon of pop or youth cults as they used to. Aestheticism is mainstream, so there's no point trying to launch an aesthetic rebellion. Under New Naff, the point of pop is inverted. A transsexual wearing a gladioli dress, singing a song called "Diva," wins Terry Wogan's Eurovision Song Contest and the *Top of the Pops* studio and presenters have a glam makeover, while the performers become ever more dowdy. By the same token, New Naff has also murdered camp—since nothing is serious anymore, you can't have any failed seriousness. And since everything is silly now, you can't use superficiality as a subversive strategy.

Paradoxically, the gaying of straights is very bad news for gays. Now that "gay" is the mainstream aesthetic, homos have nowhere to go. Gays complain that Pride and the gay districts like Manchester's

Gay Village are being overrun by straights. But then, calling anything "gay" these days is just an invitation to be invaded by lots of New Naff heteros looking for imported bottled beer, designer drugs, swanky toilets, and Eurobeat. Perhaps homos should just vacate The Village, and in fact the whole "gay" thing, and leave the heteros to get on with it, while they take up some hobbies like fishing, pigeon-fancying, or car maintenance, instead.

Such a drastic step may not be necessary, however. There's a glimmer of hope on the horizon. There are signs that that the children of the New Naffs may leave the poor harassed queers alone and stop nagging them for fashion tips. A recent survey of eight- to fourteen-year-olds found that they used the word "gay" to mean "crap," "uncool," "deeply unhip," or "naff."

Which sounds about right. Think about it: NaffTime TV, Naff Pride, naff bars, naff discos . . . and naff jokes about naff quiche in naff sitcoms.

Attitude
May 1999

The Pittfall of Being Brad

What do you do with a bit of rough who was fun for an hour or so but overstays his welcome? You know the ones—they tend to become more and more annoying the more they open their mouths. Instead of pissing off in a taxi when you've had your way with them, they moon around your home as if they were permanent fixtures. As if you had a future together. As if you were interested in anything they had to say.

Brad Pitt is the ultimate clingy one-night stand. Geena Davis has a lot to answer for. Ever since she picked him up off the side of the road in *Thelma & Louise* in 1991, we've had to put up with his delusion that he's some kind of *movie star*. Yes, lots of us would like to give a boy like that a ride. But does one evening of passion justify eight years of boredom?

Okay, so he was passable in *A River Runs Through It* (1992). Even if he didn't get his kit off much, he did look lovely in a white shirt and braces, the river light catching his face from below making him look even more like a fallen angel than he did in *Thelma & Louise*. A young Robert Redford, but dumber and therefore cuter. But really, the best thing about all that fishing was that he didn't have to do much *acting*.

However, in the rather silly *Kalifornia* (1993), where he played a psycho serial killer, poor Brad was already out of his league. It's difficult to be menacing when you look like an ad for men's moisturiser—even if you grow a beard, wave a gun around, and shout a lot.

In the rather sillier *Interview with a Vampire* (1994), he was cast opposite Tom Cruise and poor Brad's dullness became all too apparent. You could understand why Tom might want to suck Brad's lovely neck but not why he'd want to spend eternity with him, no matter how lonely being undead might be.

Interview illuminated the difference between Tom and Brad and why, despite the fact that Brad is seen by many as the 1990s' Tom Cruise, in this instance today's trade *wasn't* about to turn into tomorrow's competition. Thing is, Tom, in addition to actually having some acting ability, is a tart who works hard for his money, charming and flirting with the camera like it was the last punter before Christmas, and showing just enough vulnerability to make the experience of watching this shameless display of male narcissism sadistically pleasurable. Brad's vanity, on the other hand, is just arrogance. It seems to say, "Oh, yeah, I know everyone wants to shag me." Which of course is true. But if you let the world know you know, it stops being true very quickly.

Even when Brad really tries to act, it just looks like a way of showing off his expensive coaching. In the very silly *12 Monkeys* (1995), he was so annoyingly *studied* in his performance of the tics and jerks of a madman that electroshock therapy seemed like humane treatment. Then there was the matter of his Irish accent in *The Devil's Own* (1997), which would have single-handedly made a comedy out of the movie if the script hadn't got there first. Saying "aye" a lot and pronouncing "back" with about twelve long Celtic vowels doesn't help much if you also pronounce every third "back" with a single, short American English vowel.

Appropriately enough, Brad's most convincing accent was the one in *Seven Years in Tibet* (1997), where he plays an irritating, arrogant *German*. However, it becomes strangely *un*convincing later in the film, when he is supposed to be learning humility and abandoning his ego. This transformation is supposed to happen in the Tibetan wilderness—a place where ego and arrogance can kill a man. But Brad looks like he's still in Malibu, where these qualities get you an eight-bedroom extension to your beach house.

Brad probably agreed to appear in *Seven Years* because he thought it was a sequel to *Seven* (1995). A hit at the box office, *Seven* was a clever suspense movie whose cleverest move was typecasting Brad as an annoying little brat wannabe and Morgan Freeman as the actor. Even the decapitated head of Brad's "wife" in a box does more acting than he does in this movie.

To be fair, it isn't all Brad's fault. He's the victim of something largely beyond his control: his beauty. It's what made him and it's what unmakes him. In *Kalifornia*, his chiseled, hairless naked body beneath the full moon screams "Culture" when he's supposed to represent trailer park Nature run riot. And in *Seven Years in Tibet*, his six-pack stomach and pert pecs do somewhat belie the notion that he's starving to death thousands of miles from the nearest abs machine.

In *12 Monkeys*, when he moons us with his smooth, finely muscled ass it doesn't signal madness and excremental rebellion but instead hours of disciplined dedication in the gymnasium. Despite being on-screen for only a couple of seconds, Brad's ass steals the film (and Bruce Willis's desperate gambit of flashing his own flabby butt every five minutes fails completely) and probably landed him his Oscar nomination. This is because Brad's ass is so much more expressive, so much more characterful, so much more articulate than his face.

Come to think of it, Brad's best performance was in that jeans ad he appeared in years ago where he wakes up in a Mexican prison with no trousers on, being eyed up by fat, sweaty, moustachioed prison guards. After making puppy eyes at his captors, who keep his jeans as a memento of the night, he is released and whisked away by an attractive woman (with an extra pair of jeans) in a convertible—to a photo shoot. And the reason this is his best performance ever? *Brad doesn't utter a single word.*

His latest movie, *Meet Joe Black* (1998), could be something of a make-or-break picture for our one-night-stand-that-became-a-decade. After a number of recent flops, Brad, who is now well into his thirties and thus negotiating a very tricky, uncharted territory for the male bimbo stars that were spawned by the early 1990s, needs to prove that he can still hold our interest. Make us *care*.

Everyone knows Hollywood does strange things to beautiful young women, but it does even stranger things to beautiful young men. Brad's ailing brunette doppelganger, Keanu Reeves—someone who has also failed to yet make the transition from sex object to character actor, boyhood to manhood—was recently cast as Satan's/Al Pacino's son in *The Devil's Advocate* (1997) in a desperate attempt to make him interesting. It didn't work. Alas, Hollywood doesn't seem to have learned its lesson; in *Meet Joe Black* poor Brad has been cast as a blond Grim Reaper.

Let's pray he doesn't try a Swedish accent.

Guardian
November 1998

Elvis Has Now Reentered
the Building

Elvis didn't want to be black; he wanted to be Tony Curtis. A natural blond, Memphis's belle boy dyed his hair in imitation of his idol's shiny black pompadour and continued tinting it that unnatural-supernatural blue-black colour until the very end (though later it was probably merely to hide the grey). Even those virile sideburns, which by the early 1970s seemed to be bracketing the world, were deceivingly dyed too.

This is a shocking, indecent thing to bring up, and not just because of the way Tony Curtis's "hair" looks now. We like to think of Elvis as rock's Unmoved Mover, The King, the original, the alpha and omega—the fount of all pop cultural sovereignty. "Before Elvis there was nothing," as John Lennon famously put it. In a world where popness has become the measure of everything, we're all Elvis impersonators now, and we don't want to think that we might be inadvertently "doing" Tony Curtis.

As the parade of celebs lined up for the premiere of the reedited, remastered, rereleased 1970 Vegas gig movie *Elvis: That's the Way It Is* bears testimony, all the new pretenders want to be seen in His presence, even if it's only a celluloid one. Maybe it's just the PopStars in Your Eyes, but Elvis seems to keep on getting bigger, while those that came after him keep getting smaller. Elvis was the first truly giant pop star created by postwar consumerism and its attendant media. Since then, consumerism and the media have swallowed everything, and Elvis has become the personification of the looking-glass world we inhabit now, a latter-day Narcissus who drowned in his own reflection (on his bathroom floor)—but was granted immortality in a universe of surfaces and permanent (shallow) memory. "Elvis" is fame's first name in an age when "fame" is something we're increasingly overfamiliar with.

Perhaps this is why in Elvis' face we can see an angelic/demonic premonition of the faces of so many of those stars that have come since: Tom Cruise, Mick Jagger, Michael Jackson, Jim Carrey, Madonna, Bill Clinton, Princess Diana, Jeffrey Dahmer. Elvis' masculine androgyny and animal smartness seem even more modern today than when he launched his career. In footage of The King in action, all the male faces—and many of the women—in the crowd seem strangely frozen and meatish next to his, even when he is clearly half-paralysed by downers, the eyes all hooded and sleepy. As lesbian Elvis impersonator k.d. lang observed, "He had total love in his eyes when he performed. . . ." It only makes his "total love" all the more potent that when he sang, he didn't mean it, or didn't know what he meant; *we* are left to sort it out, like the swooning victims of a passionate but exquisitely totally careless lover (which is the condition of human subjectivity in a mediatised world).

Elvis the Lover is also, however, the archetype of the postwar male pervert. Radiantly narcissistic and dramatically unable to negotiate his oedipus complex, he is the prime idolatrous icon of a decadent, postpatriarchal age. Again, he may not have invented virile degeneracy (Clift, Brando, and Dean, whom he also imitated, have a prior claim), but he patented it. True, it may have been campy Liberace who was accused by the British press of being the "quivering distillation of mother-love," but it was good ol' boy Elvis-the-Pelvis who got away with it and, in fact, made it cool. Elvis, the beautiful boy who loved his mammy and almost forgot he had a daddy (as we did too; we always call him by his first name), is the patron saint of the New Matriarchy.

Even today, twenty-four years after his death, as we stumble into a century he never actually swung his hips in, Elvis the rock star, pop star, stand-up comedian, and self-medicating Vegas showgirl remains the acme of the mediatised male, and also of male desirability. Male love-me-tender passivity and vulnerability was legitimised by Elvis, helpfully preparing men for the (prone) role that consumerism had in store for them.

Tony Curtis fixation notwithstanding, Elvis really is "the original," the template from which everything else is stamped, because he has become the ego ideal of an image-led, "perverted," dyed-sideburns culture. Since his death, through a process of global mourning and melancholia and constant reruns and revivals, the lost lurve-object has been introjected into our Collective Unconscious so completely that we don't have to be lonesome tonight or tomorrow or ever again. His absence has become an overwhelming presence. Elvis really is alive. It's just the rest of us that I'm not so sure about.

Independent on Sunday
April 2000

All Hail Dame Liz

So now Ms. Taylor is officially supposed to be addressed by her first name, as in "Dame Elizabeth will open an exhibition of portraits of herself today at the National Portrait Gallery" or "Dame Elizabeth will attend an AIDS charity benefit this evening and be introduced to a lot of gay men who curtsey nervously and promptly faint."

For once, this feudal familiarity reflects a trend of contemporary culture—these days everyone is on starstruck first name terms with all those special, "divine" women—not just Liz and Julie—in gay men's lives: Bette! Judy! Joan! Marilyn! Liza! Barbra! And attuned to all those signifiers—big hair! exaggerated cigarette movements! tragedy! strength! psychotic stares! impossible bosoms! excessive femininity!—which made them so obviously "camp." In an era riddled with and addled by postmodernism, everyone wants to be in on the smirky joke, as well as on their knees at the altar of false gods. The "gay icon," once the jealously guarded ancestral secret of the gay subculture, belongs no longer to gays but to everyone.

Liz played a big part in this. By devoting so much energy to AIDS work, Dame Elizabeth "came out" about her special relationship with gays and made her "gayness" public property. It also made her tangible to gays themselves (for gays, the gay icon is a mother-goddess, so when she actually intercedes on their behalf it's like Lourdes at Happy Hour).

In the old model of gay iconery, the dependence of the fading starlet on aesthete bachelors was something that had to be kept discreet—even as she increasingly devoted herself to her most forgiving, most *cloying* audience. This would ultimately be the ruin of the diva: the more Judy faltered, the more words she forgot to "Somewhere Over the Rainbow," the more of a mess she became, the more the gays loved her. Theirs was a dance of the doomed—the rejected and the dejected slow-waltzing in a suffocating embrace (rather like Wimbledon Football Club and its supporters).

In the 1970s gays got liberated and the songs they were dancing to changed from "The One That Got Away" to "So Many Men, So Little

Time" (even if the latter disco ditty turned out to be too true). In the 1980s another aspirational disco diva captured the hearts of gays— Margaret Thatcher. Yes, in the early part of her reign Maggie cast herself as a slightly dowdy nanny whom the country needed to spank its bottom and dispense unpleasant medicine. But by the latter part of her reign she had mutated into a serious diva with shoulder pads, hair, and ambition that outgunned even Joan Collins. (Though, of course, now she resembles more the Judy Garland-type of gay diva.)

But Margaret in the 1980s turned out to be just a bad dress rehearsal for Madonna in the 1990s. As a pop star completely in control of her career, her image, and, most important, her sexuality, Madonna represented the culmination of a new kind of career woman—one who was spending more and more time with gay men. In addition to epitomising the gay daydream of the mother-goddess who would come and rescue them, the Madonna cult epitomised the new alliance between gay men and independent, straight career women looking to learn how to live single lives—which at times threatens to take over the world. Or at least the gay disco on a Saturday night.

Madonna not only directly acknowledged her gay audience, she directly addressed them ("Justify My Love"), stole from them ("Vogue"), and even said she was one of them: "I'm a gay man trapped in a woman's body." She transformed fag haggery from fatal diva faux pas to fashion statement and even, for a brief flirtatious moment, managed to make lesbianism interesting to gay men (remember "lesbian chic"?).

In her wake, the gay icons who have come after her are mostly jokes—gay men's investment in them is largely *campy* or self-consciously comic: e.g., Patsy and Edina, Margarita Prakatan, Kathy Burke, Jennifer Aniston. Which means, of course, that they are, like everything else these days, *democratic*. They are icon-lite. Their "gayness" is there for everyone to buy into. Of course, the greatest example of this is Geri Halliwell, a cliché trapped in a Basingstoke bargirl's body who can't, it seems, be seen in public without a brace of oiled gay go-go dancers. She's a flat-packed fag-hag, a dot-to-dot diva.

Liz, however, as an icon from a time when such things were taken very seriously indeed, has managed to survive long enough to escape the Judy effect—more or less—*and* reap the benefits of the Geri effect without being contaminated by it. Liz is a monument to a past we don't believe in anymore and to a future we can't imagine. Her films radiate with a femininity we now know was impossible to embody, and as her eight marriages demonstrate she has, like most people these days, proved to be very bad at performing traditional heterosexuality. She may even have married a gay man, as a recent disputed biography of Richard Burton suggested (lending another layer of irony to their bitchfest performance in *Who's Afraid of Virginia Woolf* [1966]).

Dame Liz: truly, a "gay icon" for everyone.

Independent
May 2000

What Kind of Man's Man
Is Guy Ritchie?

"Do you have big brave balls?" asks human rottweiler Vinnie Jones in a standoff moment in Guy Ritchie's new movie, *Snatch* (2001). "Or mincey faggot balls?"

We don't entertain any doubts about the circumference and virility of Vinnie's testimonials—and not just because he flashes a semiautomatic handcannon big enough to make Linda Lovelace gasp. And now, with the birth of his son Rocco Ritchie, the whole world knows that the thirty-year-old writer-director who has been described as "the Orson Welles of his generation," has balls big and brave enough to impregnate Madonna.

But is this middle-class gangster-groupie so sure himself about what kind of family heirlooms he dangles? On the basis of his curiously sexually ambivalent output, it seems Mr. Ritchie—like his vast, appreciative young male audience—has more than a little anxiety about the possibility that he might have mincey faggot balls, after all. Emasculation and masculinity, for Ritchie and the laddist culture he represents, are constant if uncomfortable bedfellows.

Like his first film, *Lock, Stock and Two Smoking Barrels* (1999), *Snatch* is obsessed with buggery. The mockernee geeza dialogue is thick with references to "'aving me pants pulled down," being "bent over," "full penetration," and being "fucked." Maybe this isn't so surprising, since, again like his first film and the TV series *Lock, Stock & . . .* he executive produced, women don't really exist in this testosterone-flavoured world. The only snatch in *Snatch* belongs to other men. Hence the obsession with "hard men" and "pussies"; those who take and those who are taken. The erotics of Mr. Ritchie's cinematic universe seems to be that of the prison showers (or public school dormitories).

Ritchie is so "hot" because he is the preeminent example of a rising phenomenon in an age of masculine confusion: the homo-hetero. Exclusively and adamantly heterosexual in the bedroom, the homo-

hetero is nevertheless entranced by masculine images, forever fanta-
sising about a world of homosociality that is just a dropped bar of
soap away from homosexuality. Is Guy Ritchie—the man who lives
with the woman who famously proclaimed herself a gay man trapped
in a woman's body—a gay man trapped in a straight man's body?

As a kind of answer the new film actually *begins* with a jokey disavowal of homosexuality. Turkish, the central character and narrator,
(played by the very handsome, man's man suedehead ex-diver Jason
Statham) introduces himself and "me partner, Tommy." Adding quickly,
"now, I don't mean 'partner' in the sense of 'olding 'ands."

Certainly, there's a lot to disavow. The nearest thing to a sex scene
in the first film was the lovingly shot, soft-focus, all-male pub party
where the lads get very drunk, wrestle, horseplay, and light each
other's farts before falling into a blissful, exhausted postorgasmic
group slumber. In the first episode of the TV series, the "lads" are trying to flog some dodgy porn to a fence. "They're not gay, are they?"
he asks, worriedly. "Do we look like a couple of rear gunners?" the
pretty boys retort, in their £600 knee-length leather jackets.

Let's not beat around the old bull and bush here. The *Lock, Stock
and Two Smoking Barrels* genre—and the lad mag culture from
which it seems to have sprung—is a kind of gay porn for straight
men. Mr. Ritchie's relationship to masculinity, as shown in his dodgy
films, is rather "gay"—it seems to mix up a desire to *be* his heroes
with, well, *desire*. Like the new lad sensibility of *Loaded* and *FHM*,
used to sell a commodified, aestheticised masculinity back to a generation of young men alienated from it in their own lives, it's the
supplicatory, hungry, nerdish, and slightly masochistic perspective of
the *wannabe*.

Mr. Ritchie's idolatorous camera-worship of "hard man" Vinnie
Jones and his big brave balls borders on the erotic. The most memora-
ble scene in *Lock, Stock* features Vinnie repeatedly slamming a car
door on a man's head in slo-mo to uplifting music. The power of this
religiously intense scene stems from the way that much of it is shot
from the POV of the victim; Ritchie and the audience are looking up
admiringly—and open-mouthed—at Vinnie doing his "nut." It's a
moment which could have been directed by Jean Genet (if his taste in
"hard men" had been less exacting).

Perhaps this is why Mr. Ritchie can be so touchy about his image.
Asked a few worshipful questions recently about his taste in clothes

by *FHM*, he became a tad defensive, spraying out the words "fruity," "queeny," "fucking fruit tree," and "mincey," and declaring that he would be happiest "in a gladiator outfit" (a leather skirt).

But then, Ritchie's disavowal is deep-rooted. He famously reinvented and relocated his past: "I've lived in the East End for thirty years," he was quoted as saying last year. "And let's just say that I've been in a load of mess-ups. . . . I've been poor all of my life. . . ." It was revealed that instead of hanging around York Hall in Bethnal Green, he spent much of his childhood at Loton Park, the seventeenth-century home of his baronet stepfather.

Like any public schoolboy, Ritchie understands that nowadays what is "street" is sexy—and that middle-class balls are mincey faggot balls. "They're poufs. Soft as shite . . . faggots," is the verdict of one of Ritchie's crims in *Lock, Stock* on the clownish public schoolboy ganja growers—who are humiliated, mutilated, and dispensed with early on in the film.

A recent interview in *Time Out* glossed over the exposure of his privileged past as a classic example of British "inverted snobbery" (well, yes, but *Ritchie's*), and somewhat desperately trumpeted instead his dyslexia as proof that he really was an "outsider" after all (despite the fact that dyslexia has tended to be a privileged disability—working-class dyslexics are just "thick"). Ritchie really is an outsider, however, in one area: his relationship to "authentic" masculinity; it's what makes him such a good "reader" of it—and appropriator.

But then, he isn't the only one. In a consumerist, postfeminist, divorced world, most men are on the outside looking in, wondering what a masculine world might look like. As Brad Pitt puts it in another homo-hetero movie *Fight Club* (1999): "We're a generation of men raised by women. Maybe another woman isn't what we need." (Appropriately enough, Pitt makes an appearance in *Snatch*, reprising his *Fight Club* role as a bare-knuckle fighter.) A generation of men feel emasculated and threatened by women's advance into the public realm—no wonder they are so interested in seeing big brave balls at the cinema.

But an interest in big brave balls on the part of men is itself anxiety producing. Throughout *Snatch* the nasty top-dog gangster (as with the first movie, the only father figure in the film) insultingly refers to lead-guy Turkish's partner as "your boyfriend"—contradicting the reassurance Turkish himself gave us at the beginning of the film. Of course, as in the first film, the Bad Daddy is the one that "gets it" in the end.

The wrong kind of homosociality can be lethal. In an episode from the TV series, a gangster leaves prison (a world of men) and has to collect a bag of money from a locker in a gay sauna (a world of men). The bag turns out to be a bomb and explodes (moral: a gay sauna is the wrong kind of world of men). Interestingly, this episode aired around the time that another nerd with an interest in "hard men" (fascists) and a "gay" past (he was called a "poof" at school) to disavow was sentenced for exploding a bomb in a London gay pub.

Ironically, it's the squeamishness of Mr. Ritchie in particular and homo-heteros in general about actual homosexuality that betrays their lowlife fantasies as essentially middle class, suburban, and "pussy." In *Lock, Stock* one of the lads explains the perfect scam, which involves placing an ad for "arse tickler faggot fan club anal-intruding dildos" in gay magazines, and waiting for the cheques to roll in. Then you send out letters saying that you're out of stock and enclose a cheque, stamped "Arse Ticklers Faggot Fan Club." "Not a single soul will cash it!" we are told. Somehow, I doubt that Ronnie Kray, for example, would have had a problem.

Actually, Ritchie—and lad culture—have been running that scam ever since *Lock, Stock,* selling homo-heteros a promise of something phallic and titillating that never quite arrives.

All in all, it seems both a paradox and entirely apt that big brave ball-fixated Ritchie lives with the ultimate gay icon, a woman who many men would consider to be the biggest ball buster in the world, and one whom many men would imagine/worry had her own collection of "anal-intruding dildos"—an older woman whose own success and fame easily dwarfs his own. But then, Ritchie's interest in her is entirely consisent with what we know about him from his films: "I like her," he explains, "because she's ballsy."

Independent on Sunday
September 2000

Eminem Melts in Your Mouth

Eminem, aka Marshall Mathers, may have won only a few consolation prizes at the Grammys yesterday, but clearly the white rapper behind *The Marshall Mathers LP* has the Album of the Year in every other sense. Em is the hottest property not just in the music business, but in pop culture itself. And, like Big Gay Al, aka Elton John, who duetted with him onstage at the Staples Center, no one—the fans, the press, the critics, the police, the vice president's wife, the gay activists—can leave him alone.

Especially, of course, the gay rights activists, 200 of whom picketed the Staples Center in protest at his "violently homophobic lyrics" (and what they saw as gay Elton's "betrayal"). Afterward, the Gay and Lesbian Alliance Against Defamation solemnly issued a statement expressing "gratitude" that Em was not awarded Album of the Year but complained that the three minor Grammys awarded Eminem showed that "Academy members were willing to place their stamp of approval on lyrics that promote hate, prejudice, and violence."

Amen. But the rather important point which the protestors appear to have overlooked is: Sure, Em's music is violently homophobic. It also happens to be *violently homosexual.* The two facts are not necessarily in contradiction of each other. Actually, in the world beyond the Care Bear sexuality of GLAAD, they're inseparable. It might even be the case that the Grammy didn't go to Em precisely because his lyrics are *too queer.*

To understand this, you just have to pay attention to the *music* instead of the press releases. Sodomy never sounded so seductive, or seditious. When fellow Detroit rapping duo Insane Clown Posse wittily renamed Slim Shady "Slim Anus" on their last album, the squeaky blonde bombshell responded quickly and explicitly. *"'Slim Anus'? You damn right, Slim Anus / I don't get fucked in mine like you two little flamin' faggots,"* he retorts on a track on *Marshall Mathers,* the CD that lost the Grammy. But then in the track "Ken Kaniff," he all-too-enthusiastically impersonates the voices of the Insane Clown Posse frontmen engaging in lip-smacking fellatio, complete with very convincing grunts and groans and backed by cheesy porno muzak: "Fuck, yeah! Suck it! That's good!" In response, Insane Clown Posse have placed a downloadable track on their Web site featuring an Eminem-on-poppers-soundalike getting reamed by his hip-hop producer, Dr. Dre.

Am I the only one who got aroused by all this "homophobia"? I suspect not. After all, sodomy—and graphic sodomy at that—is really the only sex you'll find on Em's record-selling CD; whether in the form of invitations to the listener to "suck my fucking dick, you fucking faggot" or dismissing his critics as bitter queens: "He's just aggravated because I won't ejaculate in his ass." If Em really is the "New Elvis," it seems that "Jailhouse Rock" is his starting point (which would at least explain his "prison punk" look). Even when he leaves the violent sodomy alone for a moment and turns to romance, it's of a rather queer "homiesexual" kind, as in the hit-single "Stan," in which a fan sends a series of unrequited love letters to his rap-star hero—the song he chose to duet with Elton John at the Grammys.

Em himself "comes out" and acknowledges his obsession/passion in another skit on *Marshall Mathers* in which a furious record exec complains that he can't sell his records because instead of rapping about his wide-screen TV, Eminem is "rapping about homosexuals!" Of course, the joke here is that Eminem's records "about homosexuals" could hardly sell better.

Now, if all this "fuckin' homo" stuff seems adolescent, that's probably because it is. It's *meant* to be. Adolescence is a time of hormonal anxiety about identity for boys, but nowadays it's not just a phase, it's a career. And what is it that boys are supposed to grow into these days? Masculine certainties have vanished, in many cases, along with dad, family, and blue-collar jobs. The only certainty left to bastard boys like this is that they are "not a fag." It's a negative identity that can't sustain a sense of self, let alone sustain one in a world which has made boys useless—i.e., faggots—by making mature masculinity redundant.

Rapismo like Eminem's articulates that frustration, then soothes the anxiety the articulation produces. Eminem's own story—now the stuff of legend—is instructive. A poor, pretty, blue-eyed white boy growing up in a depressed black area of Detroit without a dad, he left the house the definition of "different." He claims that he was neglected by his mother, which she vigorously disputes. Perhaps the truth is that, like many sons of single mothers, he was spoiled and fussed over and then ended up hating his mother for turning him into a "sissy": *"I used to be mommy's little angel at twelve,"* he sings in "I'm Back."

To avoid complete emasculation, he rebelled against his mother and chose to be fathered by pop culture, in the form of hip-hop and what he took to be the humongous phallus of black street culture. To Eminem (and other "shady" white boys of uncertain paternity from better homes) the world seems like a postfeminist nightmare where Mom is the law—and political correctness is merely "wash your mouth out with soap" writ large. The irresistible conundrum of homosexuality for boys like Em is that it represents not only a kind of (seductive) surrender to emasculation and weakness, it also seems like the ultimate machismo, the ultimate rebellion against "bitches"—as well as a solution of a kind to the problem of being fatherless, easing as it does the ache for male intimacy. But easing that ache means acknowledging it. And that means weakness. So, in a vicious but passionate circle, homosexuality has to be constantly "stabbed in the head," to use one of Em's more infamous lines, even as it is constantly being evoked.

Every stab just leads to another target. After all, homos are everywhere nowadays in pop culture. And the blatancy of male passivity in a world where males are coveted as sex objects only makes this "stabbing" more imperative—even when you're not, like Eminem, a pretty bottle-blond boy with what might be called "cocksucking lips" and more than a passing interest in having your picture taken. *"All I see is sissies in magazines smilin',"* groans Eminem, and: *"Staring at my jeans, watching my genitals bulging / (Ooh!) That's my motherfucking balls, you'd better let go of 'em / They belong in my scrotum, you'll never get hold of 'em."* Look at the pictures of him in his book *Angry Blonde* (interesting spelling, that). Skim past the one of him in blonde pigtails to the ones showing him surrounded by a crowd of bottle-blond Shady clones looking at him with shining, hungry eyes. Has pop culture ever looked more disturbingly queer?

Slim Shady is famously a character Em invented to express his "dark thoughts." But maybe Slim is himself just a screen. This is not to say that Mr. Mathers is "really gay" (just as he clearly isn't "really straight") but just "really fucked up." Perhaps the "real" Em is as neurotic, mother-identified/mother-hating, homeless, vulnerable, narcissistic, and passive (-aggressive) as the lyrics and the picture of him on his album cover suggest. In other words, all the things that make a great star, from Elvis to Lennon to Cobain.

And, alas, he's all the things that can make young men these days who will never be stars sad and sullen—and sometimes suicidal. A seventeen-year-old white Eminem fan in Devon, England, recently killed himself by throwing himself in front of a train. Apparently, he was depressed by the "dissing" he'd experienced from friends after a gay boy said he fancied him at a party. The liberal coroner thought the lad's anxieties foolish and misplaced: "He appears to have been unusually worried over his sexual orientation, which really should not affect people a great deal either way." Maybe. But Eminem and the sexually shady, not to say confused, world of white hip-hop show that such a preoccupation is anything but trivial for many boys today.

It's all they have left.

Nerve.com
March 2001

Banal Rape

Buggery ain't what it used to be. In 1980, *Romans in Britain* provoked a scandal with its representation onstage at the National Theatre of the anal and oral rape of a young, naked male Celt by Roman soldiers. The tabloids were apoplectic with sweaty-palmed rage and veteran morality campaigner Mary Whitehouse brought a private prosecution against the play. It may come as a surprise to some younger readers, but this wasn't because the anal sex scenes were unconvincing, or because the Celt lad was unattractive, but because its critics thought it corrupted public morals.

Twenty-one years later, in what might be interpreted as staged sodomy's coming of age, next month sees the opening, also at the National, of Mark *Shopping and Fucking* Ravenhill's new play, *Mother Clap's Molly House,* which he promises will feature "plenty of buggery," and aims to turn the stage into an eighteenth-century all-male sex party. Will anyone even bat a jaded eye?

Oh, you can bank on an outcry, for old-times' sake, from the good old *Daily Mail* about "subsidised sodomy," and the toothless successors to Whitehouse's moral junta have already made some muttering noises, but the bottom line is that in the theatre anal sex has become commonplace. Banal, even. The shocking truth about simulated anal sex between male actors onstage is that it's not, of itself, terribly shocking anymore—any more than the idea of it going on for real *backstage.* However, Ravenhill reckons he has an ace up his, ahem, sleeve—he aims not just to show men "fucking" each other onstage but show them *actually enjoying it.*

"I think that sex between men has tended to be represented as either a kind of sexless romanticism, such as in *Beautiful Thing,*" explains Ravenhill, "or as a climactic moment—usually in the form of violent anal sex, bordering on rape." He cites plays such as Antony Neilson's *Penetrator* (a squaddie victim of bullying is buggered with a broom handle), Simon Bennett's *Drummers* (a young criminal rapes his brother for betraying him), and Sarah Kane's *Blasted* (a male journalist is raped by a soldier), but cheerfully admits his own culpability: "I've tended to be one of the greatest culprits." At the end of *Shopping and Fucking* one of the rent boys begs for "a knife or screwdriver" to be shoved up his arse (perhaps he was a fan of the film *Cruising*). Ravenhill argues that what's missing from representations of bum sex is pleasure. "What we don't have is portrayals of it onstage as something done for fun, which is, after all, the usual motivation."

If *Mother Clap's Molly House* succeeds in showing what he sees as the shockingly pleasurable side of anal sex at the National, perhaps it might prove as much a cultural watershed as *Romans in Britain*. Since it was staged in 1980, using anal sex as a metaphor for imperialism, anal sex has been completely colonised by violent cliché—and not only in the theatre, but in films and even on TV soaps.

Time was when you had to be sent down to see a man's sphincter stretched. For some years now, prison movies have had no chance of being taken seriously without the statutory shower gang-bang scene—a proud rite of passage for many a young actor from Timothy Robbins (*The Shawshank Redemption*) to Ed Norton (*American History X*, 1998). Interestingly, despite the fact the the typical white male fear/fantasy of prison is usually expressed as "I don't want to share a cell with some big black motherfucker who is going to make me his bitch," we never see it happen. It's *always* white guys fucking other white guys.

Perhaps this is because to show a white guy being fucked by a black guy would be too shocking, too close to the "bone"—too arousing, in every sense. And not just from a right-wing racist point of view but also a right-on racist perspective. If it's a liberal cliché that rape "is about power" and all anal sex in the movies is rape, it's also a liberal cliché that white racist men's relationships are homo-suspect and unnatural, whereas "the bros" relationships—and by extension, which is the main point really, groovy white guys' relations with black guys—are authentic and natural and pure. In *The Shawshank Redemption* Tim Robbins is gang-raped by white guys and falls for Morgan Freeman; in *American History X* white supremacists ball Ed in the showers and he falls for a black inmate *and* his black English teacher.

However, anal sex has become so "popular" that it is no longer confined to white-on-white shower action in prison movies. *Pulp Fiction* teased us with the possibility in that very curious basement redneck "gimp" scene (a *Deliverance* flashback?), in *Your Friends and Neighbors* (1998) Jason Patric reminisced fondly about how he took part in a gang bang of a boy at high school, and in *Me, Myself & Irene* (2000) a policeman has a live chicken's head inserted into his anus. Some gross-out comedies are perhaps already anticipating, in their sniggersome disavowing way, Ravenhill's desire to acknowledge the fun of anal sex: in *Me, Myself & Irene* a split-personality Jim Carrey wakes up to find he's used a dildo on himself while having sex with a woman, and *Road Trip* (2000) features a young man getting turned on to the pleasures of anal sex when a nurse assists him in providing a sperm donation with her gloved finger(s).

Ass attacks have even made it onto TV. Not only is there an HBO series practically dedicated to them (the male prison drama *Oz*), anal sex has even reached the young person's soap *Hollyoaks,* in the form of a male rape hour-long "special" where, after a long exciting car chase, a lad was violated over the bonnet of his Mini Metro by a young footballer.

What's truly scandalous, however, is not just how often this meta-anal cliché has been deployed onstage and screen, or even the way that the audience just lies there and takes it, but the way in which every playwright/scriptwriter lazily reaching for it seems to think that they are being so original, so fearless, so *visceral.* Possibly the worst practitioner of the meta-anal cliché is Irvine Welsh. In his play *You'll Have Had Your Hole* the audience is violated by a monstrous, unlubricated conceit. Oh, and two men kidnap a young man, tie him up, torture and rape him. One literally fucks him, while the other *metaphorically* fucks him by fucking his girlfriend (calling out his name while doing so). Nor was this Welsh's first foray into the colon of the popular unconscious. The film of his novel, *The Acid House* (1999, film), for instance, has three anal intrusion moments—a bloke watching his dad being buggered blind by Mam's strap-on, a nasty squatter who fucks the soft upstairs neighbour's worthless wife up the arse and then, just in case we missed the significance of this, knocks a hole through the soft man's *floor* from below and plugs an extension cord into his socket to steal his juice. And let's not even mention that the film *Trainspotting* (1996) begins with some eye-wateringly large suppositories and a character called 'Renton' diving into a shit-filled toilet bowl.

Why do they do it? And why do we let them get away with doing it to us? Partly because in a "sex-positive" world, anal sex is the last naughty, filthy thing there is, and partly because it's the easiest way to literally dramatise the "crisis of masculinity" and the ambivalence of relations between men. The anus is the "weak spot" in the masculine body—and God saw fit to add temptation to vulnerability by giving all men a prostate gland. However hard or phallic or good at spitting a bloke may be, he still carries a "manhole" with him wherever he goes. In a consumer culture which is encouraging—nay compelling—men to say "yes" to pleasure and sensuality, there is an anxiety about the "yes" of sexual passivity which still needs to disavowed. Men are still saying "no" to being penetrated—but it happens anyway. The depictions of "male rape" are really a kind of a rape of the male. "No" always means "yes," at least in plays and films and soaps.

"Fundamentally," it comes back to Sodom and Gomorrah. Sodomy is a biblical crime, defined as non-penile-vaginal intercourse—it is not gender specific or, in fact, anal specific. Nor is sodomy sexuality specific. The important thing about sodomy is not whom you do it to but that it's nonreproductive, sex-for-its-own-sake. This is what the Cities of the Plain were levelled for—and why Lot's kinky wife was turned to a pillar of salt: she couldn't resist "looking back."

Male homosexuality in general and male anal sex in particular might be the epitome of hot, bestial lust—mostly to those who've never tried it—but in a postpill, postmarital, postmonogamy society we're all—male and female, gay and straight—tangoing in Sodom. Anal sex is such a "hot" issue, not just because it represents anxious identities, but also because it symbolises the nonreproductive, nonromantic use of sex we're all making. As the old, pre-AIDS adage has it: "One up the bum for fun—no harm done."

Or, as Ravenhill points out, "Before the advent of reliable contraception in the twentieth century, anal sex was the only kind of intercourse which didn't involve the risk of pregnancy. The Molly House was a place where men could go and have fun without any consequences, or responsibility." This, of course, is why women like Mary Whitehouse think we're all doomed. Other women, however, might take a more pragmatic view; women, for instance, like the madame who appears at the end of Ravenhill's play to buy the Molly House. Because of the popularity of Molly Houses her female brothel has gone bust. Says Ravenhill, "She announces that God came to her in a dream and told her, 'It's a bugger's world. Arse will always triumph over cunt.'"

Independent on Sunday
August 2001

Beyond the Valley
of the Mardi Gras

"So, what are you travelling to Austrayy-lyah for," asks the pretty male Quantas trolley dolley, somewhere over Southeast Asia, as he collects the plastic remains of my meal. "Bizniss, or . . ." his eyes flick almost imperceptibly down toward my trackie bottoms and up again, "pleazure?"

I've been asleep in this emergency exit seat with my legs stretched out. I really should have used a blanket. Or worn some underwear. I reach for my jumper and hastily throw it over my crotch. "Punishment," I reply. "I'm being transported for crimes against gays." Well, okay, I don't actually tell him this. Instead, I tell him I'm going on holiday.

"It's such a shame you've just missed the Mardi Gras," he says.

"Yes, it's a terrible shame," I agree, not very convincingly.

"Yer'd reely love the Mardi Gras," he enthuses. "It's a febulous perayde and pardy, with floats, drag queynes, and strippers." Adding hastily, covering his bets, "It's reely mixed these days.'"

I don't have the heart to tell him that I've heard the "yer'd reely love the Mardi Gras" speech from almost every gay Sydney boy I've ever met. Don't get me wrong; I'm sure it really is a febulous pardy, and I'm sure they're right to be proud of it. It's just that if you're a homosexual, running around off your tits/with your tits out is something you can do in any major Western city. You don't have to go to the other side of the world to do it (especially since by 3 a.m. you usually feel like you're on the other side of the world anyway).

Besides, there seems to be a self-defeating dimension to visiting Australia during Mardi Gras—aren't you just going to bump into the same people from New York you scored cocaine off/sucked off at the Miami White Party a few months earlier?

No, I've come to Australia for much more . . . perverse reasons. *History.*

*   *   *

"Thomas Morton and Isaac Stott, both aged sixteen years, were discovered in an empty ward during the day, committing an unnatural crime with two men whom they refused to name." I'm reading (avidly) the punishment records at Hyde Park Barracks, the former convict centre in Sydney, now a splendid museum. For some reason my eye has been drawn to the numerous entries recorded for "unnatural crimes."

Gloriously, the sexual arithmetic of early Australia doesn't add up. In New South Wales in 1828 the population was 36,598. Of these, 16,442 were men and only 1,544 were women (a bit like the old door policy at Heaven). According to the joke, Australians are descended from convicts and rabbits. Truth be told, the rabbits had no need to be nervous, as convicts were rather busy trying to propagate with other convicts, regardless of whether they had wombs or not.

In an attempt to discourage sodomy, many of the convict women were encouraged into prostitution—something which was reportedly not too difficult as many of them had been transported for being "naughty" ladies in the first place. Perhaps this is part of the reason why many Australian women today have a refreshingly direct approach to sex. A straight male friend of mine once picked up an Australian lady who announced breezily, "Oim on the blad at the moiment—but yer can put one up the shitta, if yer like!"

Alas, the valiant and patriotic efforts of early Australian women to save their men from Sodom were largely in vain. A parson from that period bewailed albeit in excited terms the "nightly indulgences" by convicts in the "horrid, debasing, disgusting, detestable sin of the Cities of the Plain." (Obviously *she* was just bitter coz she'd not been invited.)

According to the diligent records in Hyde Park Barracks (HPB), our naughty convict boys Thomas and Isaac were "given 34 lashes each on the breech," a relatively mild punishment. A couple of years older and they would have had twice as many and on their naked backs, the lash flaying off the skin, leaving the meat exposed and bleeding. (The chances of a lashee avoiding an even more agonising— and terminal—infection depended on the twice-daily salt-water ministrations of a trusted mate.) Reading on, I note that the boys were "confined in separate cells until the mens' names were provided."

HPB itself is a solid, imposing colonial structure, commissioned by Governor Lachlan Macquarie, the man who built Sydney—or rather, the man who built Sydney with (white) slave labour. Downstairs are brightly lit glass cabinets exhibiting the heartbreakingly modest artefacts such as rusty, bent spoons, tobacco tins, and fragments of tunic excavated from the hundreds of rat's nests underneath the barracks, where they were secreted by the vermin after their night sorties. Upstairs are the long rooms of rows and rows of hammocks where convicts slept like trussed animal carcasses, swaying slightly in the fetid night air, sides occasionally touching, after toiling all day in the alien Australian heat building Macquarie's monuments, as the rats scurried beneath them. A spot of sodomy must have been the only thing to look forward to; a bit of fun and tenderness in a world sadly lacking both of these qualities. Thomas and Isaac and boys like them must have been very popular lads back then, and men may have fought one another to sleep in the hammock next to theirs.

There's no record of what became of Thomas and Isaac or their "partners," or whether they squealed in the end. Although male rape was probably common in penal New South Wales, it was not the only kind of sodomy that went on, nor, it seems fair to speculate, the most commonplace (the parson's horror seems to be implicitly about *mutual* immoral pleasure). Given how the lads were found and their refusal to name names and the lashings that were inflicted on them, it seems likely that whatever kind of unnatural act was taking place between these boys and their elders was consensual.

HPB is a solid, sobering reminder of Australia's origins and, ironically, of the reason why the "Lucky Country"—probably so dubbed to try to erase the memory of the time when it was once so *cursed*—is nowadays so relaxed in its attitude toward homosexuality, and sex in general. There's no getting away from it: Australia was built on sodomy (and prostitution). The colony on the wrong side of the world slept on the wrong side of bed; the Upside-Down Country had inverted sexual mores. Despite the best efforts of the parsons and the politicians, and despite its highly middle-class luxurious lifestyle today, Australia never really became culturally bourgeois. She was never civilised by wife and mother—and priest—in the way that other Western countries were.

A desire to stamp out sodomy was one of the reasons why transportation to Australia was ended—the growing numbers of free men and women of Australia wanted a respectable future that didn't look back to a disreputable past. Ironic, then, that in the world's eyes, apart from the 2000 Olympics, Sydney's and Australia's greatest claim to fame is the annual lesbian and gay parade (and a series about a lesbian-rich women's prison made out of balsa wood).

* * *

The day after visiting HPB I attended a pride parade which, for most Australians, is of much more significance than Mardi Gras, despite the fact that there are no floats, no drag queens, and the participants tend to wear clothes. On a wet autumn morning, I watched what's left of the "Diggers," or war veterans of both World Wars, parade proudly and stiffly through the shiny streets of downtown Sydney, resplendent in their medals and blazers, accompanied, and in some instances literally supported by, the new generation of young Australian fighting men. It's a moving sight—enough to make you dye your hair grey and mug some Digger for his walking stick and medals.

The Anzac Day Parade held each year on April 25 marks the Gallipoli landings of the ANZACs (Australian and New Zealand Army Corps) in southern Turkey during World War I. The landings were a complete disaster—the Turks, trained and armed by their German allies, were dug in and waiting (like the Brits, the Aussies love a noble defeat more than a glorious victory). Australia's most famous son Mel Gibson played a Digger in the midst of the pointless slaughter in the 1981 film *Gallipoli*. All the same, the Dardenelles debacle represented the isolated, exiled, and despised antipodeans' first entrance onto the world stage.

This is part of the reason why Anzac Day is not any old remembrance. Unlike, say, Armistice Day in the U.K., which tends to be shunned or go unnoticed by anyone not old enough to travel free on the buses, Anzac Day is something that young Australians get worked up about. Not only are many of them lining the streets on this grey rainy morning cheering, but thousands of miles away, hordes of young Aussie backpackers turn up at the Anzac graveyard in Gallipoli, Turkey, every year to respectfully attend the dawn service and reverently read the inscriptions on the tombstones of the fallen. Such as those reprinted in today's *Sydney Morning Herald* which talk of the dead Australian soldiers "lying side by side," as "friends in each other's arms," who may now "sleep in comfort and peace."

Even more than a statement of Australian identity, Anzac Day is about the Ozzie tradition—no, national religion—of "mateship." Mateship is considered such an important concept in Australia it was nearly enshrined in the new constitution, but was vetoed by jealous feminists. If male friendship—and tenderness—was the only thing that made life bearable for the convicts who built Australia, it was also the soul in a soulless world for the sons of the convicts who found themselves working in the bush, alone in the wilderness, with only their mate to rely on. And whilst it is hardly ever discussed, no Australian can be ignorant of just how far—and how physical—mateship often went for young men facing an untimely death thousands of miles from home and wife/girlfriend.

The Diggers are celebrated because they are seen as the last link with that world. It's a form of nostalgia. Australia, like every other Western nation these days, is a consumerist country competing in a global marketplace that has no place for guts or for fellow feeling (in the literal, traditional, chaste sense).

At the ANZAC parade I ask a couple of cheering beefy-blokey lads in their early twenties in damp knee-length shorts and sweatshirts why they had come to see a parade of old crumblies and young squares. "Oh, it makes yer proud," says the smaller one, smiling with that open-faced friendliness Australian men are rightly famous for. I ask why. "Well," says his chum, "it keeps the tradition of mateship alive. It's an Australian thing."

"If you talk to most people outside of Australia about a parade in Sydney," I say, hoping to provoke a reaction, "they think of Mardi Gras."

Disappointingly, they just laugh and shrug. "Yeah, I suppose. We go to Mardi Gras as well, though." Adding quickly, "With our gerlfriends. It's a reely grate perdy. . . ."

Not everyone shares the groovy tolerance of the younger generation. A ragged veteran not on the parade, wearing the Digger hat and his medals but also wheeling his possessions in a shopping trolley (not a sight you see often in Sydney), is yelling at the parade and the spectators from the sidelines: "Men today—they're all a bunch of pouftahs! They don't know what it is to be a real man! That died on the beaches of Gallipoli!" Everyone pretends not to hear him. Except me.

The parade ends at the ANZAC memorial in Sydney's Hyde Park—opposite HPB, appropriately enough. Within the monument—its inner sanctum and the highest official shrine of Ozzie mateship—is a crypt containing a remarkable sculpture by Raynor Hoff (1894-1937), which happens to be a study in homoerotic passivity and male idolatry. Presented on a kind of altar in the centre of a burst of bronze flames, surrounded by flags, it depicts a limp, young naked male warrior borne on his shield, crucified by his own sword. The sacrificial post would not look out of place in some of the funkier basement bars on the Mardi Gras strip on Oxford Street.

* * *

The evening before I left Sydney I attended a service at another, more modern temple to mateship and the male body. At the Sydney Cricket Ground an Australian Football League (AFL) match was taking place between the Sydney Swans and the Geelong Cats. Now, of course, all non-Aussie homosexuals are familiar with AFL, even if they have absolutely no interest in their homegrown sports. I could describe AFL as a mixture of rugby and soccer, but actually it more closely resembles a fight in the showers between wrestlers over a particularly slippery piece of soap.

Of course, AFL is not actually played in the nude. It just seems that way. The players wear sleeveless, pec-hugging shirts showing off bulging, sculpted torsos and (waxed?) shoulders that seem to have burst out of the suffering fabric. Already fiendishly skimpy pants are stretched even skimpier by tight, round buttocks and large, firm, golden thighs which run down to grapefruit sized calf muscles (breakfast anyone?). Veins pulse on thick, brown necks, while graceful, balletic kicking movements are sexily underscored by aggressive hand-to-hand contact. No wonder that AFL—along with lifeguards—is the main reason why the Aussie male is idolised by homos everywhere.

However, I have something to report which will cause international gay consternation on a scale not seen since those killjoy body-length swimsuits were accepted by the Olympic Committee. Your actual, everyday, humdrum, chip-eating, bad-haircut-wearing, under-exercised Aussie male does not live up to the gay/Hollywood fantasy. Maybe I'm too strict in my criteria; maybe I need my eyes tested—but in this vast full-to-capacity-with-Aussie-masculinity stadium, I can't see a single stereotypically "sexy" Aussie male. Except, of course, on the pitch. In fact, it seems as if in Australia the only men that fit the Oz-hunk fantasy are professional sportsmen, professional actors, or just pros.

You see, we've already seen the "good-looking" Australians—either on *Sky Sports, Home and Away,* offering hot towels on Quantas flights, or in the back of *QX* magazine flashing their cocks and mobile numbers. In fact, there are so many Australian actors, models, and masseurs because out-of-the-way, rejected-dejected, chippie Australia is terrified of being overlooked.

Of course, the worship of masculine prowess and the masculine body that is such a part of Aussie culture still wants, despite Aussie liberalism, to separate itself from gayness. Thank goodness. Tonight, the Geelong Cats' supporters aren't missing any opportunity to needle the Sydney supporters. "Don't go all *Mardi Gras* on us!" one of them sitting next to me keeps shouting out whenever a Cats' player drops a catch. "Does your *husband* play?" taunts his fat mate when a Swan fucks up ("Oh, that's just *typical* of those *ignorant* Geelong oiks!" an indignant gay Sydneyan complains to me later).

Whilst queueing for a beer (sold freely in Aussie sports stadia), a gawky teenage lad in front of me strikes up a pally conversation in that way which happens as casually in Sydney as a "die-scum!" glare does in London. "Enjoying the game?" he asks. I tell him I am, but wonder about the beer and the fact that there is no attempt to separate the fans. "In Britain there would be a riot by now," I explain.

"Reelly?" asks the lad, genuinely puzzled. "Why are the Brits so violent?"

"Well, maybe it's because they enjoy a good ruck," I suggest. "Or maybe," I say, arching an eyebrow, "it's because English footballers don't give their supporters as much to look at." Perhaps deliberately, he misinterprets my remark and embarks on a long discussion about the technical differences between soccer and AFL.

On the way back from the game to my hotel I walk along Oxford Street, Sydney's Mardi Gras strip, past the Beauchamp Hotel, the gay sports pub, festooned with Swans' regalia and full of men in rugby shirts, past a bar pumping out house music and atwitter with the chatter of fashionable young gays. I ignore their blandishments and head instead for an "adult" video arcade. According to safer-sex educators (who need to know about these things), there is a very large group of men who have sex with men in Australia who don't identify as gay.

Maybe it's all that AFL. Or maybe it's Australia's nongay/pregay sodomitical past. Or maybe it's the arrival on these shores in recent years of large numbers of Mediterranean men (Italians, Greeks, and Turks and their "fuck anything" machismo). Whatever the reason, there are countless "beats" in every large city, where nongay men go cruising for cock. Or so I've been (easily) led to believe.

Inside the video arcade "beat" I notice that glory holes have been cut into the sides of the booths. Professionally. Large enough to get a dick, balls, a couple of hands, and a marriage contract through. Like I said, Australians are very friendly. But not tonight. I wait a while in the gloom, inhaling the smell of cheap disinfectant, dropping coins into the hungry video machine slot (apocalyptic and embarrassing alarms go off if you allow your credit to expire but fail to leave the booth). Eventually I decide this isn't the kind of mateship I was looking for and head back to my hotel, wishing—just for a moment—that it was HPB.

So, if you want to go to Australia to get in touch with its sodomitical past, or just for a spot of sex tourism, then my advice would be to go as part of a visiting rugby team. Failing that, arrange to go during Mardi Gras, when all the escorts are back in town.

Attitude
January 2001

The Return of Metrosexuality

I'd like you to meet Pete, Steve, and Sean. Salt of the earth East End builders, they are not perhaps what you might expect Cockney geezers to be. Perfectly groomed, immaculately dressed, their meaty bodies sculpted in the gym, always sipping protein drinks like infants at Narcissus's tit, these impeccably working-class boys live in IKEA catalogue flats, where they like to entertain cooking fashionable meals or mixing cocktails (make sure you put your glass on that fuckin' coaster!). They live for the weekends—which they spend dancin' dahn the rave club with their shirts off and their arms in the air, taking home a different partner every week.

Thing is, as far as anyone can tell, our lads only fuck women, and are football hooligans to boot (when they're not busy remodelling their flat). In their mid- to late twenties, they are already married-divorced and have fathered their quota of kids somewhere along the way—though none of them seems keen to make *that* mistake again. Pete, Steve, and Sean represent a new generation of proudly vain young men who seem to be saying with their tidy, beautiful flats and tidy, beautiful bodies, "we don't need women" and, what's more, "we don't care if we're mistaken for poufs."

In fact, next to them, Rupert Everett, Hollywood's professional homo whom *Talk* editor Tina Brown recently proffered as the role model for hetero men, looks decidedly shoddy, out of shape, and, well, *straight*.

Now, if you think that I'm making this up, you'd be right—but for the wrong reasons. Back in 1994, in an article in the *Independent* newspaper, I deployed the term "metrosexual" to describe a new kind of male: the single young man living in the metropolis (because that's where all the best shops are) who may be gay or may be straight, but it's immaterial since he openly takes *himself* as his own love object. Old-fashioned (re)productive, repressed, unmoisturised heterosexuality was redundant to late capitalism, I argued. The obsolete, stoic straight male didn't *shop* enough (his role was to earn money so his wife could spend it for him), and so had to be replaced by a new model, less certain of his identity, less altruistic, more interested in his image—programmed to consume.

To be entirely too honest, I was not being completely serious. No one has been more surprised than I have by the rapidity with which metrosexuality has conquered the Western world. The Cockney geeza builder blokes obsessed with aesthetics are real. The men's glossies they read as closely as their dads scrutinise the racing papers are now a bigger market in the United Kingdom than women's magazines. Meanwhile, the most desirable role model for working-class (and middle-class) boys is also the biggest, proudest, outest metrosexual in the land: England football captain David Beckham. (Obviously he's not single, but give it time. After all, he's only twenty-five.)

Gay men were the early prototype for the metrosexual which is perhaps why straight metrosexuals like Beckham are so keen to hang around them. Decidedly single, definitely urban, dreadfully uncertain of their identity, "emasculated" gay men had pioneered the business of *accessorising* masculinity in the 1970s with the clone look—enthusiastically taken up by the mainstream in the form of the straight band The Village People (*yes,* only one of them was gay). In the 1980s the moustaches were shaved off, and the male body became more smoothly, *invitingly* aestheticised than an issue of *Athletic Model Guild,* by the likes of Bruce Weber and Calvin Klein. Two decades on, and the hairless (i.e., inviting the gaze and perpetually adolescent) muscular masculine template is still with us, simultaneously a cliché and de rigueur in an Abercrombie & Fitch world.

Perhaps this is because nowadays straight men are also "emasculated." *Female* metrosexuality has seen to that. No longer is a straight man's sense of self and manhood delivered by his relationship to women; rather it is challenged by it—their independent finances and sexuality mean they aren't interested in playing house for their men anymore and file for divorce instead. Even a man's children, once seen as the ultimate proof of his virility, are taken away from him (women almost always get custody). To make matters worse, he finds himself competing—and increasingly losing—to women in the job market.

Female metrosexuality is the complement of male metrosexuality (except active where the male version is passive), as well as the cause of it. The more independent, wealthy, self-centered, and powerful women become, the more they are likely to want attractive, well-groomed, well-dressed men around them (see Tina Brown). Equally, the less men can rely on women, the more likely they are to take care of themselves. Many years ago Norman Mailer described homosexual men as narcissists who occasionally bump into one another before realising their error. Which was true, of course. But now that everyone's gone metrosexual, it's true of heterosexuals, too.

In fact, metrosexuality is so ubiquitous these days that even that silly old slapper Miss Hollywood has finally latched onto it. Films like *Fight Club* (1999) and *American Psycho* (2000) (to be found in the brushed aluminium pull-out DVD rack in our metrosexual East End builders' homes) exploit the anxiety created by metrosexuality's impact on masculinity—whilst, of course, employing all the advertising techniques which have been used to convert young men to metrosexuality in the first place.

Fight Club, a film which looks like a feature-length glossy men's magazine fashion shoot, is so ironic it hurts. One of the chief recruiters for metrosexuality, Brad "six-pack" Pitt, smooth Calvin Klein model turned Hollywood actor, leads a rebellion against the emasculation of consumerism. Beginning with bombing Ed Norton's pristine IKEA home, Brad offers a funky, more than slightly erotic male camaraderie as an antidote to the feminisation and empty narcissism of contemporary culture which Ed, helped by some lovely lenswork on Brad's perfect body, falls head-over-heels for. Unfortunately, the film throws it all away by a facile, if narcissistic, resolution: "So he was, like, just a part of me, and I wasn't turning queer after all? Gee, hold my hand, entirely superfluous chick, while we watch these phallic skyscrapers blow."

American Psycho, *Fight Club's* prequel, correctly locates the origins of metrosexuality in the 1980s and documents very well its symptoms: the bodybuilding, the myriad self-loving emollients and balms, the main character's indifference to his girlfriend except as someone to be seen with, the scene where he fucks a couple of prostitutes while gazing at himself flexing in the mirror. And yes, there *is* something psychopathic about metrosexuality—the metrosexual is not institutionalised by (capital "H") Heterosexuality, with its roles and responsibilities, rituals, and romantic deceits *("I am your laydee and yoo are my maan")*. The metrosexual pursues (what he thinks are) only his own desires, replaces socialisation with consumption, and is in this sense potentially a bit of a beast.

In *American Psycho* the antihero serial killer's problem is clearly presented as consisting of the fact that he doesn't recognise the woman that could civilise him (with obligations): "Have you ever wanted to make someone happy?" asks the doting good-wife-waiting-to-happen secretary, sitting with bunnylike innocence in the wolf's apartment. He doesn't hear her; he's too busy getting out his giant nail gun. Making someone happy is, of course, an even more impossible quest than making yourself happy—but in this case it *is* less likely to stain your white silk sofa.

American Psycho does, however, spotlight another aspect of metrosexuality, one which is increasingly pronounced: its hostility to women—or at least its imperative to declare that it doesn't need women rather than doing away with them. The social meaning of male vanity is self-sufficiency, at least in regard to the opposite sex.

As the ending of *Fight Club* also shows, this is a trend which Hollywood, built as it is on boy-meets-girl storylines for Saturday night dating rituals, finds very difficult to cater to. TV, however, has no such scruples. The hit series *Oz* is set in a men's prison, where the romantic storylines are necessarily monosexual. In fact, this is probably *why* it is set in a men's prison. Despite all the shower rapes and stabbings with sharpened toothbrushes, it seems like a sanctuary for men from the sexual voraciousness displayed by the women in, say, *Sex in the City.*

South Park offers another world where girls don't really exist, by returning to a boys-together childhood—where the "boys" are forever trying to get away from their domineering, monstrous, matriarchal mothers. In the movie spin-off, sarcastically titled *Bigger, Longer & Uncut* (1999), Kyle's castrating mum installs herself as commander-in-chief (and the most sympathetic character is Satan, hopelessly in love with a dildo-wielding Saddam Hussein).

Perhaps it shouldn't be so surprising that in a postfeminist (i.e., postpaternal) culture of single momism, some boys seem increasingly misogynistic in their attempts to break free of their mother's massive gravitational attraction.

The public world may be getting used to the integration of the sexes, but the private world is entirely feminine and frequently feminist. The frantic, frenetic mother-hating/mother-identified rap star Eminem is clearly Kyle fifteen years on, plus a shit load of drugs and maybe a disturbing homosexual encounter or two. Next to this hysterical pathology, the vain, commodified self-sufficiency of male metrosexuality seems a *relatively* mature and benign response by men to the New Matriarchy (if a whole lot *duller*). The East End metrosexual builder geezers, bless 'em, still love their mam; as someone once said, "Oedipus-schmoedipus—who cares so long as a boy loves his mommy?"

After all, the way things are going, straight men may soon find themselves living the ultimate gay cliché: the only woman in their life will be their mum.

Vogue Hommes International
Spring 2001

It's Only Shock 'n' Roll

Marilyn Manson inducted into the Church of Satan! The Happy Mondays measure the success of their tours in terms of how much drugs they scored! Keith Moon shoots up and Mick Jagger gropes himself in banned sleazy video! All presented from the toilet where George Michael was caught short! (Or long, depending on which rumour you've heard.)

Channel Four's *Rock Babylon,* billed as a "compendium and celebration of decadence and sleaze that lurks behind the supposedly glamorous and sophisticated world of rock" and featuring the above shockers, is a scandal. Not that anyone's complaining, mind.

"Seeing the high and mighty with their trousers down has always been a natural human desire," says *Rock Babylon* producer Mark Ford of Rapido TV, also makers of the cult testes-tits-n-kitsch show *Eurotrash.* "But until recently it's been cloaked in hypocrisy and moral righteousness. Now it's just entertainment." Knowing a good trend when they doorstep it, Rapido TV is planning a series of *Babylon* films, including *Sport Babylon, Royal Babylon,* and *Politics Babylon.* (Although the latter programme, post-Lewinsky and Ron Davies, has obviously already run as the nine o'clock news.)

Rapido is on the money to begin a sightseeing tour of scandal in the rock world. Rock bends over backward—and frequently forward—for bad publicity. The decadents and the surrealists may have pioneered it, but it was the rock business that really understood the commercial importance of *pour epater le bourgeois.* In the 1960s that archetypal rock band, The Rolling Stones, managed to associate themselves with just about every transgression going: drug abuse, transvestism (the sleeve to "Have You Seen Your Mother Standing in the Shadows, Baby?"), troilism (the groupies), and sodomy (the lyrics to "Cocksucker Blues"). The Stones also discovered a marvellous truth about scandal: if you're any good at it, people help you out—as the police kindly did with that story about Marianne Faithfull and the Mars Bar.

149

Bowie in the 1970s merely recapped these themes, albeit in an impressively precise, poised, psychotic way. Punk tried to crank things up by mainlining anarchism, theatrical violence, and using swear words on telly, but was effectively the crash-dancing coda to rock and roll transgression. All that was left by the late 1980s was the Happy Mondays' white-trash-with-hard-cash nightmare which makes Oasis look like those grammar school boys who wear the knots on their ties big to look like secondary modern boys.

In the United States, God bless, scandalising people is still relatively easy, demonstrating some of the advantages of living in a country founded by religious maniacs. All-American Antichrist Marilyn Manson presses all the Right buttons: Satanism, gender-bending, cops kissing in his videos, and—most scandalous of all for an American audience—*pessimism*. As his recent topping of the U.S. charts has shown, becoming Tipper Gore's worst nightmare is commercially effective, if rather time-consuming—shaving your eyebrows and spraypainting on that mascara every morning must be a real chore. But even in America, it's all been done before. In the 1970s Christian fundamentalists picketed Bowie's concerts on his U.S. tours wailing, "He's the *Antichrist!*" In the 1990s their children are outside Manson's concerts wailing the same warning. Obviously, there's a credit-card hotline you can phone when you want to order this kind of scandal: 1-800 MUTUAL PUBLICITY.

Of course the Christian crazies wouldn't have heard about Manson or Bowie or cared much about either if it hadn't been for the very proliferation of media that made rock, and attention-seeking antics in general, so profitable. But it's a truism that the more scandal there is, the more difficult it is to be scandalised. In a sense, Lewinskygate was the scandal to end all scandals. Once the holder of the most powerful and prestigious public office in the whole world has been paraded naked in a cage through the streets of the world's media, has had his oral sex life discussed in the Senate and uploaded onto the Internet as if he were a member of Aerosmith, every other revelation about the private lives of public people is bound to be a bit of an anticlimax. Especially as it only increased his ratings.

It's significant that the U.S. Congress should have tried to assassinate President Clinton via the Internet. This electronic viper's nest was the origin of many of the initial rumours about his intern interference. Being unregulated, irresponsible, and somewhat at a loss to find a use for itself, the Internet is the perfect medium for malicious gossip about celebrities and politicians (who are much the same thing these days; that's the flip side of scandal being entertainment). Frequently this takes the eye-popping shape of seedy porno images they never wanted you to see. A home video made by Pamela Anderson and Tommy Lee (ex-Mötley Crüe) showing them "rocking and rolling" in the most intimate and explicit way went missing from their house last year. Not to worry though; it turned up on the Internet where anyone with a modem and a couple of hours to kill can download it.

Trouble is, the rock business has taught us to be so media savvy and cynical these days that we can't enjoy a good scandal when we watch one. No sooner had the Pammy & Tommy Show started than rumours abounded that Anderson and Lee deliberately released the video themselves and were secretly profiting from it. Which spoils at least half the fun. Even though the rumours were false, they obviously represented a certain kind of truth. One not lost on Vince Neil of Mötley Crüe, who made a video of his antics with a Playboy Playmate and released it, pretending it was done without his consent. It was a "blue" video in the modern sense of the word: it made an obscene amount of money. Crucial to our enjoyment of the private details of celebrity life is the malicious idea that it shows us something they don't want us to see. This, we think, makes it *real*.

Which is why George Michael's arrest in an LA toilet caused such glee. It was so obviously *not* what he wanted us to see. For a pop star who had made such strenuous efforts to keep his sexuality enigmatic and his image iconically glamorous, being caught cottaging was hilariously bathetic. Significantly, *The Daily Mail* aside, no one seriously pursued the moral indignation that used to accompany the reporting of such arrests. Instead, it was acknowledged for what it was: popular entertainment. *The Sun's* headline said it all: "ZIP ME UP BEFORE YOU GO-GO."

Perhaps this is why Michael was able to use the scandal-merchandising machinery of the pop business to turn his abjection into production. By playing the media game to the utmost, by offering fulsome confessions (but not apologies), by making himself the butt of his own jokes (his greatest hits album is called *Ladies and Gentlemen*), and by turning his acute embarrassment into a saucy, transgressive, and clearly vengeful pop single, "Outside" (the video features some more kissing cops, probably on loan from Marilyn Manson), Michael has spun scandal into hard sell. Something which could have made him a dirty joke for the rest of his life was used, instead, to revamp his ailing career.

Of course, that original British pricker of bourgeois convention, Oscar Wilde—another Mr. Smooth who turned out to be into Bits of Rough—was not so lucky. His tragedy was to be postmodern before anyone else. He lived in an age before the pop promo allowed you to fast-forward the humiliation and ruin that scandal could bring. In true rock-star fashion, Wilde courted the disaster that befell him, but he never recovered from his conviction for gross indecency and had to rely on posterity, not pop promos, to rescue his name.

Some students of rock's school for scandal, however, seem to have taken the lessons altogether too literally. Post Punk Noise Rocker GG Allin would perform naked, covered in his own shit, bludgeon himself with his mike, and viciously assault members of his audience. His last gig turned into a riot which erupted out onto the streets of New York in 1993. For his coup de grace, he heroically died that night of a drug overdose.

Alas, to no avail. GG Allin missed the point that you have to *be* somebody before you can scandalise anyone. Poor GG Allin's only real claim to fame is that he appears on *Rock Babylon*.

Guardian
December 1998

Cock Star

"Are you wearing eyeliner?" an amazed office clerk asks Mark Wahlberg as he repairs a photocopier in *Rock Star* (2001). "I'm in a rock band," Mark explains testily, as if pointing out the obvious. Of course, he isn't really. He's in a "Steel Dragons" tribute band and he's a facsimile of its lead singer "Bobby Beers" (who is, as it happens, a poor facsimile of the gay former Judas Priest frontman, Rob Halford)— but one so eerily accurate that he ends up taking his place (just as, in real life, a fan ended up taking the place of Rob Halford). And *Rock Star*, like most Marky Mark films, isn't really a film but a facsimile of one.

Perhaps this is why Mr. Wahlberg always seems to be cast as a photocopier repairman: in *Three Kings* (1999), this was his job when he wasn't a Reservist pretending to be a soldier in the Gulf War (a war which, we are solemnly informed by Marky Mark's CO, is a "media war"). In *Planet of the Apes* (2001), he's essentially trying to solve a jam in the cosmic photocopier of evolution. Even when he's the star, Wahlberg seems to be tinkering away in the background.

As the oddly yet fondly duplicitous nickname "Marky Mark" suggests, Mr. Wahlberg is the facsimile star of a facsimile world, a plastic icon for a Planet of White Trash, an extra who appears to have blundered into the lead role. But it's a lead role that seems always to have been written with his story more than half in mind: a white boy who became a rapper, a "hustler" who became a Calvin Klein model, a novelty act who is now hailed on the cover of *Vanity Fair* magazine as "Hollywood's leading man" and "the next Cary Grant." Not bad for a failed white rapper who used to have to drop his pants to get our attention.

Wahlberg of course achieved global fame in the humongously successful Calvin Klein underwear poster campaign of the early 1990s—in which he was depicted masturbating on the side of buses. Or more precisely, grabbing his bulky lunch basket through his Calvins and showing off his pumped pecs—stimulating millions of men around the world to buy Calvins in the especially vain hope that they might look like Marky Mark in them.

So it was either ironic or simply a case of more photocopying that Mr. Wahlberg's big-screen breakthrough was in *Boogie Nights* (1997), in which he plays a mega-hung hustler who "jacks off for men" and who is "talent spotted" by a porn director played by Burt Reynolds. Of course, the main reason anyone went to see *Boogie Nights* was to finally get a butchers at Marky Mark's lunch packet—one which was already much more famous than that of John Holmes, the unfeasibly penised 1970s' pornstar that Dirk Diggler was based on. Which is why the director made damn sure that you don't even catch so much as a glimpse of it until right at the end—and then all we get is a deliberately plastic-looking prosthetic.

Which serves us right, since Wahlberg has made a career out of a perpetually deferred, postponed, polymorphous, plastic manhood. This is also the reason why he is so closely associated with homosexuality and homosexuals, who are after all experts in facsimile masculinity. It was media regents David Geffen, Calvin Klein, and Bruce Weber who pimped Marky to the public and launched his career into the stratosphere with posters that looked like they'd cut and pasted an Irish altar boy's face onto a gay hustler's body. Marky is the man-boy for a man-boy age of facsimile manhood in which men no longer grow up; their chests just get bigger instead.

Hence in his "adult" movie career, Wahlberg never plays a healthily heterosexual role. In *Boogie Nights,* he's a freak show surrounded by failed men and mad women; in *Rock Star,* he replaces a gay star and ends up trading Jennifer Aniston for a life of sad, groupie debauchery. But the way we know he's *really* hit rock bottom is not that he loses Jennifer but because *he actually loses his six-pack.* Meanwhile, in *Planet of the Apes,* his main romance is with a creature that is a cross between Michael Jackson, Bubbles the Chimp, and Helena Bonham Carter. (Apparently, in what passes for "real life," Mr. Wahlberg, who is now thirty, avoids relationships and still lives with his mum.)

And Marky always seems to be a *victim* in his films, as if he has to pay for his narcissism—or at least pay for *our* interest in *his* narcissism. In *Boogie Nights,* he's a sad loser who is exploited by other losers and ultimately falls victim to his own vanity—even ending up being queer-bashed. In *A Perfect Storm* (2000), he is the victim of terrifying, gigantic special effects. In fact, *A Perfect Storm* is ninety minutes of watching Marky Mark drown, deliciously. Even in *Planet of the Apes,* in which he was supposed to be playing an action hero, he was the passive victim of circumstances: just when he thought he'd saved the world, he discovered he'd lost it (the "Apeman Lincoln" moment).

In *Three Kings,* he is captured by the Iraqis and stripped down to his underwear (again) and tortured by a rather nice-looking but very cruel young Iraqi officer. Poor Marky is beaten up, electrocuted, and has oil poured down his throat—though of course we worry/wonder whether they might not want to use the oil at the other end. Fortunately, George Clooney comes to the rescue in the nick of time and Marky escapes, but alas not long after he gets shot and has to have a valve painfully inserted into his famous chest in extreme, invasive close-up to stop him from suffocating in agony.

All this is very peculiar—especially when you consider that Wahlberg is definitely *not* a victim or a homo; he is a multimillionaire success story with hordes of powerful women and screaming Hollywood directors pursuing him everywhere he goes. Moreover, Marky has a proven track record as a *bully.* This former dissed rapper is much "badder" than that contemporary street-bred white rapper with another double "M" moniker who is all mouth (could it be that Eminem is a Marky Mark wannabe after all?). Marky "Motherfucka" did time when he was *sixteen* for taking out a Vietnamese man's eye with a stick during a robbery. More recently, his bodyguard filed a lawsuit against Mr. Wahlberg claiming that he was beaten up by the man he was supposed to be protecting—and bitten. (In the light of these allegations, perhaps Marky would have been better suited for Tim Roth's role in *Planet of the Apes*).

In other words, our facsimile film star really *can* act. It's just that his act is convincing us that he's more altar boy than hustler, more lovable loser than wily winner, more bottom than top; the photocopier boy with eyeliner rather than white trash with plenty of cash. The tag line for *Rock Star* proclaims: "A wannabe who got to be, but discovered that he didn't want it." That we believe for one moment that Wannabe-who-gets-to-be (over and over again) Wahlberg *doesn't* want it is much more convincing proof than the ending of *Boogie Nights* that he really does possess a whopping great talent after all.

Independent on Sunday
January 2002

The Sex Terror

In the midst of all the overdiscussion—and all the overexposure—of the Republican show-trial of William Jefferson Clinton, the real charge against him remains curiously underreported. In fact, it's not reported at all. Oddly, the media is thunderously silent to the point of *discretion* about it.

What is this crime of crimes that can lay someone so high, so low, and which can't even be mentioned? It isn't perjury, the obstruction of justice, or the betrayal of his oath of office. It isn't even being a successful Democrat president.

No, it's having the effrontery to resist the most magisterial, sovereign, and powerful force in the land: the "sex" terror. Clinton is being made an example of—one that everyone, even editors of academic journals, should fear.

In January 1999 the American Medical Association impeached George Lundberg, editor for seventeen years of the AMA journal. Lundberg's high crime and misdemeanour? He included in this month's issue of the AMA journal research from 1991 which showed that 60 percent of college students did not define oral intercourse as sexual relations. A spokeswoman for the AMA explained his sacking: "Through his recent actions he has threatened the integrity of the journal by inappropriately and inexcusably interjecting the journal into a major political debate that has nothing to do with science or medicine."

Who can blame the AMA for purging Mr. Lundberg's heresy? Everyone, of whatever political hue, whether they think Clinton should be censured, impeached, or impaled, seems to agree on one thing—that Bill Clinton is a liar, that he *did* have sexual relations with "that woman," and that his distinction between sexual intercourse and "inappropriate intimate contact" (in this case, fellatio) is pure sophistry and legalese.

In fact, this point has become the crux of the whole scandal (which, as I'm sure the AMA knows, has *everything* to do with science and medicine). Clinton's "crime," the justification for all those

"LIAR!" banner headlines, the approval of the articles of impeachment, and now his constitutionally unprecedented Senate trial has boiled down to his refusal to agree that fellatio constitutes "sex." After the broadcast of his four-hour inquisition in the Starr Chamber, in which he admitted "inappropriate intimate contact" with Lewinsky, many liberal papers cautiously applauded his forbearance but still called on him, for the sake of Mother's Milk and Western democracy, to either throw himself on the Republicans' sword and resign or admit to Congress "what we all know"—that he lied, and that orogenital contact constitutes a "sexual relationship" (in other words, fall on his *own* sword).

But is Clinton really a "liar"? Is it really absolutely clear what "sex" is? Isn't "common sense" a fickle, not to say tyrannical, mistress? Aren't we just joining in the shouting because we want to distract from the necessary hypocrisies and disavowals that make our *own* lives bearable—because we don't want the Sex Terror to come for *us?* Isn't Clinton's trial more than just a farcical accident of history? Isn't it perhaps the clearest sign anyone could ask for that no-one is safe from the Sex Terror?

It is a measure of how bad things have become that this has to be said at all: *Everyone makes distinctions about what "sex" is.* Prostitutes, for example, know very well that most married men distinguish between "full sex" and fellatio and "hand relief," often opting for the latter two because it doesn't feel like they're *really* cheating on their wives; while prostitutes themselves don't even acknowledge vaginal intercourse as "a sexual relationship": they regard it as "business." Good Catholic girls in Latin countries often masturbate or fellate their boyfriends or even allow them to bugger them so they will remain virgins on their wedding night. Of course, nowadays it is de rigueur to smirk at their "naivete" and "denial," and congratulate ourselves on *our* sophistication and honesty, but who are we to say they're wrong to make that distinction? Isn't it a form of erotic totalitarianism to insist that *all* sensual contact is "sex"? That the "meaning of sex" can never be incoherent?

The only indisputable "fact" about sex is that the meaning of it changes entirely with the context. What happens in private, in the dark between two people, takes on a different meaning—or just a meaning—when put under the spotlight. The "Oh boy, was I drunk last night! I don't remember a thing!" line is not the recourse of someone who did something they regret the night before, but someone who doesn't wish to regret, or even think about, what they did the night before. Of course, this can be the refuge of a scoundrel or worse, but the difficulties prosecuting so-called "date rape" cases merely demonstrate the difficulties in trying to draw one unambiguous meaning out of an intimate exchange between two people in the dark (or windowless, locked corridors off the Oval Office).

Of course, Clinton occupies the most sober, most brightly lit office in the world. In a sense, he's not so much the victim of his own stupidity, mendacity, promiscuity, or even Republican hostility, but of the late twentieth-century mania for dragging everything private out into the open. The more the meaning of that private activity changes once it is put in the public sphere, the more imperative it is to expose it. And what could be more private, and therefore more worthy of being made public, than the sex life of the President of the United States? The Starr Report was a $40 million, half-ton tabloid scandal sheet, though, alas, not so well written. But this is not to downgrade its importance. As tabloid editors and Kenneth Starr know very well, despite the protestations of the public to the contrary, everyone wants to know the "truth" about sex and in particular the "truth" about celebrity sex lives. More than this, everyone thinks that the "truth" about sex is the most important truth about us.

This is why pretty much everyone, except the Pentagon and Pat Buchanan, seems to want private homosexuals to come out as public gays these days. After all, gays are the living proof that the truth about our sex lives is the most important truth about us. They are literally *defined* by it; Telling the Truth About Sex is what they're *for*. Even the uptight, soul-of-discretion Brits, for goodness sakes, want them to come out. Disgraced British Minister Ron Davies' crime wasn't cruising for sex on Clapham Common but refusing to "come out" as "gay" after this emerged. He was berated by a sneering press for being "hypocritical" and "dishonest" (the tabs) and "in denial" or "mentally ill" (the broadsheets). However, it seems worth asking—and no one did—if he had been caught in a red-light district visiting prostitutes, would he have been called upon to announce to the world that he was a congenital visitor of prostitutes and confess that this "truth" about his sexuality was more important than, say, his relationship with his wife and children? (Of course, prostitution and homosexual cruising grounds are both age-old, "secretive," "hypocritical" institutions which have made the public virtue of marriage tolerable to millions of men who otherwise wouldn't have been able to meet its demands.)

By way of contrast, George Michael, ever the showman, knew exactly what the public wanted after his entrapment by the Beverly Hills PD's finest—and Fleet Street's sleaziest—and gave full confessions earning him the approval of the press for cooperating with their enquiries. This despite the fact that for several years George Michael had been fairly open in his work and interviews about not being *straight*. What the world wanted was for him to come out as "gay"; to stop being equivocal about sex and recognise instead its irresistible sovereignty in all our lives.

Interesting that many gay activists in the United States have been largely silent about the Lewinsky affair, despite the fact that they know all too well how salacious and vicious moral crusaders like Starr can be behind their smiling respectability and constant invocation of The Law. As the shock troops of Telling the Truth About Sex, who originally elected Clinton so they could go on telling the truth even more, they are ideologically hamstrung.

Barney Frank, the outspoken and openly gay senator who is a close political ally of Clinton's, exemplifies this dilemma. Although, unlike many others in the Democratic Party, he has consistently fought in his President's corner, he has nevertheless called on him to be "truthful" about his relationship with Monica Lewinsky and abandon his pedantic "sex" distinction. In other words, to "come out."

Frank has, however, pointed out one of the curious paradoxes of this whole affair—that those leading the inquiry into Clinton's sex life and publishing their findings on the Internet are the very people who told Frank to shut up about his sex life and keep it private.

Putting Clinton's behaviour into the context of America's history and his own Baptist background, the charge against him (that he is a "liar" because he didn't consider having non-penile-vaginal relations with Lewinsky, "sex") becomes even more confused. The Starr Report effectively brands Clinton a "sodomite." Under the antisodomy laws still on the statute books of many U.S. states, "sodomy" is defined as orogenital or anal-genital contact between members of either sex. That is, pretty much anything that isn't penile-vaginal intercourse. This is because the Puritan founding fathers regarded missionary-position sex within marriage as "real" sex. Everything else was a perversion, or "inappropriate intimate contact," to use Clinton's telling phrase, and had to be fiercely discouraged. This is why gay marriage is so fiercely resisted in the United States today—including by Clinton who signed into law a bill banning gay marriage—because it bestows recognition and respectability on an act which is by definition unrespectable.

Sodomy was, until quite recently, not only unlawful but a crime against the American State. J. Edgar Hoover, who together with Senator Joe McCarthy, begat (spiritually) Kenneth Starr, kept secret files on public figures who were reported to engage in "oro-genital contact," as they considered this meant they were subversive and "un-American." McCarthy's hysterical—and probably *jealous*—view of oral sex as a form of treason is echoed today in the repeated shrieks of a Republican spokeswoman on a recent TV debate: *"He was having a blow job when he sent troops into Bosnia!"*

Of course, since Hoover, we have had Kinsey, the 1960s, gay liberation, and feminism, and the meanings of what "sex" is have been widened enormously. Hoover himself has been "outed" posthumously as a "closet gay." But the effect of this "sexual liberation" is not unambiguously "progressive" or "liberating" as most liberals seem to think. You don't have to be Michel Foucault to see that the old imperative to control people's erotic lives by prohibition has not been abolished. Instead, it has been supplanted by a compulsory, puritanical *transparency* in people's erotic behaviour—and indeed their whole sense of themselves is controlled, defined, and produced through the ritual of public confession (i.e., *Protestant* rather than Catholic confession). Everyone must submit to "sex" and "sexuality," even, and especially, presidents.

The modern, "scientific" discourse of "sex," à la Kinsey and Masters and Johnson, which demands that sex be confessed, exposed, and measured, allied in the 1960s with the explosion of personal politics. That alliance was in turn given an irresistible momentum by the exponential increase in media and exponential decrease in respect for privacy since then. The rise of political correctness and battles over sexual harassment has only intensified the need to confess "sex" in the courts, the workplace, and the television studio in the 1990s.

Now, at the end of the twentieth century, this Sex Terror has made its way into the highest office in the land. It has become a Scylla to America's puritan, scolding, sodomy-hating Charybdis. With "Elvis," the 1960s' baby-boomer, liberal, Baptist, telegenic talk-show president in the middle. The supreme irony is that the Republicans, who believe that the distinction between sex and sodomy should be maintained in life and law, are trying to impeach a president on the grounds that he made that very same distinction in life and law. The Grand Old Party which once was the party of discretion in matters of eros is now a party of sexual Jacobins in the service of the Sex Terror, branding popular presidents Enemies of the People for not confessing every detail of their private life—even outing *themselves* as adulterers on the steps of Capitol Hill—and turning American public life into one gigantic, insane Denunciation Box.

Prophetically, ironically, Clinton, whose presidency began with an uproar about his intention to lift the ban on sodomites serving in the military, now seems to be ending with him being branded a (heterosexual) sodomite himself. The compromise solution he came up with for that first crisis has turned out to be the most apt—if most hopeless—solution for what may turn out to be his last. As well as a romantic resistance slogan in an era where "sex" is a sign we must all submit to. "Don't ask. Don't tell. Don't pursue."

Seattle Stranger
January 1999

DIRTY TALK

Alexis Arquette

Fierce drag queen in Last Exit to Brooklyn *(1989), hysterical rejected fag in* Threesome *(1994), trembly sniper in* Pulp Fiction *(1994), dipsy dithering boyfriend in* I Think I Do *(1998) brother to family thesps Patricia, Rosanna, and David, Alexis Arquette, arthouse Hollywood's favourite sissy, is actually something of a* dude *in the flesh. Within minutes of meeting him I just want to go out and down a crate of Bud with him and talk baseball scores. But, you'll be glad to hear, like most fags all he's interested in is talking about sex.*

ALEXIS: I'm a lot like John Malkovich's character in *Dangerous Liaisons* (1988). I just talk about sex all the time. Actually, John's a lot like that character, too. He wants to know all the details about your sex life and what you got up to last night. You'll be on the set and he'll go in that weird, wavery voice of his, "Alexiss, last night I was having sssex with a wo-man and she put her fing-er up my asssshole." "Did you like it?" "Yeah. It was really great!" It was a revelation for him! I said, "Well, of course you did! It's like the male fucking G-spot, dude!"

I like talking about sex, but don't really like talking about sex beforehand, if you know what I mean. But then, I do like talking *during* sex. . . .

MS: You like abuse?

AA: Well, I've not really had that yet, but maybe it's something I want. Part of me thinks it's the slave gene that's in us all. At some point all of our ancestors were enslaved, or something. I don't think it's a bad thing. But on the other hand, if I was in love with a boyfriend and saw him get tied up and fucked and slapped around by six guys it might hurt my feelings. . . .

So you're old fashioned?

I guess I am. On the other hand, if he really, really wanted it, it might turn me on!

Who's your ideal lay?

Henry Rollins is pretty fucking hot, man!

So you're at a party with Henry. You're introduced. How do you chat him up?

[Pause.] I don't know. I'd have to find out what he was into. You see, that's the only thing I don't like about myself. I think I would have more success if I just went for what I wanted, instead of trying to please people.

Isn't that the paradox of being an actor? You exist for others...

Yeah, it's a problem. You begin to wonder if you really *feel* anything. "Am I acting, or is this really me?" Something I can't handle is rejection. That makes me insane. Someone rejects me, that makes me want to kill. I suppose that's real.

So if Henry wanted you to be a sadist and whip his ass, would you?

Yeah, I would. And I'd probably enjoy it.

How about Stephen Baldwin? Didn't you make a movie with him which is basically all about his ass?

Oh, yeah, *Threesome*. Oh man, I love Stephen. He like totally loved showing off his butt in that movie. When we were making that movie he was drinking a lot. He's sobered up now and become more respectable, but back then he was always getting trashed. He was always getting his dick out and waving it at me. He wanted to get blown by some chick while I watched. Crazy shit, man.

So what does Stephen's dick look like?

Not very long, but very, very thick.

That figures.

Yeah, and I think he likes to be brutal with it.

I loved the climactic scene in *Threesome* where the cool liberal straight guy played by Stephen selflessly allows the sad fag to touch his arse whilst he balls the bitch . . . .

Yeah! It's even funnier when you know Stephen. During the filming of *Last Exit to Brooklyn,* we were drinking in the bar, like, really fucked up. Then we went out into the lobby and, for some reason, he went to me, "I know what you want." "Oh yeah, what's that?" He turns around and shows me his ass—in this brightly lit hotel lobby with people behind the desk and everything—*"You want to fuck my ass, don't you?"* I laugh, but he's *serious,* man. "You do, don't you?" he says, bending over, rubbing his behind. *"You want to fuck my ass!"* I was like, "What?" But he was like, "Oh, dude, this ass is *something else!* You'll fucking *love it,* man!"

He's right, of course. He does have the best ass in Hollywood.

Yeah, it's a fucking bubble-butt, man, I'm telling you. But he's a fucking monster. He just really loves to be desired. If he even thinks you're into him, he'll want you to be around all the time. I think that Steve is a sexy guy. But he's not the kind of person I'd try to get into bed; I know him too well. He's like a brother to me. . . .

Yeah, right. You're sharing a motel room and he sneaks across to your bed in the middle of the night and starts slapping your face with his fat cock and grunting—you're absolutely going to call the front desk and demand your own room. . . .

[Resignedly.] Okay. Well, if he made all the moves, then yeah, I probably wouldn't stop him.

But that's not going to happen because he wants all the attention.

And he gets it. Brian, a Hollywood director, was in love with Stephen. One night the three of us were together in some punky club in LA and I made the mistake of introducing him to Traci Lords. Afterward Brian, Stephen, and I were on the bench seat of Stephen's pickup truck. Brian was in the middle, really off his face, and out of nowhere he turned to Steve and said, "Oh God, I want you sooo much!" and starts fucking crying on his fucking shoulder! And Stephen's like "Er, it's okay, man . . ." all the time with this "Oh, Jeez!" look on his face. I told him, "You started it, dude! This is what you get for leading boys on!"

Stephen needs to be taught a lesson.

Yeah, and I think he's fair game. I think you'd probably have a good shot with Stephen. I don't think he's one of those straight guys who's into drag queens. I think that if he opened himself up, he could be genuinely bisexual, y'know what I mean? I think that if he slept with a guy, he'd wanna get fucked.

I'd like to help Stephen "open up." Besides, it would be criminal for his prime rump to reach wrinkly, saggy old age without being put to the purpose which God obviously intended. . . .

And you know what? Even if you never get fucked in the ass ever, that's the male G-spot. It's the prostate, y'know what I'm saying? My best friend in LA, a straight guy, very open minded, he says he's never wanted to get fucked, but every time his girfriend sticks her finger up his butt, he shoots, like, *everywhere*. He's totally cool about his male vagina. But most guys would be, "Ohmigod, I must be a fag!"

So are you a bottom, Alexis?

I think it goes beyond that. I remember one of my first sexual-energy things as a kid. There was this cartoon I saw, where Colonel Custer was forcing some Indian to kiss his feet. I remember getting a fierce little woodie instantly. Poingg! Then I got together with a friend of mine when I was six and we'd play this game where he was the king and I was the slave, and all I really wanted to do was kiss his feet. It just made me feel completely . . . *opiated*. I didn't know what sex was, but I knew I really, *really* liked that. And y'know what, since then, no matter how wild the sex, I've never experienced anything like that. Nothing that's come even close.

Are you a good little bottom?

There's no one that likes giving pleasure more than I do, but y'know what? When I'm done, when I've busted, you'd better take your dick out, and you'd better get those shackles off me, master, because this little pussy boy's gonna kick your ass, *Daddy,* cos I'm done.

[Alexis pauses and thinks.] On the other hand, maybe I *want* to be taken to the point where I'm having sex with someone and not wanting it anymore. I don't know. . . .

Jeez, *where does all this stuff come from?*

Attitude
April 1999

Henry Rollins

Henry Rollins is not gay. Okay? Can we get that straightened out right now?

The ex-Black Flag front man, stand-up comic, author, actor, weightlifter, and leading exponent of penitentiary chic á la *Cape Fear,* may come across like the American Mishima, but he's into *chicks.*

Though not that much.

"There was this rumour going round," says Henry in his oddly articulate jock/jarhead/jeffstryker way. "Fucking MTV called me up and asked me if I'd like to come out on some show of theirs. 'So I'm gay, huh? I think I'd remember some guy fucking me up the ass!' The thing that bummed me out about it is that when you have the 'he's gay' fiction spread around the media about you it's only to slander you. Everyone is like, 'That guy, he's a *fucking fag!'* But for me, being gay is just such a nonevent. You are into what you're into. End of story."

MS: Why do you suppose people think you're homo?

HR: I asked my gay friends why people thought I was gay, and they said, "You're thirty-seven and in shape. You are thoroughly focussed. You have a great ass."

Maybe the rumours have something to do with the fact that you don't have a girlfriend?

Well, yeah. That's possible. I don't want a girlfriend because I don't want to have to call someone every day. The only thing I miss on tour is my bar. I got a precision-engineered York powerlifting bar. I miss that fucker because it feels so good! I've had enough girls in my time, but I've slowed up lately. I'd rather jack off than get into something shallow. But I think the problem is that I don't make a song and dance about the women I do fuck. I don't go out on the town with them on my arm. I go to the bookstore.

That's faggy.

Yeah, "He must be a fag—he's *literary!*"

On the other hand, you are gay in the sense that you've built yourself your own masculinity.

Is that a gay thing?

Not specifically. But characteristically.

Yeah, you do get some gay guys who are like hypermasculine. Look at that guy in leather! Hell, that's two guys in one man! He's really getting his point across. When I was in high school I was very skinny. It was a Vietnam vet that got me into weightlifting. It was the first time in my life when I achieved something. I put on fifteen pounds of muscle mass. In life you've got to have a bit of the "Come on, motherfuckers! I got something for your ass!" mentality.

Tell me about it. Do you get offers from men?

Oh, yeah. Sure. All the time. And I go, "Well, that's cool, but I'm not from that bolt of cloth," and they go "Really? I thought you were." And I go, "No, no I wouldn't kid you about that." "Are you *sure?*" "Yeah." "Not even maybe just this once?" "Nah, really I don't want to go there." One guy hit me with a really great proposition. He said, "Well, close your eyes and you really can't tell the difference. And I'd do it a lot better than any chick you've been with." "Well, since you've got a cock, I bet you would." But you know, it's just not my scene.

Your look, the tattoos—have you done time?

Nah. But other convicts—other *convicts!*—come up to me. One man I'll never forget. Nebraska, 1988. Old-school prison tattoos. Guy walks by and goes, *"Brother!"* "Scuse me?" "Soledad, '85, right?" "Er, no." "Chino?" "No." "Hell, I've done time with you somewhere. . . ." [Rollins puts on nerdy bookworm voice.] "Well, no, sir, actually not."

How do you think you'd do in prison? Do you think you'd be some motherfucker's bitch?

I don't know, man. You're looking at me about eight pounds under-
weight. Usually I'm two hundred, but I can't get the lifts because I'm
touring so much. I think that kind of keeps me out of little-bitch
mode. I'm not anybody's idea of a piece of chicken, and as far as
fighting goes, I know a little bit about that. But in prison, I'd probably
be fucking terrified, man.

**But hasn't your whole life been a kind of preparation for prison?
No family life, no time off—you even weightlift . . .**

Well, other people tell me where to go; because I want to go there, I
let them structure it for me. But yeah, I see what you're saying. I went
to a military school for seven years and that had a big impact on me.
My dad was also ex-military. My dad would say stuff like, "Fall out
for McDonalds." Fall out for your fucking Happy Meal. Shit like that
gets to you after a while.

A shrink would say that you have a very punishing superego.

[Rollins shrugs his shoulders.]

**What I mean is, it sounds as if a part of you is always watching
over yourself, policing you, always demanding better.**

Oh, that's true. A lot of my work is result orientated. I'm always trying to do a better show, a better CD, a better book. I have to grade myself nightly. I come off the stage and I often kick myself . . .

**I've heard that you were recently "watched over" by someone
else.**

Oh yeah, well [He acts out the scene like a college jock at the frat
house bar], this guy is standing next to me just staring at my dick, and
I'm thinking, this is cool, I can deal with this, and my bladder's
fucking bursting, but I can't go, man! I said to myself, Watch me take
a leak with this guy watching me and me not give a fuck. But this guy
totally took me. He won. Maybe he was some kind of urine comptrol-
ler. Fucking crazy shit, man.

Attitude
May 1999

Dana International

"It is very hard for a man to admit it. They think that if they are attracted to me that they are homosexual. How *come!* I am representing all that homosexuals *don't like!* They don't like makeup, they don't like dresses—*how can I attract a homosexual?*"

Very easily, is the answer that occurs to me, lying on a queen-sized bed barely a goosepimple from the gorgeous man-made lady that rendered the Eurovision Song Contest redundant, Richard breathless, Judy jealous, and Orthodox Jews apopleptic. Dana International—despite a name which sounds like a 1960s Irish airport—is very, very sexy. She's tranny tall—her legs pour over the edge of the bed—and elegantly pointy: all elbows, shoulders, and long, ruby-red fingernails. Her black hair is spikey too, in a relaxed, cool kind of way. A kind of Jewish Souxsie Sioux, more camp than Goth.

This distillation of diva-ness, whose Eurovision winner, a tribute to strong women, was itself called "Diva," is, it seems, a bit bored with the subject. "When I grew up in the Seventies there were no strong women celebrated in pop songs. So I was determined to change that. But, y'know, I don't like titles. For me, everyone is the same. There are exceptional women, but they are women; they are not angel dust—they laugh and they cry like everyone else. It's the same with 'transsexual.'"

Dana's back onto territory she's more interested in. Herself. "Think of me as a cow. Think of me as a chicken. I *don't care* what people think I am, so long as they are attracted to me. [She uncrosses and recrosses her legs.] What is a transsexual? It's a *word*. Do you know how many men made passes at me in the street today? They see a beautiful girl. I say to them one word: 'transsexual.' *Do I not look attractive anymore? Do I grow two heads?* No!"

MS: In a way, a transsexual is the ultimate symbol of sex . . .

DI: Yes, that's the problem. *Just* sex.

Do you have a boyfriend?

I've had several. But I can tell you that it is not a problem of the man. Human beings don't fall in love with a pretty face. Love is very wide. Everyone can love everyone. If you have an attractive personality and you know how to make your boyfriend fall in love with you, you'll be successful. But most transsexuals are too preoccupied with the way they look. They think, "Why doesn't he love me? I'll have my nose fixed, then he'll love me! Or I'll buy a Versace dress. Then he'll be at my feet!" They don't understand that you have to work very *hard* on your personality.

Yes, and you clearly have, but do you have a partner at the moment?

[Dana goes quiet, dropping her feisty, lecturing tone. For a moment.] No, I don't. I used to. Three years ago, the love of my life. He said in a newspaper interview, "Fuck all the Israelis—I don't care what they think. She's more of a woman than all the women I met before put together." He told me, "I didn't want to fall in love with you. I just wanted a lay." But one date led to another . . . before we knew it we were a couple.

How did it end?

He was very brave, but his family abandoned him. He still wanted to marry me, but I felt stranded. I loved him very much, but I couldn't spend too much time with him—I need my freedom. I want to do what I want to do every minute of my life and once you are connected to another person you have *commitment*. He wanted me to give up my pop career, live a normal life, have a normal job. In the beginning it was great—but he met me before I became famous.

Do you think it's possible to combine love with fame?

No, no, no, never. [Dana, shaking her head.] Not even for a natural-born woman. The other party is always jealous or unhappy. If you were a magician and you said to me, "You will be poor, ugly, and unknown, but you will have a man and you will love him for the rest of your life," I would say—yes, do it, *I agree*. Human beings are only 100 percent happy when they are in love.

But it never lasts, does it?

And I'll tell you why, Mark. You can't be 100 percent happy all the time. You have to be unhappy sometimes to appreciate being happy.

So it sounds as if your offer to trade fame, fortune, and beauty for eternal love is quite a safe one to make . . .

Well, I did say "if you were a *magician* . . ."

Are effigies of you still being burnt at the stake in Israel?

You have to understand, Mark, that the Orthodox, intolerant people, the bigots who say I am mad and sick and sinful are in the minority in Israel. They are loud, but a minority. If you go to Tel Aviv, you will discover that everyone is very open and tolerant. And tolerance and understanding are extremely important, of course.

Why do you still refer to yourself as gay?

Why not? This is the family I come from. They understand how I feel; they are not always questioning me. They know what it is to be attracted to men.

I ask because I wondered if your homosexuality was still "active." I know a male-to-female transsexual who is now finding herself attracted to other women . . .

[Dana sits up suddenly, shaking her head and banging her hands on the bedcover.] This is *very crazy,* this kind of thing! *I DON'T UNDERSTAND IT!* I don't like it! But . . . [she catches herself] I respect it because it's their own life . . . but it doesn't sound logical to me! Maybe their changing sex was a mistake. You go through all this trouble to have relationships with men, and then you want to have relationships with *WOMEN?*

But perhaps it isn't so illogical. After all, they're simply remaining attracted to the same sex.

No, I cannot understand why a transsexual would want to sleep with a woman. *I THINK IT IS MADNESS!*

Forgive me for saying so, Dana, but you sound a little intolerant . . .

But I cannot understand it! *If you cut off your penis and afterwards you want to sleep with a . . .* Ah! I know why! You want to know the answer, Mark? *THEY ARE NOT ATTRACTED TO WOMEN!* They want to prove that they are women. If a lesbian is attracted to you it means that you could never be a man! Lesbians are totally feminine!

Perhaps you have different kinds of lesbians in Israel. But it sounds as though you're saying that your gender is about who you're attracted to, not who you are.

No, I have never felt comfortable as a man, never felt comfortable in a man's clothes. It is something in your genes, maybe. When you are born, a soul combines with you and my soul is feminine. A transsexual is a feminine soul in a man's body. People suggest that it is a choice, but if you are not attracted to women, what can you do—what can you take? There is no cure . . .

* * *

Except a career in pop music.

In the taxi home, the driver was very chatty. When he found out who I'd been interviewing, his first question was, "Would you give 'er one then, mate?"

"Oh yeah, definitely," I said.

"Yeah, I would too, mate. Fit bird."

Attitude
October 1998

Bruce La Bruce

A skinhead is stealing an old woman's purse as she dozes on a park bench. A middle-class gay catches him in the act, but his look is more of a cruise than an accusation. So the skinhead follows him home and then, with his mates, breaks in. It turns into a night of sexual terror. And, of course, the gay's lover is black—and the skinheads are racists.

Welcome to the world of Bruce La Bruce's latest. And if it sounds a little heavy, let me lighten the mood by mentioning that it's also a hard-core porn movie. The exhibitionist Canadian auteur behind *Super 8 1/2* and *Hustler White* has returned to his *No Skin Off My Ass* roots with *Skin Flick,* a film about bad white boys with no hair that will, he hopes, bring together audiences in both art house and bathhouse. Shot on location in Britain, *Skin Flicks* is *A Clockwork Orange* crossed with *Looking for Mr. Goodbar.*

MS: Do you finally get to play Diane Keaton in this movie, Bruce?

BLB: Ha ha. No, not exactly. I get to play the part that Marc Almond turned down—the fag that gets beat up by skinheads in the opening scene in a cemetery.

Sounds just up Mr. Almond's street.

Yeah, they're kicking the shit out of him—in slow motion of course, with romantic music—they lean over and give each other a big tongue kiss over the fag's prostrate body.

So why on earth did he turn it down?

I probably shouldn't say this, but he said he wanted to do this but his management advised him not to do it. Apparently, it "went against his new image."

I see. A little bird tells me that another famous Brit fag turned down a role in your movie . . .

Oh yeah, that would be Aiden Shaw. He was going to play the bourgeois gay. But he turned it down, saying he thought that the script was "racist, misogynist, juvenile, pretentious . . ."

That good, eh?

Yeah, apparently. Actually, this movie is a much more conventional narrative film than my other self-referential, camp numbers. . . . To be honest, I kind of blew my *own* mind with this movie really, because it was also a hard-core porn movie. There's a scene where a new initiate into the skinhead group has to masturbate over a picture of Adolf Hitler . . .

An act of sacrilege or reverence?

Oh, reverence. A lot of the art direction was very Forties fascist nostalgia. I tried not to think too hard about the meaning of what I was doing; I just wrote it. What the film is about is encapsulated in that first scene. Yes, they engage in homosexual acts, but they hate homosexual culture and don't see themselves as gay.

It's the perfect economy of desire: "We hate you, we beat you, you love us, but we love each other." Why do you have this "pathological" interest in skinheads?

Well, as you know, Mark, I had this whole *boyfriend* thing with this hustler who was quite socialist, but after we split up he turned into a Nazi skinhead. He wasn't gay identified at all. He always had girlfriends when I was going out with him. He encapsulated every conceivable contradiction. He's probably dead now. He contracted full-blown AIDS. He was going to the bathhouse in a *wheelchair*. Of course, when he was younger he was stunning. He looked like a young Morrissey crossed with a young Robert DeNiro . . .

Yes, that would have helped to render some of his more "contradictory" qualities romantic and enigmatic. . . .

. . . When if he'd been fat and pig-ugly, he would have just been a headcase loser. I know. Obviously, skinheads are sexually fetishised objects for me. But I can live with that.

But can you live with your audience? You do realise, don't you, Bruce, that this film will be marketed to "gay skinheads and their admirers"?

[Winces.] Yes. To be honest I wanted to get away from the gay skin-head look. To style them, I thought it would be interesting to make them more Sixties—put them in Abercrombie, short boots, button-down shirts, long coats, even walking canes.

Ted or Dandy skinheads—aspirational working-class youth cults, instead of downwardly mobile middle-class gays.

Exactly. This film is heavily influenced by *A Clockwork Orange*—es-pecially the scene where they break into the house. When I got here I realised that the budget wouldn't support a proper stylist. So the fash-ion ideas went out of the window and we had to use just the Fred Perrys-and-braces kinda thing. And then the night before shooting we went to Bar Code in Soho, and everyone was dressed *exactly* like that.

So how do you feel about all these Bar Code skinheads going out and buying your film to wank over?

I don't know. There *is* a serious psychodrama angle to this film. And the acting is pretty incredible. But I suppose people who just want the porn will fast forward to that. We shot, like, eight hard-core scenes using the conventions of American porn—rimming, cum shots, shots from below—it's all there. They won't be disappointed.

High production values in a Bruce La Bruce movie?

It sounds strange, I know. To be honest, in *Hustler White* I was al-ready bored with the porn scenes after the first cum shot—it was like, "Oh, how am I going to make the next one look any different from the last one?"

So why the return to porn?

Well, I'm actually very influenced by Seventies film porn. Back then the people making porn were very aware of the whole tradition of avant-garde porn, which had a lot of sex and nudity in it. For me, *Skin Flick* was an attempt to try and force two genres together and down the throats of the audience. I have nothing to lose. I already have the baggage of being a "pornographer." I used to make a lot of pop videos in Canada and then I won an award, and the headline was "Pornographer Wins Music Award" and my phone totally stopped ringing.

So pornography has saved you from selling out?

So far, yeah. It bugs me that so many "underground" directors have crossed over and now they're making mediocre multimillion dollar shit. Mind you, I'm trying to get a million dollars for my next film, which is about pornography. Actually, it's a *condemnation* of pornography.

Of course.

That's the other reason why I'm making another porn film. So that I can say, Look, I know what I'm talking about. There's nothing like a reformed whore . . .

Or as Oscar put it, before he became a reformed whore himself, "A moralist is someone who lectures on the evils of the sins of which he has grown tired."

Exactly.

Attitude
September 1998

Aiden Shaw

An LA friend of mine once answered an ad placed by Aiden Shaw in one of the LA gaypers. They talked about money. Mr. Shaw did not, as you might expect, come cheap. My friend took a deep breath, thought of England (up his ass), and agreed to the fee. "But then I asked him if he would fuck me. And you know what he *said?* 'Well, that depends on what you look like, *whether you turn me on enough.*' Well, fuck *that!* I can get rejected all over this city for free. Shit," he spat down the phone, "I can get rejected without leaving my *house.*"

"I can't control my dick," explains Aiden Shaw, sitting behind me in the minicab taking us across London to his flat in Chelsea, "so I'm very fussy about who I work with. They have to be someone I have some interest in." He's talking about shooting his "comeback" flick in the United States recently.

"But surely as a pornstar and ex-prostitute you're paid good money to control your dick?" I ask. (The minicab driver, an ordinary-looking married-man type, is now hanging on every word.)

"Well, I can't control it," says Shaw. "I can't just get it hard if I don't like the other person. It's not as if I can just get off on myself. There was one guy in the film doing a solo jerk-off spot—and he was wild. He just became this total sex beast on set, jacking off in front of a mirror. Everyone was blown away; they said they hadn't seen something like that in years. But I can't do that. When I look in the mirror I don't get off on what I see."

"Besides," he adds, "in this video they were paying for my name on the box. I was a label. So they had to indulge me."

"Why did you decide to go back to porn? Was it money?"

"No, it wasn't money," says Aiden dismissively. "I have an allowance from a friend in New York. I did it because I was fed up with people calling me an ex-pornstar. As if I was an ex-alcoholic or something. I went back to make this film because I wanted to combat this antisex attitude there is in the U.S. at the moment."

"Are you sure you didn't go back because 'ex-pornstar' sounds like 'over-the-hill?'" (Aiden is now one year on the wrong side of the now-you-are-dogmeat-in-gay-years age of thirty.)

The voice behind me is silent for a precisely timed, significant moment. "No," he says finally. "That wasn't it at all. I just love sex and wanted to make a pro-sex statement."

"Excuse me," he says to the minicab driver, "could you stop at a toilet if you see one? Look out for a little man with his legs apart."

The driver laughs embarrassedly, "Yeah, okay, mate—but you'll be lucky round 'ere. They've closed 'em all down." Unfortunately, he doesn't add, "Because of people like you."

But luck is on Shaw's side again and we pass London's last remaining operative public toilet and Shaw goes to piss. After he comes back the conversation turns to LA, a city he likes but which I don't. "LA is the worst thing that could happen to you—especially if you're English. To have your every whim indulged is a disaster. You end up completely cut off from the world, from life, from your national heritage of frustration."

"This sounds very moralistic to me," says Shaw.

"Yeah, maybe," I say. "But what's wrong with that?" No response.

When we arrive at Shaw's flat in Chelsea, the minicab driver surprises us by announcing, "Thanks, lads. As a matter of fact, I really enjoyed this fare." Difficult as he may be, Aiden Shaw always gives a good performance.

Even if he won't always fuck you.

*   *   *

Aiden Shaw, (ex-)prostitute, (ex-ex-)pornstar, poet, artist, novelist, singer, and one-man multimedia experience, was born in 1966 in leafy Harrow, North London, the second youngest in a large Irish Catholic family. Like Aiden, his parents seem to have been uncertain where they belonged. His builder dad and housewife mum emigrated from Ireland to Chicago when they were sixteen, then moved to London to start a family but ended up spending much of their time in Ireland. Getting noticed in such a large family turned little Aiden into a budding star, dressing up, wearing makeup, and being outrageous generally. He even told his dismissive careers advisor that he wanted to be a pop star. So after he left school it seemed natural that he should take a performance and visual arts course at Brighton College. Prostitution, which he discovered around this time, turned out to be another way of singing for his supper, of being a pop star on a one-to-one basis.

In 1997, several years and countless punters and porn videos later, Shaw is a "gay icon" and on happy-clappy, fluffy-wuffy *Gaytime TV*. His book of poetry, the snappily titled *If language at the same time shapes and distorts our ideas and emotions, how do we communicate love?*, bubbly poems about death, disease, loss, longing, and dilated arseholes. Funnily enough, it isn't going down very well. To be honest, it's excruciatingly embarrassing to watch. But there's something admirable about it too. Shaw's willfully casting his seed on stoney ground, doing something much more perverse than he's ever done in his videos.

It's clear that he relishes discomfort. His eponymously effective novel *Brutal,* published the year before, had him book-signing in Clone Zone. A book signing in *Clone Zone.* It's difficult not to fantasise how the phone call that booked him went:

> "So, will Aiden be demonstrating our sex toys whilst he's here?"
> "No. He'll be signing books."
> "Oh. Will he be signing them with a penis print?"
> "No, a pen."
> "Oh. Will he be at least signing them with no clothes on?"
> "No, he'll be fully dressed."
> "Oh. *All right then.* Maybe I can get off with him afterward . . ."

Sitting on the sofa in his sparsely furnished housing association flat in Chelsea, I find it's my turn to feel uncomfortable. I'm not sure whether it's because of the self-conscious artiness of his "living room"—one wall is pasted with manuscript pages from his novel—or whether it's because of the unsettling mixture of intelligence and beauty of Shaw himself (whose looks *hurt,* even though he isn't my type), or his surprisingly soft, slightly mid-Atlantic way of talking which has me straining to catch what he's saying. Whatever it is, I feel very uneasy. I start by asking him what the feedback has been from fans of his porn, the audience that "claps with one hand" as he once put it, to his other work.

MS: They're getting a bit more than they bargained for, aren't they? They obviously want you and your big dick, but they don't actually want the whole "package," do they?

AS: [Shaw laughs.] Well, part of the deal with me is that you get the whole thing eventually. The mail I get is all supportive, though.

So you don't get anyone complaining that they just want to fuck you and you insist on talking, singing, reading your poetry?

No, but I expect there are people who say this to their friends. But I want to be there for those who want more. When I was younger I would have jumped at the offer of something more than just a pair of tight jeans and a bulging crotch.

Isn't there a contradiction between your making a career out of being gay and your artist/outsider persona?

I've made a career out of having *sex.* You can do that whether you're straight or gay. If I wanted to make a career out of being gay, I'd have worked in a gay pub, bookshop, gay magazine, but I never did those things, which are much more specifically gay than having sex, either with punters or on film. Number one, I'm sexual. Number two, I'm gay. It's a question of timing. When I got involved in prostitution and porn it was very Other. Yeah, seven or eight years down the line it's very much gay mainstream.

It does seem there's a tension between you and gayness.

Well, that's not so surprising—but there's no more tension between me and my gayness than there is between me and my membership in society in general. I was aware of being "other" much earlier than I was aware of being "gay." It's not something I cringe about; it's just something I accept as a part of what I do. It's also not who I am; it's not my identity. They're just places I go. If I was more insecure in myself about it, then I think it would make me cringe. But I'm pretty comfortable about it.

Have you seen the 1980s' Jeff Stryker movie *Matter of Size,* where he plays a rock star and actually performs a song—well, half a song—in the middle of the movie, before getting sucked off outside the stage door . . . ?

[Shaw interrupts abruptly.] So what are the comparisons you're drawing?

Well, he had a big penis; he was a pornstar . . .

No, he was a little guy. Proportionately, he looked like he had a big penis.

Oh, right.

Apparently he was an excellent performer. And people liked that sort of boyishy look he had.

Why do they like you?

I think they see me as an honest-to-goodness top.

Jeff wasn't much of a bottom. Not until his *career* bottomed out.

I think he was too pretty to be a top, d'you know what I mean? From what I hear, even early on, people were calling me "Daddy-boy" instead of just "boy." I think they think it's more real, or something—I don't shave my chest, I don't have pearly white teeth, y'know? And I'm gay. Jeff isn't. [Shaw pauses.] I'm sure he has many more fans than I do.

But he's over, as they say, and apparently you're not. Even if there are some pornstars that earn more money than you—

[Shaw interrupts again.] No, that's not true. I think there's probably only one star that commands a higher fee, and that's Ryan Idol. And that's only because he has an agent and plays the game for all it's worth. I'm a top who doesn't play by the top rules—I'll suck and rim, and you're not supposed to do that as a top. I did everything except get fucked. I think they put up with it because I was European, or something.

Is your Englishness part of your attractiveness to the American audience?

Well, if Englishness is measured in foreskin-ness, then definitely.

Ah, right, another thing you've got that Jeff doesn't have. Whatever it is that you do, they certainly like you in the United States; but in Britain there is no real porn industry.

Yeah, people over here don't recognise me, but when I tell them my name, they've heard of it.

When you were younger, did you ever want to be an American?

I wanted to be a gay icon. A long time ago.

Who was your model?

No one. I was cutting the groove myself. There didn't seem to be any at the time. I suppose there was Brad Davies or Joe Dallesandro. But it would've been kinda nice to be a gay one, y'know? To be gay and a gay icon. D'you know what I mean? But I'd say that my whole masculinity is completely contrived. I don't believe in separate genders at all. I believe it's all conditioning. But I took on this stud persona because I just wanted to be successful in life. I wanted to get what I wanted—which was a certain amount of sex and a certain amount of attention. I am very well aware of what a huge influence this contrivance has had on my life.

This kind of honesty isn't the sort of thing that porn careers are made of. Nor is being honest about having HIV. How much of a problem has that been?

Well, it's supposed to be a big problem. But it's all about demand. The first company I called, they wanted me. And I said, well, I only want to work with other models who are positive. They said, "That's great—and we really appreciate what you're trying to do." So, did I change the industry overnight? Maybe. People like Chi Chi LaRue were saying that they would never work with models who were HIV positive—which I think is downright dishonest, cheap, and vulgar because she knows that probably all her friends are positive. Then along comes someone in demand enough to do that. And then, of course, I quite like the idea of taking people places they don't want to go again—y'know, look at this! It's that more-than-they-bargained-for thing again.

The reality is that a lot of people in the porn industry are positive. A lot of people are positive full stop. And a lot of people had problems with identity when they were younger, especially gender. I'd rather give my audience more than they bargained for than less.

There's been no backlash in the United States?

Well, in the opposite direction to what you might have expected. After my piece appeared in the November issue of *Poz* I guest edited, apparently Chi Chi had the nerve to complain that I was *his* model and that I shouldn't be working for another company. I suppose it's just another illustration of if they want you enough, you can pull it off. On the other hand, I've seen people's careers die after they tell other people in the industry that they're positive. You've got to make people want you.

When I ask Shaw about his band, Whatever, he starts to play me one track from a tape and then, as if dissatisfied with the impersonality of this, sings another song in front of me a capella. It's a touching moment, but also rather uncomfortable. I feel, like Shaw's porn fans, I'm getting more than I asked for. Another display of honesty, Shaw has discovered, is the best form of defence; interpret yourself before someone else interprets you. This certainly seems to be what his poems are doing. Shaw explains how most of his poems were written at a time when he was "hungry for love" and that they came out of "desperation." When asked where this desperation might have come from, Shaw offers a long list of possible explanations: ten years of prostitution, living in the city, being gay. I ask whether there isn't a trade-off between being an artist and/or an outsider and having happiness.

"You make it sound like a choice."

Well, it's not exactly a choice, but it's not exactly a totally unattractive deal, either. There's a certain narcissistic consolation in being an outsider.

I don't think it's about narcissism. [He says this very quickly, visibly bristling.] I think it's about trying to communicate more honestly. I want people to read my work. To say it's narcissism is to say that it's narcissism to help somebody up in the street . . .

But, for example, in your poems I think there are only a couple that don't use the "I" word.

I use the "I" a lot in my work because I want to communicate. In my third novel, *Boundaries,* I've gone back to it because I feel you can't get much closer than that . . .

But "narcissism" doesn't simply mean selfishness of vanity, but self-love—the kind of self-love and self-sufficiency that's necessary for all living things to survive and for all artists to produce things of beauty.

Well, people are going to pick up on the negative meaning of narcissism, so if you don't want people to misunderstand you, I suggest you choose your words more carefully . . .

Maybe I touched a nerve.

I guess that would be a simplistic enough interpretation. [Shaw pauses.] I've picked up on several questions you've asked this evening, not just this one. I don't think you should read too much into the fact that I've picked up on this question.

But why is it so strange that I should mention the word narcissism?

Because it's too obvious. Because I'm a pornstar, there must be a connection between my being onstage and my writing. It's like saying that all self-expression is narcissistic. Is that what you're saying?

Well, obviously there's an *element* of narcissism in all self-expression . . .

Is there narcissism in all communication? Surely that's all you're trying to do with self-expression. I couldn't have this discussion by myself, remember that. You're giving me these lines to work with. It can't be blamed on me. It's a two-way street.

What does that mean?

I'm saying you're a part of this discussion, that when you say "why are you doing this?" it's not just about me.

Well, what *I'm* asking is why, when I bring up the word "narcissism", do you immediately try to do away with it by saying all communication is narcissistic?

Well, I guess that's my way. With words.

I find it difficult to believe that people haven't brought the word up before when interviewing you.

Of course they do. But they usually use the word "self-obsessed."

Shaw's right to be wary of resentful attempts to dismiss him as an egomaniac—"Oh, *her,* she's just up her own arse, that one." That other narcissist, Gore Vidal, famously once defined a narcissist as "someone better looking than you." But there is an important point at stake here. You can't be a romantic outsider without being at least half in love with the idea of yourself as a romantic outsider. In an article for *Poz* magazine, Shaw wrote:

> I have a fantasy. It goes like this: I would never have had to rebel against my family simply to justify my existence. I would be allowed the luxury of a God who didn't reject me. I wouldn't need solace in a culture created in response to hatred. My relationships would be complicated, but not because of oppression and damage. And the sexual-outlaw mentality I once had might seem manic, even neurotic.

However, the fantasy is just as much, if not more, his image of himself as a sexual outlaw.

I have a theory that Shaw went back to porn because he's trapped inside the porno stud persona he's created and is clearly very proud of. Like Anita Pallenburg who played the Black Queen in *Barbarella,* it's a role he can't shake off. Or, more obviously, like Richard Gere in *American Gigolo,* he imagines himself in control of his universe but is trapped inside other people's image of him. While he's perfectly well aware that he's playing a role, I think he's less aware of how such roles can stick. No matter how much success Shaw has as a writer—and he is talented, in more ways than just the eye-watering one—I suspect it'll never give him the kick he got out of being a *pornstar.* As he said himself, "You have to make people want you." People in general and gays in particular don't *want* writers; most don't even read.

But Shaw isn't desperate or unhappy anymore. He's in love with someone else this time. With a fellow pornstar that he had to fuck in his latest porn movie. Talking about him, that smiley dreamy look that people get when they talk about their beloved crosses his face. "This is the first time I've been in love," he says emphatically. "For a while I thought I was too damaged by my experience of ten years of prostitution to be able to love someone. He gives me so much care and attention. I didn't know that someone could give that much care and attention."

Then his smile fades and turns to the more familiar frown. "And it makes me angry to realise that people weren't giving me that care and attention before."

Attitude
June 1997

Julie Burchill

Julie Burchill is more famous than any journalist dares dream. Which means that she's much more successful than any scribbler deserves to be. She's a household irritant. She's achieved a celebrity status by getting under the nation's skin. We've all had to share her loves and hates, fashions and fads—whether we've wanted to or not. Hence her career needs no account, just a list of things that we probably shouldn't have heard of if it wasn't for her: Bristol. The *NME*. Tony Parsons. The Groucho Club. *Ambition. The Modern Review.* Toby Young. Charlotte Raven. Lesbianism. Brighton. Smorgasbords.

Ms. B is the most successful stalker of the public imagination that British journalism has ever produced. As the marvellously objective title of her autobiography—*I Knew I Was Right*—suggests, there is no escape from her arrogance. Julie's psychosis *will* become your reality. So there.

As if to rub salt into the wound, the thirtysomething woman responsible for redefining journalism has a helium voice that sounds put on. When she picks up the phone at her house in her beloved Brighton I'm tempted to ask, "Is Mummy there?" Transcribing the interview later, the flat batteries on my tape recorder, which made me sound like Sher Khan the tiger in *The Jungle Book,* made her sound almost normal. (And eerily like Suzanne Moore.) But a girl with a squeaky voice can get away with almost anything. As indeed Julie has.

Her new novel sensitively explores the complex and delicate arena of human relationships, acceptance, and commitment. It's called *Married Alive.*

MS: Which one of your two marriages is this book based on?

JB: It's not based on any of my marriages. In the book, she's the injured party, but in my marriages I'm afraid I was the injuring one. I was a bit of a . . . SLUT! Ha ha ha ha ha ha! You're either the dumper or the dumped, and I've never been dumped yet and I don't plan to be either!

There's an awful lot of dumping around these days . . .

Yeah, well it's kicks, innit? Ha ha ha ha ha!

What do you think the future is for men and women?

Don't believe in mixed marriages! Ha ha ha ha ha! I don't know, Mark, you tell me. I think we'll muddle along the way we always did. But you know, I don't know why all these Bridget Jones women are complaining about not being able to get a boyfriend. I've never had any trouble! What fucking planet are they on and how crap are they in bed? Ha ha ha ha! I think that they pretend they can't get a boyfriend. I think they're afraid of not appearing feminine. They think that if they admit that they've got a career, a life, and are getting laid regular that people might not think they're a LAY-DEE.

Or interesting.

I don't think it's interesting to whine.

Which reminds me, what do you think about the idea of gay marriage, as advocated by people like Andrew Sullivan?

Oh! Andrew's LUV-LEE! I ate his chewing gum once to prove I'm not homophobic. . . . He's very conservative, though. But he's Catholic, isn't he?

Very much. And apparently running for pope.

I think he's looking to marry a doctor. You know, Mark, it's different strokes for different folks. Andrew's the sort of person who'd be completely happy to live in a kitchen in a plastic pinny, but it's not for all of us, is it?

No. Besides most gay relationships don't last long enough to get out of bed let alone into a pinny. Did you know, by the way, that there's an event at the ICA this spring called "The Girl Looked at Julie: A Queer Appreciation of Julie Burchill"?

No!! You're JOKING! That's the funniest thing anyone's ever told me! That's a total hoot! I'm an ICON, I love it!

Didn't you know about your queer following?

No, honestly, I didn't. I never thought I was enough of a mess. . . .
Hang on, it's probably a bad sign, isn't it?

I'm not sure it's quite that sort of iconic status they have in mind . . .

They think I'm bitchy, don't they?

**Well, yes, but you've also got this sensibility which is queerer
than that of a lot of queers. You're an outsider . . .**

I like that.

Yes, I thought you might.

Somebody once told me I'd have made a very good gay man, which I
think I would have done. Whereas I don't think I could make a very
good lesbian, to tell you the honest truth.

Why not?

I dunno. . . . It's just a bit too TENDER for my liking, y'know? I'm a
bit ROUGH . . .

There are plenty of rough lesbians.

Yeah, but I don't like 'em! They're all so UGLY! The pretty ones
want you to be all tender and the rough ones are just so NASTY!

**What was that quote you gave the press at the time you eloped to
Brighton with Charlotte Raven? I thought it was fantastic.**

[Putting on a very lofty, sincere voice.] "Ms. Raven and I are not homosexuals, we are simply in love." Which turned out to be about
right, actually . . .

Do you find lesbians too serious?

What? You mean humourless? I'm not going to be drawn on that!
They'll cancel my night at the ICA! Anyway, I actually think they're
not serious ENOUGH! They've given up on politics like everyone

else. They just want to go out dancing. But lesbians shouldn't, because they're better than other women.

Why?

Well, they're purer cos they don't consort with the enemy! They
should be inspiring us not to sit at home, making interesting stews . . .
GAWD! I've just realised! THREE QUARTERS OF MY FRIENDS
ARE GAY! I've just counted 'em in my head! I suppose it's because I
live in Brighton. In London, Paul was my only gay friend; down 'ere,
it's practically everybody. You know Paul, don't you? Welsh boy. He
used to let me feel his tattoos! Luv-lee Spanish boyfriend.

**Yes. Didn't you once ask him, "So, what does your *movement*
think about such-and-such?"**

OHMIGOD! What a thing to say! That's very me. Ha ha ha ha ha!
[Pause.] I wonder if I was being cute or if I meant it?

**Didn't you also once write a piece about The Great Dark Fag and
how you wished he had rescued you from Bristol and taught you
about art and literature?**

Oh, yes, that was Ned Sherrin. I had a really big crush on him and sent
him lots of gifts. But by that time it was too late. [Sighs.] I'd said all
these terrible homophobic things. But he's so LUV-LEE! He's much
bigger than you think. He's from a farm an' everything! He's a
REALLY BIG MAN. [Pause.] I went really girly when I said that,
didn't I? Ha ha ha ha ha ha ha!

Attitude
March 1999

DIRTY BOOKS

A Great Future Behind Them

NAKED MEN:
PIONEERING MALE NUDES 1935-1955
BY DAVID LEDDICK

In the twenty-first century, probably around the time that men are restricted by law to the occupations of handyman and strippergrams, it will be agreed that the image which summed up the end of the twentieth was not the fall of the Berlin Wall, nor the death of Diana, but a close-up of a man's naked bottom.

And who today can deny that the twentieth century is ending on a bum note? Turn on the TV any time after 9 p.m. and you will almost certainly be faced with several pairs of naked male buttocks, shiny and slick with baby oil, being jiggled to the strains of "Hot Stuff" in yet another documentary about working-class Northern men with fake tans forming a male strip troupe to help pay for their gym membership.

The uncovered male derriere is the most eloquent symbol of our times, representing the rise of the Rabelasian over the suburban, the expressive over the repressive, the feminine over the masculine—and the rosy financial future of Immac for Men.

Of course, it wasn't always this way. Before housewives were encouraged to bellow "gerremorff!" (and that's just during the ad breaks) such images were strictly for a specialised niche market that had little to do with women and even less to do with consumerism. They were at best bohemian; at worst degenerate.

The cover image for David Leddick's *Naked Men: Pioneering Male Nudes 1935-1955,* of a naked, muscular young male photographed from behind with his open hands resting saucily on his buttocks, might be almost a cliché today—though perhaps he should be bending over and shimmying down a pair of spangly knickers—but when it was taken in the 1950s it was intended for private collectors, not the latest advertising campaign for Levi's or Häagen-Dazs.

Now that ogling men is in the mainstream, several pioneers of male nudity have been "outed" by publishers. Last year Bob Mizer's famous Athletic Model Guild work from the 1940s-1960s, was published in one painfully loud-and-proud pink boxed set decorated with Tom of Finland drawings. The same year saw the publication of *Physique*, a life of the eccentric British male nude photographer John S. Barrington by Rupert Smith.

Meanwhile, David Leddick confesses that the inspiration for his book was *Collaboration*, a recently published book about the male nude drawings and photos of Paul Cadmus, Jared and Margaret French.

Leddick's innovation in the crowded pioneering male-nudes market is to make his book a biography of the pioneering male nudes themselves, answering that vague question that poses itself in the back of the mind when looking at old pictures of beautiful young men: "I wonder what they look like now?" by tracking down Platt Lynes' surviving models and photographing what's left of them.

Like most vague questions, it's one that's probably best left unanswered, as is demonstrated by The Gap's recent advertising campaign featuring a contemporary Joe Dallesandro, the famously angelic devil who posed for Bob Mizer and Andy Warhol in the 1960s and whose torso adorns the first Smiths album, but who now looks like a truck driver with ulcers. True, the pictures of the young men have a certain poignancy when placed alongside an inset headshot of the young man grown old; and, reciprocally, there's a certain dignity revealed in old age, too. However, while the ephemeral nature of male beauty is undoubtedly part of its appeal, you need to be able to suspend disbelief in the immortality of such beauty to fully appreciate it; a disavowal not exactly helped by seeing precisely what time had in store for them.

On the other hand, if the contemporary pictures were nudes instead of discreet headshots, the effect might have been more provocative and less precious. Two of Platt Lynes' best, most disturbing pictures actually play on this theme. In "Alexander and Diogenes" he recreates Alexander's encounter with the philosopher in a barrel. Alexander, smooth and strong, stands wearing nothing but his laurels and his youth looking down at Diogenes, wizened and wrinkled, wearing nothing but his years and his wisdom. In his famous portrait of Somerset Maugham, a fat, middle-aged man fully clothed in a dark suit looks down contemptuously/enviously at a slim, naked young man kneeling before him.

As this last picture hints, there's something slightly distasteful, slightly corrupt in the fey, 1940s New York world of writers, artists, ballet dancers, fashion photographers, and Fire Island parties that this kind of photography emerged from and which employed Greek imagery, partly in an understandable attempt to avert the intervention of the law, and partly in a faintly contemptible attempt to suggest something pure, virile, and artistic on something that—frankly—wasn't. It's a world too fey and pretentious to be erotic and too timid and neutered to be artistically impressive. As Leddick writes of one of Lynes' models, "Bill Harris was an arbiter of style. During the 1940s and 1980s, when one wanted to do things the right way—clothes, travel, lovers—one called Harris for advice."

Curiously, in all the tributes to the "brave" pioneers of male nudes there is no mention of the LA photographer Bob Mizer, who also used Greek and Roman imagery, but in a way that somehow managed to be erotic and pure, virile and artistic, as well as lighthearted. Of course, Mizer was too crude: he used Californian sunlight instead of overwrought New York studio lighting; he wasn't a friend of Cadmus; he didn't move in Café Society; and the Manhattan Mommies Boys no doubt disapproved of the rough sailor and Marine models he used, and which most of them didn't have the nerve to pick up themselves.

Moving in Café Society does, however, have its perks—you occasionally persuade a celeb or celeb-to-be to strip for you. A picture of Christopher Isherwood from the 1940s shows him undressing to the left; and one of Yul Brynner from the same era shows both his heads covered—he sports a full mane of hair and a fully un-American foreskin. But best of all by far is a picture of Tennessee Williams lying face down on a bed. We are told that Mr. Williams possessed a "taut swimmer's body."

This may or may not be the case, but judging by the picture, I have to say that that I have no doubt that Mr. Williams' bum will *not* be featured in twenty-first-century history books about the twentieth century. It certainly wouldn't sell any ice cream.

Independent on Sunday
April 1998

The Private Lives of Dr. Sex

SEX, THE MEASURE OF ALL THINGS:
A LIFE OF ALFRED C. KINSEY
BY JONATHAN GATHORNE-HARDY

Growing up in the 1970s in York, frustrated and bored with waiting for someone to invent the Internet, I got my teenage kicks at the Central Library. Dropping in on my way home from school, I would furtively rummage through the dusty sociology section looking up dirty words, especially "homosexuality" and "penis" (blissfully unaware that in the gents toilets both these words could be found in flagrant action). One of the most fertile resources for my highly subjective researches was *Sexual Behaviour in the Human Male* by a Dr. Kinsey (1948).

According to the sensational biography by James H. Jones, *Alfred C. Kinsey: A Public/Private Life,* published last year to scandalised uproar, the good doctor's interest in these words was less academic than mine. Apparently he was "a homosexual," driven by personal demons, who cruised parks, bars, cinemas, and public lavatories, and frequently had sex with the men he interviewed. In other words, the good doctor was a pervert and his research was to be handled with rubber gloves.

Gathorne-Hardy's *Sex, the Measure of All Things* aims to liberate Kinsey from the nonce wing of sexology by refuting Jones' reductive approach to his sexuality, arguing that he was as complex as his subject matter, that the sex pioneer from Indiana was a living testament to the value of his own refusal to countenance that there was such a thing as "a homosexual"; there were only homosexual or heterosexual *acts*. On Kinsey's famous 0-6 scale, where 0 = exclusively heterosexual behaviour, 3 = equally homosexual and heterosexual behaviour, and 6 = exclusively homosexual (and 7 = Harvey Fierstein), Kinsey moved in his own lifetime from a Kinsey 0 to a Kinsey 4. Gathorne-Hardy argues persuasively that Kinsey's bisexuality and proactive approach were actually a help rather than a hindrance in his research, contrasting it with that of the "blue rinse" brigade who conducted the research for a recent American sex survey (as one respondent put it succinctly, "I'm not gonna tell someone who reminds me of my mom that I suck cock").

Gathorne-Hardy also demonstrates why Kinsey's data, despite all the statistical brickbats hurled at it, is probably still more accurate than any gathered since. Recent sex surveys both here and in the United States have sneered at Kinsey's failure to "random sample." But the trouble with random sampling in regard to these sex surveys is that it isn't random. Around 30 percent of people randomly selected in the recent mammoth British sex survey refused to take part. In contrast, over a quarter of Kinsey's data was garnered from 100-percent responses from the universities, factories, and associations he visited. Even when you remove the so-called "dirty data" of prisons and homosexual groups, this has little or no effect on the findings that most people who attack Kinsey today are concerned with—that between a quarter and a third of all American males had had homosexual contact to orgasm.

And yet one can't help feeling that Gathorne-Hardy should have spent less time refuting Jones and more time reading Foucault, whom, along with Freud, he has no time for. Gathorne-Hardy, like his behaviourist subject, is allergic to theory. But this fetishism of facts, refreshing as it was in a 1940s sexologist, is simply frustrating in a 1990s biographer. What is most interesting about Kinsey is what is omitted here.

Gathorne-Hardy dismisses as "irrelevant" and a "swamp of words" Foucault-fan Thomas Waugh's intriguing observations on Kinsey and the scientific study of sex: "How can the pleasure of looking be separated from the pleasure of erotic looking . . . the drive for visual pleasure, in which knowledge and desire are interlocking terms of power?" (p. 317). And yet, on the very next page, Gathorne-Hardy, introducing Kinsey's study of the female orgasm, cites a story which graphically presents precisely this question. Beck, a pioneering sex researcher, was examining a woman for a collapsed uterus. Her cervix was clearly visible through her labia and he was about to probe here when she told him to be careful; if he touched her she would almost certainly have an orgasm. "Beck suddenly realised he might have a chance to see the female orgasm in action. He ignored her and 'swept my finger three or four times across the space between the cervix and the pubic arch, when almost immediate orgasm occurred . . . .'" (p. 318).

Foucault may have been too ready to play the French phoney, but I can hardly think of a single historical figure more deserving of a Foucauldian hermeneutic than Kinsey. Everything is there: the confessional; the integration of power, knowledge, and sex; observation as a form of control. Kinsey even insisted that his male assistants have sex with him, arguing that it would help them with their homosexual interviews. If they objected, this was taken as proof of how much they needed to have sex with Kinsey to overcome their inhibitions (judging by the plates of some of his young, beefy assistants, I can't help feeling it's an argument that I would have used too).

In effect, the Institute for Sex Research (ISR) was one gigantic sexual panopticon with Kinsey at its centre, surveying the most private, most intimate behaviour of literally tens of thousands of people. Kinsey personally observed hundreds of acts of coitus and masturbation, and his institute filmed and photographed thousands more. As an example of the whimsical power of this voyeuristic potentate, on one occasion Kinsey ordered the ISR to film a thousand different men masturbating to determine whether men actually ejaculated, i.e., threw out their semen, or whether it just fell out (most men are dribblers, it transpired).

Of course, it doesn't take a Foucault to see that the thousands of in-depth sex interviews that Kinsey conducted could themselves be interpreted as a form of sex (even if you didn't know about his habit of measuring his male interviewees' erections). One indignant NY hotelier famously made the connection. Fed up with the constant stream of disreputable types of men lining up in his foyer to be interviewed by Kinsey, who was lodged in one of his rooms at the time, he turfed the doctor out, shouting, "I will not have you undressing people's minds' in my hotel!"

Kinsey started a trend that has become unstoppable. Nowadays, any sex surveyor has to begin their interview with the question, "When was the first time you were interviewed about your sex life?" Kinsey's sexual liberationist approach has become mainstream. Turn on the television, open a newspaper, and be confronted with another "sex survey" or a new series claiming to "uncover the secret of sex." Even Republicans are at it. Kenneth Starr, the right-wing Kinsey, conducts an investigation into sexual behaviour even more ambitious and more famous than Doctor Sex's. Relentlessly making the private public in the name of the public good, he aggressively pursues evidence of extramarital, extravaginal sexual activity. And you can be sure that when Mr. Starr extracted a confession of orogenital contact from the president of the United States himself, he had no doubts about the relationship of knowledge to power. (Interestingly, 40 percent of Kinsey's respondents didn't consider orogenital contact as "sex"—nowadays, of course, the same number of men wouldn't think of sex as being anything else.)

Explicitness is now as compulsory for our age as hypocrisy was for Kinsey's strict Methodist father. Given this, Kinsey's increasing fascination with homosexuality was entirely appropriate, since homosexuality is the most "naked," most "explicit" kind of sex—i.e., nonreproductive, noninstitutionalised sex-for-its-own-sake. Interestingly, the number representing exclusive homosexuality on the Kinsey scale—six—is "sex" in Latin. Little wonder, then, that as our age has become more obsessed with sex, it has become more obsessed with homosexuality.

However, there is a huge irony here. Kinsey's ambition to demolish the category of "the homosexual" by revealing the commonness of homosexual acts has not been realised. Instead, homosexuality is, in some senses, even more ghettoised than in the 1940s. Male-male activity, precisely because it is more visible, is probably less common these days. Knowledge about sexuality of itself changes the meaning and practise of what people do with their bodies. Going to bed with your buddy after a few beers too many now means you have to move to West Hollywood when you wake up.

But, despite some admirably thorough legwork and some astute observations, you won't find these points discussed by Gathorne-Hardy. He's too busy using Kinsey as a behaviourist battering ram against theory, psychoanalysis, and religion. The end result is that Kinsey himself is lost in the noise of liberal partisan warfare.

Gathorne-Hardy repeatedly cites Richard Webster's *Why Freud Was Wrong,* like some kind of charm warding off evil spirits, and refuses to seriously discuss Kinsey's unconscious life because he doesn't want to give credence to Jones' idea that Kinsey was "pursued by demons." But Kinsey himself confided to a friend that he was afraid of psychoanalysts; apparently, he had a feeling that they could divine his "innermost and most secret thoughts."

Whether or not Kinsey might have benefited from some psychoanalysis is difficult to say, but this biography certainly would. Kinsey was himself the best example of the limits of sexual liberationism. He died an unhappy, broken, impotent man in 1957, aged sixty-three. According to Gathorne-Hardy, this was due to overwork and the result of the triumph of the reactionary forces that cut off Kinsey's funding. But perhaps it may also have had something to do with Kinsey's own driven, controlling nature and his masochistic tendencies—later in life, he liked to suspend himself from the ceiling by his scrotum, and he announced to a surprised friend that he had recently circumcised himself in the bath.

Kinsey and Gathorne-Hardy may not have had much time for theories about the superego, but it looks as if an especially punitive one had plenty of time for Kinsey.

Independent on Sunday
May 1997

Agony from the King of Cross-Reference

FREUD'S FOOTNOTES
BY DARIAN LEADER

Recent research, widely publicised in the press with the usual barely disguised *schadenfreude* that usually accompanies news that the efforts and sacrifice of other people have been in vain, suggested that therapy was no more effective than prescription drugs or "talking regularly to a friendly academic." I doubt this is the case, though I can't speak from experience as I've never been in therapy. Like a Church of England agnostic—or what amounts to the same thing, a pathologically lazy person—I don't take part myself but like to think that lots of other people do.

In my case, I like to think I can *read* myself better, or at least smarter. Certainly there's no shortage of literature these days pandering to those who can't quite make it out of their armchair and onto the couch, encouraging, however tacitly, the idea that a talking cure can be a reading cure. In fact, with practising analysts such as Adam Phillips, Darian Leader, and Raphael Samuels so keen to write for a general audience it's impossible not to suppress the uncharitable thought that perhaps shrinks are fed up with having to shut up for most of that analytical hour. One of the disadvantages of the talking cure is that someone has to do an awful lot of *listening*. Probably very few people "talk regularly to a friendly academic." Most academics I know would become very unfriendly very quickly if the traffic were one way: in the opposite direction to the one they are accustomed to.

But then, as Leader himself puts it, "anyone who chooses to devote their life to psychoanalysis be it as profession or object of academic research, has something seriously wrong with them" (p. 1). Of course, it would be cheap to deploy such an ironic confession against its author, but I won't let that stop me. I've never used prescription antidepressants, but Leader's prose strongly inclines me to try. Clearly, some of his reviewers have been trying nonprescription ones. His extraordinarily bloodless writing has been pantingly described as "coltish" by one paper and "athletic" by another. *The Guardian* described him in awe as "Oliver Sachs as agony aunt." Which does rather beg the question, who would want Oliver Sachs as an agony aunt? Mind you, Leader's last book, *Why Do Women Write More Letters Than They Post?*, also begged a few questions: the first, from every woman I mentioned the title to, being, "*Do* they?"

However, it's all somewhat academic whether Leader begs questions or asks them because he rarely stoops so low as to actually answer them. Or present a coherent argument. Or write in an accessible way (except in his introductions—which are probably based on outlines written for publishers). No, Leader doesn't need to do any of these things because Leader, as his name would suggest, is a very special kind of man, with a very special access to knowledge and a very special way of showing it off. Leader, you see, is a Lacanian.

Jacques Lacan is the French poststructuralist smoke-and-mirror-phase phallus-as-signifier chappy who "updated" Freud and rescued him from his gravest error: his accessibility. Lacanians are a perverse bunch. It is as if after Martin Luther, Protestants had decided to translate the Bible back, not into Latin even, but into *Greek,* so as to keep the *hoi polloi* and their crude misapprehensions at bay. Difficulty is not of itself objectionable, especially in an age of pop-everything let alone psychology, but something that is at once inscrutable and trying too hard is just hideously *uncool.* Someone once said of reading Nietzsche that it was like seeing the world lit by flashes of lightning; with Lacan and most Lacanians it's like seeing a library lit by a faulty fluorescent tube.

As Leader points out, Freud was the father *and* mother of psychoanalysis. With the possible exception of Nietzsche himself (whom Freud deliberately avoided reading until late in his career) there really isn't much of a tradition that goes before him. Hence, psychoanalysis really *is* footnotes to Freud, in a way that philosophy isn't footnotes to Plato, despite the famous aphorism. Perhaps this is why Leader wishes to present himself as the master of the addendum, the king of the cross-reference. His book is largely a squabble about sources, overly arcane even for someone who "has something seriously wrong with them." *Freud's Footnotes* is in fact a book-length footnote to a footnote. Moreover, almost every page has its *own* footnotes, including the very first line on the very first page of the introduction. This, no doubt, is a Lacanian's idea of a clever joke. It is, however, everyone else's idea of agony.

Sometimes Leader's observations are mildly interesting, such as when he points out that Freud's footnotes on the importance of the repressed olfactory senses hugs the bottom of the page, "just like the quadruped man they are supposed to describe." It is also piquant to learn that when Newton magnanimously described himself as "standing on the shoulders of giants," he was actually being very bitchy—Hooke, his chief rival, was a hunchback.

Occasionally, like a lighthouse looming up out of the nighttime fog of his obscurantist prose, Leader produces an important contention, albeit one which goes against the grain of his own style: "Freud's idea that desire generates states of wishing and of expectation as well as all forms of thinking only emerges in the most garbled form, in most of the translations . . ." (p. 41).

And there is a curiously fascinating case history Leader touches on to illustrate how Freud may have put too much emphasis on guilt/self-punishment as a function of the desires of the child, instead of a response to the parent's own desires. Leader tells the story of a two-and-a-half-year-old boy, fussed over by his mother, who continually banged his head against inanimate objects because his father had greeted his first bruise with the exclamation: "That'll make a man of him!" ("Or," I found myself adding out loud as I read this passage, "a Lacanian.")

Certainly Leader is always well informed and bafflingly well read, but unlike the Viennese master (as opposed to the French pretender), he has a tendency to come across as a pedantic show-off. Worst of all, Freud himself seems to be largely missing from "his" footnotes. Unless you are mightily interested in what the Kleinian and Lacanian schools might have in common despite their recent falling out, *Freud's Footnotes* isn't worth looking up.

Independent on Sunday
February 2000

Platonic Time Travel

THE SMITHSONIAN INSTITUTION
BY GORE VIDAL

The jacket cover of *The Smithsonian Institution* is a piece of work. Before the Gothic splendour of the Smithsonian, surrounded by roses, a young blond Adonis stripped to the waist embraces a brunette (eyes closed, lips parted) with ample bosoms proffered by a silk and lace ballgown with plunging neckline. It seems to promise an historical romance of the gooier, gushier variety. Until you spot the huge bold typeface over a nuclear mushroom head emerging from the institute spelling out the name GORE VIDAL. Behold Gore—destroyer of worlds (of sentiment).

The blinding flash of Vidal's wit, the searing heat of his irony, the supersonic shock wave of his archness are irresistible, Vishnu-esque forces which have threatened the pax Americana ever since he was dropped on New York in the 1940s. Over the years, however, we have grown accustomed to him and the awful threat of the emotional winter that would surely cover the earth if he were read in enough places simultaneously. And as we have learned to love The Vidal, he has learned to up his megaton yield.

Having vaporised Christianity in *Live from Golgotha,* Gore's latest novel sets out to incinerate something even more sacred: the American Empire. Set in the national museum of the same name in 1939, it tells the story of a humpy teenage math prodigy and baseball star called simply "T," who is called to the Smithsonian to help with their programme to build an atom bomb, but whose special gift for visualising complex mathematical equations also allows him to travel in time. Glimpsing himself dying in World War II, he then tries to change history to keep America out of the war and his future self alive.

In addition to the time-space-continuum malarkey, the dummies in the exhibits come to life after hours, providing T with the opportunity for a (purely pelvic) underage affair with President Grover Cleveland's lusty wife, and Vidal with an opportunity for goosing the grandees and immortals of American history. In another, parallel America, General Douglas MacArthur is passed over for promotion and in a fit of pique becomes a Tokyo Rose, urging American soldiers to surrender. Meanwhile, Abraham Lincoln has fallen in love with Carl Sandburg's pompous hagiography of him: the prime mover of American (imperial) history is but a mannequin mouthing someone else's idea of what he should be and is bought by Walt Disney as an animatronix.

All good fun, but perhaps, given Vidal's own habit of using his characters as nothing more than mannequins for displaying his ideas, setting *Smithsonian* in a museum of dummies which come alive at night is maybe an irony taken too far.

There's also a tad too much showing off—not something you usually complain about in Vidal's work because high-wire intellectual egotism is what we look to him for. But here the scholarship slips. The physics is very wobbly, and Darwinian ideas are confused with Lamarckian ones. Even the history is occasionally off-beam: In one passage, Charles Lindbergh, who really should know better, states that the U.S. Navy's aircraft carriers were sunk at Pearl Harbor. In fact, the carrier fleet, the main target of the Japanese torpedo planes, happened to be out at sea on exercise at the time and were largely spared. Perhaps these points would be mere pedantry—if they were about a novel less convinced of its own intellectual unassailability.

What saves *Smithsonian* is the warm realisation that it *is* a historical romance after all, that Vidal is actually more love-bomb than A-bomb. The central character, T., could be "Time" but is almost certainly a fusion of Gore and Jimmie Trimble, the blond, baseball-playing, belly-rubbing, school-buddy love of Vidal's life who was unveiled in his memoir *Palimpsest*. And who died tragically and somewhat conveniently on Iwo Jima in 1944, building the American Empire, aged nineteen.

In *Palimpsest,* Vidal interviews Trimble's mother, telling her, "I'm thinking of making a little book about Jimmie, photographs, letters, what people remember. . . ." If *Palimpsest* turned out to be that memorial, *Smithsonian* is the resurrection. It would seem that all that messing around with timelines, all that buggery-pokery with physics, is so that Jimmie Trimble can survive the war, pursue his baseball career, get married, and have kids.

As he made clear in *Palimpsest,* Vidal considered Trimble his true "twin" (he subscribes to the Platonic idea of love as a union of two halves that make a whole): "What I was not, he was and the other way around." In *The Smithsonian,* it is the math prodigy T. who saves his alter/future-ego, the baseball-playing T., by substituting himself just before the Japanese attack that killed him. T. is able to save his "twin" because he has enough imagination to visualise the equations that make time travel possible. In other words, he's a novelist.

It's a moving idea. Vidal, in what he has described as "the departure lounge of life" and already being measured for inclusion in the wax-work museum of Great American Men of Letters, wishes that he had been able to give his life for that of a Marine. But quite who is being saved by whom is unclear. The ultimate paradox of this novel of paradoxes is not one of time, but of the heart. Is it the American Empire which cuts T. off from his destiny by throwing away his life on some rock in the Pacific, or is it the childless, ageing Vidal who wields the gelding knife by denying the lad a dignified death and commissioning him to live in his stead?

Whatever the answer, this historical romance is assuredly about the greatest love the world has ever known. *L'amour propre.*

Independent on Sunday
October 1998

Sex in the Afternoon

THE MARRIED MAN
BY EDMUND WHITE

"Please," I begged a trusted friend shortly after reading White's 1997 book, *The Farewell Symphony,* "if I should ever turn into Edmund White, *shoot me."*

It wasn't that I didn't rate his artistry. Anyone who can render twenty years of meaningless sex in the Parisian afternoon even more tedious than twenty years of meaningless sex in the Parisian afternoon actually is, must be possessed of a great talent. Nor was it that I didn't rate him as a person: I met him once at a dinner party a few years ago and found him, like his prose, disarmingly charming and candid. No, it was the *idea* of Edmund White that I couldn't bear.

I found it almost as unappealing as much of the serious book-reading public appeared to find it *aspirational.* After all, as "Austin," the middle-aged American living in Paris with a snobbish disdain for Americans (who, like all White's protagonists, bears more than a passing resemblance to White) puts it rather smugly: "Europeanised Americans are the best sort of people."

Edmund White is a literary brand which promises salons, boulevards, and buggery in garlic-scented backrooms; a highbrow Anglo tourism of Gallic lowlife with plenty of disposable income and an indispensable sexual identity. A *Queer as Folk* for those who won't watch television (and have never heard of Manchester). George Orwell once complained that, to Americans, Paris represented a cross between a brothel and a museum. *Plus ça change.* For American and British fiction aficionados, White represents a cross between a bathhouse and an antiques shop.

The jacket blurb to his new novel reads like an especially precious article from *Condé Nast Traveller.* It gushes about how Austin and Julien, a young architect, "dash between Bohemian suppers and glittering salons . . ." and how their quest for "health and happiness drives them to Rome, to the shuttered squares of Venice, to Key West in the sun, Montreal in the snow and Providence in the rain—landscapes soaked with feeling which lead, in the end, to the bleak, baking sands of the Sahara." If only we could all arrange for the scenery to match our moods so tastefully!

Oddly, apart from the hint about a quest for "health and happiness" and a cryptic "dark cloud on the horizon," there is no mention that this is an AIDS novel. A slightly ironic "closetedness" given the Anglo/Protestant habit in White's work of decrying the lack of honesty and openness in Latin countries. It's a shame, because even though AIDS novels are hideously unfashionable these days, *The Married Man* is a good one—as AIDS novels go. Largely because it avoids the sentimentality and melodrama which drowns most of the others so much more fatally than pneumocystis pneumonia.

If *The Farewell Symphony* was a confession of sorts of a plague survivor's guilty if entirely predictable and human irresponsibility (in it, White seemed to admit that he has HIV and that he had deliberately unsafe sex with a bisexual man after learning of his status), *The Married Man* is an admission of a plague survivor's guilty *responsibility*. Set in the early 1990s, before the arrival of the protease inhibitor cavalry, *The Married Man* tells how an ageing but immature writer for glossy magazines abandons his life of selfish indolence to take on the crushingly heavy responsibility of caring for his terminally ill bisexual boyfriend—whose condition he may have brought about—not out of love, but *duty*. It anatomises unflinchingly not only the progress of the disease, which turns Julien into "a death's head shaking on a stick," but also his own ambivalence, self-delusion, and questionable motivations. Its autobiographical nature is advertised by the fact that Julien's end parallels almost exactly that of Brice at the end of *The Farewell Symphony*.

Perhaps corruption of the flesh and of the soul are handled so well here because White is an undisputed master of a slightly sickened-sickening sensuality—managing to evoke tastefully the distasteful truth of our own desire (in *The Married Man* he appears to have controlled his habit of taking a sniff of self-justifying 1970s gay-lib poppers every few pages). In one passage he describes a twenty-four-year-old lad with "an intense stare and the strange smell of an old well, as though his fillings had started to rust in an excess of saliva." And later, Austin reminisces about "the hot, bitter taste of his anus, like stale cucumbers . . ."

Despite his tendency to never use one adjective when three will do, White can be very droll and to the point when he allows himself to be vulgar, especially in his observations of national foibles. Illustrating what he aptly describes as the "sing song complacency" of the Dutch, he recounts an experience in an Amsterdam bar where a "a lantern-jawed, gum-chewing blond with bad skin had asked him in a bored voice, 'And would you like to be beat?' just as if he'd been saying, 'And would you like more fries?'"

White was accused of being "self-obsessed" by some when *The Farewell Symphony* was published. Part of the (self-obsessed) reason why I read *The Married Man* was to reassure myself that I hadn't turned into Edmund White in the intervening years. The answer I found within its unflinching pages surprised me—even if it was perhaps intended to: No, I told myself, you haven't turned into Edmund White. And you never will. You don't have enough heart.

Independent on Sunday
March 2000

Genital Blending

MY GENDER WORKBOOK: HOW TO BECOME A REAL MAN, A REAL WOMAN, THE REAL YOU, OR SOMETHING ELSE ENTIRELY
BY KATE BORNSTEIN

Self-described "gender outlaw" Kate Bornstein is apparently beyond gender and hence is a fan of politically correct, not to say sexless, *Star Trek: The Next Generation*. I, on the other hand, am clearly not beyond gender, just beyond hope, and prefer the original, sweaty, sexist, sexy 1960S series. Perhaps this is why, after totting up my score on the "Gender Aptitude Test" in "hir" (sic) *My Gender Workbook: How to Become a Real Man, a Real Woman, the Real You, or Something Else Entirely,* I found myself in the top-scoring (i.e., oppressive), "perfectly gendered" (i.e., reactionary) category and was mockingly informed, "You're Captain James T. Kirk!"

Obviously my role model should have been the "transgendered" android, Data. On the other hand, Kirk is not exactly most people's idea of a "real man." He wears a corset, tight trousers, lots of makeup, and the camera lens is slathered in Vaseline every time it goes in for yet another close-up. Moreover, he has a suspiciously intense friendship with his odd-looking science officer who goes into a sulk every time Kirk falls for one of those alien beehive drag queens. So perhaps I'm not so happy to be told that my gender is Kirk, after all.

The problem with Bornstein's book is that like most efforts at "re-education," it only succeeds in reingraining your worst prejudices. Its finger-wagging, Maoist approach to the "false consciousness" those of us unfortunate enough not to be transgendered like Bornstein labour under tends to make you rather fond of gender—that "obsolete" system of oppression that Bornstein rails against. Arrogantly incompetent sentences such as: "Gender over the past couple of millennia has been twisted into a very lop-sided power arena as represented by the gender/identity/power pyramid" (p. 38), don't exactly charm, either.

Nor, frankly, does the faux cutesy style of this harangue—presented in the form of a school exercise book, with tests, diagrams, role-play/sex-talk conversations from the Internet, "wacky" fonts and "fun" exclamation marks and campy tone—succeed in disguising its essentially serious looniness.

Faced with the goody-goody characters in *Star Trek: TNG*, you can't help but side with the baddies. Likewise, who, faced with the multiple choice questions here, would have any choice at all?

Do you have a 'type' of person you regularly fall for?

A. Definitely, yes
B. I try to keep my mind open about this sort of thing, but I usually fall for one type.
C. I seem to fall for lots of "types" of people, but usually they're all the same gender.
D. What? You want to know if I fall for typists? What a silly question. I fall for anyone I can connect with and who connects with me.

Upon reading the "D" (right-on) option, anyone with a modicum of self-regard will immediately go back and tick the "A" (right-off) option.

There are countless such exercises in this book. After a while—about five minutes—even the *schadenfreude* of ticking the "wrong" box isn't enough to inoculate you against the kind of boredom that will make your genitals pack their bags and leave home, slamming the door on their way out so hard that your nipples fall off.

But perhaps this is the point. Kate Bornstein is neither a man nor a woman but "hir" own special transgressive creation—and, inevitably, something of a travelling circus. "Ze" was born male, raised as a boy, opted for a sex change in adulthood, and became a woman. A few years later, she got tired of being a woman so she stopped—but didn't want to become a man again. And I think many of us can identify with that. Perhaps this is why since then ze has become an evangelist for the joys of being transgendered.

Gender, which used to be a polite euphemism for sex, has come to stand for something separate from (if related to) the fact of internal/external genital organs. Being a "man" or a "woman" is not dependent on the shape of your squishy bits anymore, apparently. In other words, "male" is not the referent of "man." More than that, to take the postmodern/gender studies line, they are *both* signifiers without referents, since even "male" and "female" are not unambiguous, concrete terms, given the hermaphrodite tendencies of many babies who have to be surgically altered to fit the categories, and the sex-changing tendencies of certain adult humans, not to mention certain fish that have been in the news lately.

But acknowledging that gender is constructed, and that the relationship between sex, gender, and sexuality is not as adamantine or natural or coherent as most of us like to think is one thing; but to suggest that you can "work through" gender and simply reconstruct it to match your shoes—or dispense with it altogether—is quite another neutered thing (unless you happen to be David Bowie and it's the early 1970s). "The way you live without gender is you look for where gender is, and then you go someplace else" (p. 25), says Bornstein. Yeah, but where do you get hold of a flying saucer at affordable rates?

Freud suggested that the first question we ask ourselves on meeting new people is "are they male or female?" It may be that the question we should be asking is, "Are they sci-fi fans?"

As my preop tranny (i.e., *not* transgendered) friend Michelle, who is obsessed with *Star Wars,* told me after dipping into Bornstein's book before tossing it aside in frustration, "Bleedin' 'ell. I suppose my gender is *Wookie!*"

Independent on Sunday
January 1998

A Soldier King with Some
Dodgy Fans

FREDERICK THE GREAT: KING OF PRUSSIA
BY DAVID FRASER

Frederick, like a lot of "greats," has some dodgy fans. Most famous of course is his historical stalker Adolf Hitler, who hero-worshipped the general king who established Prussia as a first-rank power and saw himself, as really scary fans do, as his true heir. And in fact, the unmarried Austrian corporal's military and diplomatic genius *did* manage to arrange for a twentieth-century replay of Frederick's heroic eighteenth-century battle against a combination of most of the major European powers (Hitler's masterstroke consisted in the truly inspired addition of the United States to the list of opponents ranged against him). As we all know, Adolf the Shortarse's reign achieved the opposite results to Frederick the Great's: abject defeat, devastation on a scale unimaginable in Frederick's time, partition, and a Berlin occupied by *Russians*.

And then there are Frederick's other "dodgy" bachelor fans who wish to claim him for their cause. After all, he spurned the affections of his wife, Wilhelmina; he sired no children; women were almost invisible at court; and his name was *not* linked with famous mistresses as most other princes of the period worth their codpieces were. Instead, he collected statues of Antinous, Hadrian's lover, and Ganymede, and "was known to caress, tickle, pinch the ear of some favoured page" (p. 40).

So it is entirely understandable and perhaps even commendable, that David Fraser, a former general in the British Army, should want to save Frederick from both these kinds of Fans of Freddie. After all, Hitler and, until very recently, homos were the two things the British Army knew it was against. However, Fraser's brusque dismissal of both of these kinds of claims in the early part of his authorititive, impressive, if occasionally gruelling tome *Frederick the Great,* is not entirely convincing. He claims that because Frederick was an En-

225

lightenment man, cultivated and an aesthete, he could not therefore be any kind of progenitor of Nazism—but then, as Theodor Adorno argued, Nazism was not so much anti-Enlightenment as the Enlightenment's *dark side*. Besides, Hitler was an architect, a painter, and the author of a philosophical treatise called *Mein Kampf* (he was a mediocre artist; but then, Frederick was a mediocre poet).

More generally, it could be pointed out that Hitler was much more of a continuation of Prussian ideals and goals than is comfortable for many Germans to admit—now. Hitler's extremely popular—until it brought the Red Army to Brandenburg—policy of *lebensraum*, which aimed to annexe the Ukraine and much of European Russia and which was the motive for his preemptive war against France and Britain, was of a piece with the goals of the (largely Prussian) Officer Corps of World War I. Which in turn was of a piece with the Greater Germany created by Prussia's expansionism under Bismarck.

With respect to the rumours of rum bum goings on, Fraser acknowledges the "homosexual" reputation Frederick has gained, outlines his lack of interest in the fair sex, and admits that "together with his unabashed aestheticism and the delicacy of his tastes . . . gave plausibility to his alleged impotence or homosexuality" (p. 39). (The two, of course, being interchangeable.) He also admits that there were rumours that Frederick enjoyed what Fraser calls the "pathic" role in sodomy (looking up "pathic" in my dictionary, I discover, with a thrill, it means "victim" or "catamite"—presenting an irresistible chat-up line: "Are you active or pathic?"). In the end, however, Fraser is unconvinced and claims that Frederick was probably asexual, or at most a nonpractising sodomite. And then moves smartly on to the business that really interests him. War.

Now, while it is certainly refreshing in an era when everyone, especially historical figures, have to be interpreted and interpolated according to whether their nether regions pointed East or West, to find someone much more interested in the battle order of Frederick's regiments than his bedtime antics, Fraser doesn't really get away with it. In fact, as with the other Fans of Freddie already mentioned, it does seem here as if we're learning more about Mr. Fraser's foibles than King Frederick's. As, for example, in the passage where he cites, as evidence against Frederick's alleged homosexuality, the fact that he bought some erotic paintings featuring five pairs of "male and gloriously female lovers."

Especially since, a little later, our author seems keen to suggest that, despite his *philosphe*-inspired distrust of superstition, Frederick did have some religious beliefs—when there is considerably less evidence that Frederick was attracted to the idea of a deity than he was to the idea of sodomy. As Fraser puts it himself, "prejudice has too often clouded perceptions of one of the most extraordinary men ever to sit on a throne or command an army" (p. 6). Fraser is, of course, a Fan of Freddie, too. However, aside from the relatively minor lapses already mentioned, he isn't a dodgy one, but for the most part a fairly objective "straight" one.

Certainly though, Frederick proffers fertile material for some of the psychological speculation which Fraser eschews. He was terrorised by his father Frederick William "the soldier king," who beat him and declared he was "not prepared to tolerate an 'effeminate creature, with no manly inclinations,' who . . . was uncleanly in his person and wore his hair long" (p. 24) (of course today these latter two habits would be categorical proof that Frederick *wasn't* gay). A young Frederick tried to escape Prussia to England but was caught and imprisoned by his father, after being forced to watch his best friend "whom he probably loved" being beheaded. Which would be enough to turn any lad a bit odd and maybe even into a military genius (there are some interesting parallels here with Alexander, whose warlike father, Philip, was also a tyrant who tormented his son—a son who also went on to surpass his father's considerable military achievements—and gain a reputation for "pathic" behaviour). As Fraser puts it, Frederick came to manhood "in frightful circumstances, circumstances which would plead for understanding had he subsequently become a criminal, a degenerate or a lunatic rather than, as happened, a genius" (p. 30).

Certainly that criminal, degenerate, lunatic Voltaire seemed to think Frederick was a genius, or at least a "philosopher king." He also described him as "the Solomon of the North" and "the hope of the world." And perhaps it wasn't just because he had received a very large burgandy bill that week. Frederick was a Fan of France; he hated German and spoke it ostentatiously badly, preferring to speak and write in French, frequently dropping the "k" from his name in signatures to Francify it. He hero-worshipped Voltaire and they exchanged countless effusive letters in verse, in which they attempted to flatter one another to death. Voltaire was even invited to move to

Berlin and was awarded a house and a fat pension (Rousseau was made a similar offer, but made the mistake of asking Frederick, in the fashion of some do-gooding Hollywood celeb, "what was being done for those who had lost limbs in his service?"). Frederick eventually discovered the downside to French intellectuals: "He has the malice of a monkey," he declared exasperatedly after another scandal erupted involving Voltaire's greed and heinousness, "but I need him for my French studies" (p. 254). Voltaire was eventually sent packing and, characteristically, he offered his services to Maria Theresa of Austria, Frederick's archenemy. (To her credit, she rebuffed him, saying, "Voltaire belongs not in Vienna but on Parnassus.")

For all the exhaustive, often dramatic, and always conscientiously detailed accounts of Frederick's exemplary career on the battlefield offered here, dashing around Prussia fending off the Russians in the North, the Austrians in the South, the French in the West (and getting his horse shot from under him several times an hour, it seems), it is through Fraser's account of Frederick as a ruler, or "Solomon of the North," that Frederick's genius—and his modernity—is grasped by the civilian. Frederick, who frequently claimed to loathe soldiering, understood the importance of tolerance, for personal as well as political reasons. Against the custom for scorn, he defended an unmarried female servant in his household who had become pregnant. In Silesia, which had a large Catholic population, a Catholic soldier was convicted of stealing jewels from a statue of the Virgin in a Church. The soldier claimed, cannily, that Mary had given them to him. Frederick assembled some theologians and asked them whether Our Lady could do such a thing. They concluded that it was improbable but not impossible. Frederick annulled the sentence. He had, he said, no power to forbid Our Lady from giving. But, he added, he would in the future punish with death a soldier or anyone else who *accepted* such a gift.

Frederick's sense of justice was remarkably democratic for an absolutist monarch. A distinguished French traveller struck a postilion, who hit back and threw him out of the carriage with his valise. The Frenchman, as Frenchmen did, wrote indignantly to Frederick who told him to be less free with his whip in the future. "What an infernal country this Prussia is," complained the Frenchman, "where you cannot thrash a postilion without bringing blows on yourself!" Frederick's tolerance might have been borne of a desire to prove his intellectual as well as his temporal mastery. In a precursor of Stalin's famous question about how many divisions the pope had, Frederick was given reports of a man in Berlin who called him a tyrant and was proposing treason. "What resources has this man?" asked Frederick. "Can he raise an army of 200,000?" "No, sire," came the reply. "He is poor, a private individual." "Well," laughed Frederick, "*that's* all right!"

Of course, not even a philosopher king can master his legacy, or his followers. Another Fan of Freddie's, after routing the Prussians decisively at Auerstadt and Jena in 1806, visited his tomb at Potsdam. "Hats off, messieurs," Napoleon commanded his generals. "If *he* were alive we would not be here." Indeed, but on the other hand, if Frederick hadn't lived, Napoleon might not have come at all.

Independent on Sunday
February 2000

A Hiding to Nothing

A DEFENCE OF MASOCHISM
BY ANITA PHILLIPS

Apparently, a good sadist is hard to find. But, I can reveal, a good masochist is even harder to find. Whenever I hear the words, "Use me, abuse me, do anything you want with me!" my heart and my manhood always sink. This is not because I have any problem with the idea of using someone. Rather, it's that I know that not far behind this invitation to selfishness are always the words, "Not *that!* This! Not *there!* Here!"

And Anita Phillips wonders why masochists have such a bad name. It's a word that promises so much but then woefully fails to deliver. Far from being a slave to your desires, it turns out to be *their* pleasure that they're interested in, just like everyone else. Worse, not only is their pleasure even more tediously exacting than most people's, you also have to pretend that it is *your* pleasure. While the idea of having someone around the home to clean the toilet and bathroom floor with their tongue might appeal in an abstract kind of way, it always, *always* turns out to be much more work and much, much more tedious than doing it yourself and conducting a common-all-garden, nonmasochistic, missionary-position-under-the-floral-duvet-every-Sunday-morning relationship. As Phillips admits, the best partner for a masochist is not a sadist, but another masochist.

Sadomasochism, when all's said and done, is a bit of a con and should be prosecuted under the Trade Descriptions Act.

Nonetheless, there's plenty of it about these days—and it's selling like hot candle wax. Madonna's early 1990s flirtation with S&M chic seems to have sent it squeaking and creaking up and down the catwalks and into advertising ever since—to the point where a stilet-toed heel threatening a man's bumhole on a billboard hardly provokes any comment, let alone the rear-end pileup it might have caused just ten years ago. And while David Cronenberg's *Crash* (1997), a film about people who take pleasure being on the receiving end of mutilating car accidents, did provoke outrage and censorship from some quarters, many found it rather *banal*. Meanwhile the recent film *Sick: The Life and Death of Bob Flanagan, Supermasochist* (1997) seems to have elevated masochism to a kind of superheroism; how long before we hear little boys whining, "Mum, can I have a leather harness and cling-film cape for Christmas, *please?*"

Which almost begs the point of a book with the name *A Defence of Masochism*. However, a recent European court ruling asserting that assault cannot be consented to (which means, of course, an end to boxing, surgery, and supporting Arsenal) suggests that there is still an argument to be made. And even if most people who don't wear wigs and suspenders for a living are more laid back about the issue, there are still a number of common misconceptions and prejudices about masochism—most of which Anita Phillips dispatches here with aplomb. Most notably, the idea that masochism is always someone else's perversion. Phillips investigates, via Freud and American academic Leo Bersani, the universality of masochistic impulses, the thin line between pleasure and pain, and how the curdling of these impulses into a condition and a type changed what it means to be human.

Masochism is one of the inventions of late nineteenth-century sexology in the Gothic shape of Baron Dr. Richard von Kraft-Ebing. It was only ever intended to apply to men; women were "naturally" masochistic, so pleasure in pain on their part was not "perverse" and therefore not a problem to be explained or pathologised. This was part of a shift in gender roles in the West in the nineteenth century which was concerned with, we are told, institutionalising women's subjugation. As Phillips points out, from "Dante's ordeal in the Inferno to be reunited with Beatrice, to John Donne's love poetry, sacrificial masculine love has been a crucial theme, only in this century has what for many centuries seemed the natural, desirable form of male love been redefined as effeminate perversity, masochism" (p. 86).

Phillips believes that this reformulation of male identity that excluded masochism made masculinity "blatantly misogynistic, emotionally inept and homophobic" (p. 86). She also believes that it was this new masculinity which led, in part, to the "corrective" of feminism. Ironically, the exclusion of masochism from the male psyche has produced a public scenario of their punishment and chastisement by women, which continues up to the present day. The feminist *is* Ms. Whiplash.

To be sure, we can see that male masochism is now making something of a comeback—what else could explain The Verve and the tortured, feel-my-stigmata "soft lad" tendency? And while this rise of male self-dramatisation/self-obsession may or may not be good news for women in general, it is definitely good news for women like Phillips who enjoy masochistic sex. Ironically, now that men are relinquishing their grip on the whip handle, women need no longer feel like they are betraying their sex by expressing fantasies of domination.

But as with most cases of special pleading, Phillips' argument often slips into evangelism. We are told that masochists are "imaginative risk takers" and that real eroticism requires a certain "shattering of the self." In other words, masochists are on a higher sexual plane to those poor souls who don't want to get whipped, trussed up, and locked in a cupboard for three days. Apparently, "the shattering quality of sex needs to be diluted for those who cannot fully handle it . . . [and they] make a kind of civic virtue from their own necessity to retreat from the challenge of a full-blooded encounter" (p. 123).

Maybe those of us who prefer our sex weak and thin, with the gore and entrails strained out, are not necessarily so timid as Ms. Phillips seems to think. Perhaps most people refuse to indulge their masochist leanings any further than a spot of slightly embarrassed spanking or coy nipple tweaking simply because they have better things to do with their time than trying to "discover their limits" remaking *Hellraiser.*

Independent on Sunday
March 1998

The Antichrist Has All the Best Tunes

SONIC BOOM: NAPSTER, P2P
AND THE BATTLE FOR THE FUTURE OF MUSIC
BY JOHN ALDERMAN

Perhaps the greatest appeal of digital music is that, like all good technology, it doesn't only make listening to music more convenient and less irksome; it actually does part of the tiresome job of *listening* for you.

ISO-MPEG Audio-Layer-3, thankfully shortened to MP3, is the digital file format for music exchanged on the Internet and possibly the acronym of doom for the record industry. It is a form of extreme algorithmic compression of sound files that uses "psychoacoustic" models that account for what listeners actually notice when they hear music or other sounds. "Unnecessary" data is stripped away to make the file as small as possible to facilitate easier storage or uploading and downloading. In other words, MP3 anticipates and interprets music for the listener before she or he actually hears it.

Of course, this job used to be performed by record companies, with their A&R men and marketing departments. But, like so many before them, they appear to have been automated out of a job—dispensed with by algorithms, the Internet, and a bunch of geeky kids in their bedrooms.

The Internet has famously been compared to Gutenburg in its importance. However, after reading John Alderman's detailed account of the online music revolution, I have a hunch it's more like Gutenburg plus Protestantism plus Punk—all at once. Thanks to the personal computer and the Internet, every man is now at home with his god—downloading The Sex Pistols' "EMI." The corrupt, uncool intermediaries and authorities who used to intercede have been swept aside and the Word can be enjoyed directly and free from distortion, compressed by pure, clean mathematics, not by dogma. The free exchange of information—which is all that digital music amounts to in cyberspace—is the credo of the Nettist Movement.

To many Nettists, anyone who attempts to stand in the way of this Reformation Superhighway is the Papist Antichrist, or the fascist regime. And of course this means anyone who doesn't share their holy zeal—anyone who is non-Nettist. And the record companies are about as non-Nettist as you can get. After all, they have most to lose from the free exchange of digital music. All their fleets of trucks, CD printing presses, and back catalogues become near worthless at the press of a button in someone's bedroom. If indulgences no longer have to be bought but can be plucked from the air instead, then where is the temporal wealth and power of the record business to come from?

Hence, to the record companies, the leaders of the MP3 revolution are too often seen as heretics who have to be made examples of, burnt at the legal stake so that others may not be tempted to stray from the True Church. Against the cries for info freedom, their lawyers invoke the Mystery of copyright. Digitising music, just as printing the Bible in German did, puts it within the grasp—and control—of the laity. And like the leaders of the Counter-Reformation, they see themselves as acting in the interests of the people they burn.

You think I exaggerate, perchance? Listen to Edgar Bronfman Jr., heir to the mighty if not holy Roman Seagram Empire and quoted here by Alderman: "I am warring against the culture of the Internet, threatening to depopulate Silicon Valley as I move a Roman legion or two of Wall Street lawyers to litigate. . . . I have done so . . . not to attack the Internet and its culture but for its benefit and to protect it" (p. 139).

So is Shawn Fanning, the boy who at nineteen founded Napster, the famous MP3 file-sharing "peer-2-peer" online service, a Luther for our times? And is Napster his Wittenberg Theses, nailed to the door of the music industry? Well, not quite. But for a while it looked that way. Twelve months after the launch of Napster in June 1999, there were over 200,000 souls praying in his church nightly. By the end of 2000 there were over 50 million registered users and Fanning was a very famous young man indeed; his criminally young, beatific face shined out from the cover of magazines.

But Fanning ultimately failed to live up to his historical mission. He was no ideologue; merely an American boy who saw a need which he believed software could fill. From his time spent chatting on the Net, he knew that people were eager to trade music files, but finding good music was the problem. He joined with two online pals, only slightly older than himself, to solve this with smart code. Together they wrote the Napster program, which turned users' computers into a form of giant network.

Because Napster hosted no music itself (the files were stored on user's computers and traded), it was hoped by Fanning et al. that they would be free from any taint of blasphemy in the form of copyright violations. They were very wrong. In the opening blast of what was to prove a merciless barrage, the fearsome Recording Industry Association of America filed a copyright lawsuit against Napster in December 1999, six months after it had launched.

And who could blame them? Napster was a disaster of, well, biblical proportions for the record industry. Practically a whole generation of college kids, who didn't even have to pay for the college computers or the Internet connections they downloaded the MP3 files with, stopped buying CDs. Not only was Napster free—especially if you were a student—Napster was easier than going to a record store and it was easier than ordering CDs online. Emusic.com, an e-tailer of digital music, was forced to give away MP3 players (worth $150) to anyone who bought just $25 worth of music.

A year and a half on, under the weight of various lawsuits and injunctions brought by the record industry and Lars Ulrich of Metallica, who famously discovered that three unfinished versions of a song he had been working on had been traded on Napster (along with his entire back catalogue), the Church of Shawn Fanning is not what it was. Perhaps inevitably, Napster got into bed with record giant Bertlesmann—one of the few record companies to respond to the MP3 revolution with anything other than public burnings—in an attempt to turn Napster into a legal, mainstream, subscription-only service which, crucially, paid royalties to performers.

The issue of intellectual copyright and rewarding artists is a thorny one and not so easy to dismiss as "record company greed." Ulrich is certainly not the only professional rock and roll rebel to take indignant offence at the "criminality" of online file trading. Ultimately, though, the feelings of artists or even record companies may not count for very much. In a sense, file trading is what the Internet was designed for—and it was also designed to survive nuclear war: something even more destructive than a music company lawyer.

There is perhaps a tad too much jargon in *Sonic Boom* for the information technology agnostic, and the narration doesn't always quite match the raciness of the title or the import of the revolution it documents, but it's a valuable book for anyone interested in where our culture is headed.

Meanwhile, the Nettist Movement continues apace. Napster and Fanning may have recanted, but most of its massive congregation of 50 million that Bertlesmann hoped to convert into consumers have left and are now praying at lesser known online p2p sites. And there are always new, more convincing Luthers. Programmer Ian Clarke, for instance. He believes vehemently that information should be free. But he isn't going to try too hard to convince you with words; he has won the argument already with code by designing a system called Freenet which allows users to post and retrieve files with complete anonymity. Unlike Napster, there is no central server—this is a church which really has no walls and whose congregation is invisible. Clarke likes to tell reporters that he couldn't take Freenet down if someone put a gun to his head. Alas, Alderman doesn't tell us what Clarke would do if Edgar Bronfman Jr. sent a "Roman legion of Wall Street lawyers" after him.

Independent on Sunday
August 2001

All Right, but No Mick Jagger

I'M A MAN: SEX, GODS AND ROCK 'N' ROLL
BY RUTH PADEL

In a Tokyo hotel in the 1990s, a woman rock musician happened to have the room next door to a male guitarist from the LA Guns. As you might expect and hope, she was kept awake all night by the graphic sound of him entertaining groupies. Next morning his door was strewn with tiny, beautifully folded white notes from unsuccessful applicants. She opened one. It read, "I will wait for you. Room 361 on third floor. I cherish a dream The Rock God will come see me."

Ruth Padel, the mythologist and poet, is rather fond of this story, and offers it as an illustration of the divine power of rock. As a misanthrope and a cynic, I prefer the fable from the 1969 rock classic *Groupie,* also cited here, about the American girl who worked her way through hundreds of rockers only to complain after each one, "He was all right, but he was no Mick Jagger." Finally, she bagged old rubber lips himself, and the next day her friends asked her excitedly how it went. "Oh, he was all right," she drawled. "But he was no Mick Jagger."

Rock and roll, like masculinity itself, is a copy of an original which never existed. It's a passionate pursuit of something ultimately unattainable—for the performers, fans, *and* critics alike. All attempts to trace it to its source are ultimately doomed to failure—even in the gloriously allusive psychological complexity of Greek myth, where Padel valiantly, if at times somewhat confusedly, tries to locate it. Certainly rock and roll is more pagan than Christian, but it is a paganism that has no respect for antiquity or paternity. Which is just how it should be: what is interesting about rock and roll is precisely how irreverent, unscrupulous, and *fraudulent* it is.

Mick Jagger, like all rock stars, began by imitating his own (black) heroes, such as Muddy Waters, the blues singer who first croaked out the line "I'm a man . . . I'm a rolling stone." Luckily for Mick, he was so bad at it that he ended up being mistaken for original talent by white folks. This is the essential bragging adolescence of rock and roll: it's a form of male impersonation. And appropriation.

Marx claimed that every great fortune is founded on a great crime, and the rock world—which *seems* uniquely to reward creativity but actually rewards opportunism—is the greatest example of this. To complain, as Padel occasionally seems to, about the white "theft" of "blackness" is a bit like complaining about loose morals in a bordello. Of course, in the early days, white rockers cleaned up by literally cleaning up black blues. Bill Haley's "Rock Around the Clock," for example, was a sanitised cover of a seriously smutty Charlie Calhoun song (though, as Padel points out, Bill Haley missed the pornographic line, "I'm like a one-eyed cat, peeping in a seafood store").

And if rock and roll may have begun with white boys imitating or "ripping off" black men, it seems to have ended with black middle-class men imitating black homeboys for an audience of white-bread boys—which is, after all, what most rap is these days. And who can seriously doubt that after nearly two decades of dominance, rap has proved itself the true heir—and nemesis—of rock? The mythical appeal of BBC, or Big Black Cock, seems to make groupies of everyone. Apparently in Germany, where "bad niggas" are rather thin on the ground but rap is phenomenally popular, record company scouts cruise U.S. bases in search of "mean-looking black GIs with rhythm."

As Padel reminds us, the assertion of Muddy Waters—"I'm a man"—was political: he was demanding equality at a time when black men in the South were segregated, discriminated against, and routinely called "boy." Which is perhaps why it has fed into a music popular with white boys demanding equality with their fathers. Hence, Padel's use of Greek myth is closest to the mark when it touches on psychoanalytic/oedipal themes. Like the story of the birth of Venus, who grew in the foam that bubbled around Heaven's testicles, which was cut off with a sickle by his son Kronos and tossed into the sea. This myth suggests masculinity and sex itself is bound up with violence and revolution (and *theft*—the balls are stolen or "ripped off").

And also how, in rock terms, the "foam" of femininity tends to proceed from masculinity—even when it tries to assert something antiphallic. Padel goes to see a lesbian rock band in San Francisco who likes to whip out huge, black (of course) rubber penises, "masturbate" them, and invite male members of the audience to suck their

BBCs, before cutting them off (a finale which probably owes more to Lorena Bobbitt than Kronos).

In rock, as with everything else, the cock is always a disappointment next to the phallus. "Oh, it was all right," we all sigh afterward. "But it was no guitar."

Independent on Sunday
July 2000

Mummy, Mummy, Mummy!

BRIGHT LIGHTS DARK SHADOWS:
THE REAL STORY OF ABBA
BY CARL MAGNUS PALM

"No more fucking Abba!" bellowed an ageing, transsexual Terence Stamp in *The Adventures of Priscilla, Queen of the Desert,* driven to distraction by his fey fellow bus passengers' obsession with the silly Swedish 1970s supergroup. Some hope. We're all trapped on a Day-Glo bus full of drag queens squawking along to a loop tape of *Abba Gold* playing on the stereo. And that's just watching the Olympics. The Abba revival in the 1990s turned out to be not so much a rediscovery of a critically overlooked band as an ascension to pop cultural heaven and eternal airplay.

Björn, Benny, Frida, and Agnetha are all our angelic friends now—and we believe in them, something good in everything they do. We hear their sweetly harmonious voices almost every day, though they stopped making records twenty years ago. And we still see their warm, smiling, never-ageing, nonaligned Nordic faces, the epitome of benignity. They just want us to be happy. In fact, Björn, Benny, Frida, and Agnetha are not just our friends; they're our parents—not our unconvincing biological ones but our shiny postmodern ones who will never let us down, except perhaps in their dress sense. After all, the cute acronym of the name Abba means "Our father" in Aramaic (although in Sweden it's also the name of a tinned-fish company).

Abba was a fiendishly clever and catastrophically successful Scandinavian plan for total world domination. Deploying pop singles instead of longboats, aspirations instead of horned helmets, they kidnapped preteen children everywhere, ultimately making the world safe for that other Swedish four-letter word: IKEA. Abba was the ultimate suburban aspirational group, and the two crooning couples were the ultimate aspirational parents. Now that we're grown up, we are all Abba. We've all bought the dream of Swedish bourgeois classlessness, excellence and niceness, the soft furnishings, and cool green frosted glass kitchen cabinets that scratch easily if you're not careful.

It's significant that nowhere was Abba's strategy more successful than in Australia, where not just preteens but pretty much the whole country was abducted overnight. When they performed on television there, more than half of the population tuned in. *Abba: The Movie* was set in Australia. The Abba tribute band Bjorn Again is Australian. Australian films are obsessed with Abba (e.g., *Priscilla* and *Muriel's Wedding,* 1995).

Why did Australia go "ABBAustralian," as one paper put it at the time? Unkind Poms might say it was because the Ozzies identified with the Swedes' problems with the English language, but the truth was that Australia, the former penal colony, was a "bastard" country looking to be adopted by well-mannered parents with nice teeth who weren't sheep farmers or uranium miners.

The Abba makeover to which Australia surrendered worked perfectly: Nowadays Australia is a country of nice, friendly middle-class people, dental hygienists, publicists, models, lawyers, and cheery soap operas. In other words, once assimilated, Australia was able to go about the business of running the AbbaWorld. Hence that triumphal climax of last year's closing ceremony at the Sydney Olympics, broadcast around the world to billions, featured AbbaChild Kylie Minogue on a *Priscilla* float singing "Dancing Queen," the national anthem of AbbaWorld. (And a literally irresistible pop song—which is to say, it wrestles your better judgment to the floor, sits on its face, and leaves you free to make a complete fool of yourself.)

Of course, Britain was the first non-Scandinavian country to succumb to Abba, that Eurovision night with Katie Boyle back in 1974 at the Brighton Dome was when we met our Waterloo. It's probably why that nice Mr. Sven has had so much success with his makeover of the English football team, most of whom were born post-Abbassimilation and have no trouble recognizing their masters.

Scandinavian design, with its clean lines, high quality, what-you-see-is-what-you-get lack of hierarchy is the only kind of bourgeoisdom we Brits seem willing to recognize nowadays. Those satanically clever and clean Abba hooklines and impressive arrangements (praised now by everyone from Pete Townsend to Bono) were the product of craftsmanship and professionalism. The very things that made them deeply unhip in the 1970s and led to them being described as "cynical" and "icy" are what makes them the soundtrack to a careerist, managerial age. Those tunes may have sounded innocent to kids back then, but now that they have grown up they're glad to discover that they weren't—that like everything else these days, they were very, very calculated.

I'm not sure how much of this fellow Swede and uber AbbaChild Carl Magnus Palm, author of *Bright Lights Dark Shadows: The Real Story of Abba,* would agree to. The flyleaf describes him as "the world's foremost Abba historian," but really his book isn't as bad as that would lead you to believe. It's all clearly and soberly written, painstakingly detailed, and incontrovertibly definitive. Very professional. Well crafted. The prose slides in and out like a fitted kitchen drawer. But there are not enough clean lines. Some of this detail and definitiveness is not likely to appeal, unless you're the world's number two Abba historian. Thankfully, his main thesis about "the Nordic angst being there all along, just beneath the surface" isn't really borne out. So the band members turn out to be actual human beings who have rows and bust ups? Big deal. There are fewer "dark shadows" here than in an IKEA showroom. And, being an AbbaChild, the author can't contemplate the possibility that Abba itself may have been the "dark shadow."

As a pal of mine, a blonde male-to-female transsexual Abba fan ("Abba made me what I am today") pronounced, after rapidly scanning the pages of the book like a cyborg: "There's no dirt. No one's ever been able to find any." She didn't sound disappointed. Which is, perhaps, the scariest thing of all about Abba.

Independent on Sunday
October 2001

ABOUT THE AUTHOR

Mark Simpson is the author of the critically acclaimed *Male Impersonators*, *It's a Queer World*, *Anti-Gay* (Ed.), and the co-author of *The Queen is Dead*. He has been described as "brilliantly buccaneering" by *The Spectator*, "the gay Anti-Christ" by *Vogue*, "profound and hilarious—an amused, detached Voltaire" by the *Independent on Sunday*, "a brainy thug" by the *Seattle Stranger*, and "Joe Don Baker channeling Truman Capote" by *Bruce La Bruce*. Visit his Web site at www.marksimpson.com.

HARRINGTON PARK PRESS
New, Recent, and Forthcoming
Titles of Related Interest

Gay and Gray: The Older Homosexual Man, Second Edition by Raymond M. Berger

Against My Better Judgment: An Intimate Memoir of an Eminent Gay Psychologist by Roger Brown

The Masculine Marine: Homoeroticism in the U.S. Marine Corps by Steven Zeeland

Autopornography: A Memoir of Life in the Lust Lane by Scott "Spunk" O'Hara

The Empress Is a Man: Stories from the Life of José Sarria by Michael R. Gorman

A Consumer's Guide to Male Hustlers by Joseph Itiel

It's a Queer World: Deviant Adventures in Pop Culture by Mark Simpson

Macho Love: Sex Behind Bars in Central America by Jacobo Schifter

When It's Time to Leave Your Lover: A Guide for Gay Men by Neil Kaminsky

Tricks and Treats: Sex Workers Write About Their Clients edited by Matt Bernstein Sycamore

Gay Men at Midlife: Age Before Beauty by Alan L. Ellis

Finding a Lover for Life: A Gay Man's Guide to Finding Mr. Right by David Price

The Man Who Was a Woman and Other Queer Tales from Hindu Lore by Devdutt Pattanaik

Barrack Buddies and Soldier Lovers: Dialogues with Gay Young Men in the U.S. Military by Steven Zeeland

Rebel Yell: Stories by Contemporary Southern Gay Authors edited by Jay Quinn

Sissyphobia: Gay Men and Effeminate Behavior by Tim Bergling

Sex Workers As Virtual Boyfriends by Joseph Itiel

Tops, Bottom, and Versatiles: The Meanings of Anal Sex for Gay Men by Steven G. Underwood

Escapades of a Gay Traveler: Sexual, Cultural, and Spiritual Encounters by Joseph Itiel

Order a copy of this book with this form or online at:
http://www.haworthpressinc.com/store/product.asp?sku=4644

SEX TERROR
Erotic Misadventures in Pop Culture

_____in hardbound at $34.95 (ISBN: 1-56023-376-1)

_____in softbound at $17.95 (ISBN: 1-56023-377-X)

COST OF BOOKS_____

OUTSIDE USA/CANADA/
MEXICO: ADD 20%____

POSTAGE & HANDLING_____
(US: $4.00 for first book & $1.50
for each additional book)
Outside US: $5.00 for first book
& $2.00 for each additional book)

SUBTOTAL_____

in Canada: add 7% GST____

STATE TAX____
(NY, OH & MIN residents, please
add appropriate local sales tax)

FINAL TOTAL____
(If paying in Canadian funds,
convert using the current
exchange rate, UNESCO
coupons welcome.)

❑ **BILL ME LATER:** ($5 service charge will be added)
(Bill-me option is good on US/Canada/Mexico orders only;
not good to jobbers, wholesalers, or subscription agencies.)

❑ Check here if billing address is different from
shipping address and attach purchase order and
billing address information.

Signature_____

❑ **PAYMENT ENCLOSED: $_____**

❑ **PLEASE CHARGE TO MY CREDIT CARD.**

❑ Visa ❑ MasterCard ❑ AmEx ❑ Discover
❑ Diner's Club ❑ Eurocard ❑ JCB

Account # _____

Exp. Date_____

Signature_____

Prices in US dollars and subject to change without notice.

NAME_____

INSTITUTION_____

ADDRESS_____

CITY_____

STATE/ZIP_____

COUNTRY_____ COUNTY (NY residents only)_____

TEL_____ FAX_____

E-MAIL_____

May we use your e-mail address for confirmations and other types of information? ❑ Yes ❑ No
We appreciate receiving your e-mail address and fax number. Haworth would like to e-mail or fax special
discount offers to you, as a preferred customer. **We will never share, rent, or exchange your e-mail address
or fax number.** We regard such actions as an invasion of your privacy.

Order From Your Local Bookstore or Directly From
The Haworth Press, Inc.
10 Alice Street, Binghamton, New York 13904-1580 • USA
TELEPHONE: 1-800-HAWORTH (1-800-429-6784) / Outside US/Canada: (607) 722-5857
FAX: 1-800-895-0582 / Outside US/Canada: (607) 722-6362
E-mail: getinfo@haworthpressinc.com
PLEASE PHOTOCOPY THIS FORM FOR YOUR PERSONAL USE.
www.HaworthPress.com

BOF02

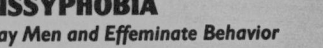

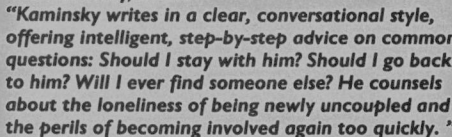
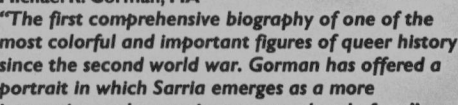